The Actor Training Reader

The Actor Training Reader is an invaluable resource for students and teachers of acting, offering access to a wide range of key texts that identify, explore, illuminate and interrogate the challenges, practices and processes involved in training the modern actor.

A companion volume to the highly-acclaimed *Actor Training* (Hodge 2010), this book collects key writings by influential practitioners of the twentieth century, introduced by essays from leading academics in the field of actor training. Key practitioners include:

- Eugenio Barba;
- Anne Bogart;
- Bertolt Brecht;
- Peter Brook;
- Michael Chekhov; and
- Konstantin Stanislavsky.

Established, widely used texts sit alongside less we development of actor training from the pioneering acting games of Augusto Boal. The texts are grot than chronologically, in order to encourage a com, similar aspects of the craft. Each section includes a specially commissioned introductory essay bringing context, critical engagement and contemporary relevance to the extracts and offering provocations for further discussion.

Mark Evans is Professor of Theatre Training and Associate Dean of the School of Art and Design at Coventry University, UK. He researches actor training and theatre education. He has published books on movement training for actors and on the work of Jacques Copeau, written several articles on theatre training, and is an Associate Editor for the *Th   ·nal published by Routledge.

The Actor Training Reader

Edited by

Mark Evans

Routledge
Taylor & Francis Group

LONDON AND NEW YORK

First published 2015
by Routledge
2 Park Square, Milton Park, Abingdon, Oxon OX14 4RN

and by Routledge
711 Third Avenue, New York, NY 10017

Routledge is an imprint of the Taylor & Francis Group, an informa business

British Library Cataloguing-in-Publication Data
A catalogue record for this book is available from the British Library

Library of Congress Cataloging-in-Publication Data
   The actor training reader / by Mark Evans [editor].
      pages cm
   Includes bibliographical references.
   (pbk. : alk. paper)   1. Acting.   2. Acting—Study and teaching.
   I. Evans, Mark, 1957- editor.
   PN2061.A32 2015
   792.02′8—dc23
                                            2014033043

ISBN: 978-0-415-82401-9 (hbk)
ISBN: 978-0-415-82402-6 (pbk)

Typeset in Joanna MT and Bell Gothic
by RefineCatch Limited, Bungay, Suffolk

MIX
Paper from
responsible sources
FSC® C013604

Printed and bound by CPI Group (UK) Ltd, Croydon, CR0 4YY

This book is dedicated to my wife Vanessa Oakes.

Contents

Acknowledgements

MY THANKS TO Talia Rodgers for commissioning this project and also to Ben Piggott and Harriet Affleck for their generous support and advice as the project has progressed. Thanks also to the authors of the specially commissioned essays for this volume – Ian Watson, Jonathan Pitches, Bella Merlin and Dick McCaw – who have provided a range of stimulating, provocative and pertinent responses to the challenges and topics raised by this selection of extracts. Their engagement with and enthusiasm for the project has been a wonderful encouragement, and the conversations we have had about the issues raised in the production of this book have enriched the whole experience. I am also grateful to Alison Hodge, who was very supportive of the idea of a companion volume to her own collection on Actor Training when this project was in its early stages.

Thanks to my colleagues and students at Coventry University, and at a number of other institutions where I have had the opportunity to talk about and reflect on the relevance of the practitioners featured in this Reader. Thanks also to several colleagues and friends who have helped track down contacts for extract permissions – Paul Allain, Jane Baldwin and Dick McCaw.

My colleagues in the Performer Training working group within the Theatre and Performance Research Association – Simon Murray, Jonathan Pitches, David Shirley, Libby Worth and Konstantinos Thomaidis – whether they are aware of it or not, have provided me with endless stimulation for this book through their passion for performer training – its histories, practices, transmissions and complexities. I thank them for their companionship on this journey.

Finally thanks to my wife Vanessa, for her love and wisdom.

The publishers wish to thank the following for their permission to publish work in full or extracts.

Jacques Copeau: Rudlin, J. & Paul, N. (eds.) (1990) *Copeau: Texts on Theatre*, London & New York: Routledge, Copeau – 'Final Advice to the Young' (209–210).

Konstantin Stanislavsky: Stanislavski, C. (1980) *My Life in Art*, London: Methuen (461–462).

Mike Alfreds: Alfreds, M. (2007) *Different Every Night: Freeing the Actor*, London: Nick Hern Books, extracts from 'Permanent Training' (29–30, 32).

Eugenio Barba: Barba, E. (1979) *The Floating Islands*, Holsterbro: Odin, 'Letter to Actor D.' (37–39).

Augusto Boal: Boal, A. (1995) *The Rainbow of Desire: The Boal method of theatre and therapy*, London & New York: Routledge, extracts from 'What is the actor?' (35–39).

Michael Chekhov: Chekhov, M. (1985) *Lessons for the Professional Actor*, ed. D. Hurst du Prey, New York: Performing Arts Journal, extracts from 'First Class: Why is a Method Needed in the Theatre of Today' (23–25, 33).

Edward Gordon Craig: Craig, E. G. (1983) *Craig On Theatre*, ed. J. Michael Walton, London: Methuen, extracts from 'The Actor and the Über-Marionette' (84–87).

Jerzy Grotowski: Grotowski, J. (1997) 'Performer', in Schechner, R. & Wolford, L. (eds.) (1997) *The Grotowski Sourcebook*, London & New York: Routledge (376–379).

Jacques Lecoq: Lecoq, J. (2000) *The Moving Body: Teaching creative theatre*, London: Methuen, 'Towards a young theatre of new work' (18–21).

Yoshi Oida: Oida, Y. & Marshall, L. (1997) *The Invisible Actor*, London: Methuen, extracts from 'Learning' (112–116, 117–118).

Konstantin Stanislavsky: Stanislavski, K. (2008) *An Actor's Work*, London & New York: Routledge, extracts from 'Ethics and discipline' (555–558, 561).

Antonin Artaud: Artaud, A. (1970) *The Theatre and its Double*, London: Calder and Boyars, 'An Affective Athleticism' (88–90, 95).

Eugenio Barba: Barba, B. (1986) *Beyond the Floating Islands*, New York: PAJ, 'Physical Training, Vocal Training' (50–55).

Augusto Boal: Boal, A. (2002) *Games for Actors and Non-Actors*, 2nd edition, London & New York: Routledge (40–41, 237–238).

Moshe Feldenkrais: Feldenkrais, M. & Schechner, R. (1966) 'Image, Movement, and Actor: Restoration of Potentiality – A discussion of the Feldenkrais Method and Acting, Self-Expression and the Theater', *TDR*, Vol. 10, No. 3 (112–113, 115–117).

Dario Fo and Franca Rame: Fo, D. & Rame, F. (1983) *Theatre Workshops at the Riverside Studios, London*, London: Red Notes, extracts (23–24).

Jerzy Grotowski: Grotowski, J. (1969) *Towards a Poor Theatre*, London: Methuen, 'Actor Training' (134, 135–136, 207–209).

Rudolf Laban: McCaw, D. (ed.) *The Laban Sourcebook*, London & New York: Routledge (233, 234–237, 276–278).

Jacques Lecoq: Lecoq, J. (2006) *Theatre of Movement and Gesture*, London & New York: Routledge (105).

Kristin Linklater: Linklater, K. (1976) *Freeing the Natural Voice*, New York & Hollywood: Drama Publishers, extracts from 'Observations and opinions on voice and acting' (202–204, 204–205, 205–206, 206).

Vsevolod Meyerhold: Bruan, E. (ed.) (1969) *Meyerhold on Theatre*, London: Methuen, 'Biomechanics' (197–200).

Michel Saint-Denis: Saint-Denis, M. (1982) *Training for the Theatre*, New York: Theatre Arts Books (115–116, 146–147, 151–152, 159–160, 170–172).

Tadashi Suzuki: Suzuki, T. (1986) *The Way of Acting: The theatre writings of Tadashi Suzuki*, New York: Theatre Communications Group, 'The Grammar of the Feet' (6–9).

Yevgeny Vakhtangov: Malaev-Babel, A. (ed.) (2011) *The Vakhtangov Sourcebook*, London & New York: Routledge, 'Subconscious Perception and Expression' and 'On Actor Cultivation' (111–112, 118–119).

Phillip Zarrilli: Zarrilli, P. (2009) *Psychophysical Acting: An Intercultural approach after Stanislavski*, London & New York: Routledge, 'Rediscovering the body and mind through practice' (22–24).

Stella Adler: Adler, S. (2000) *The Art of Acting,* New York: Applause (180–184).

Eugenio Barba: Barba, E. (2010) *On Directing and Dramaturgy: Burning the House*, London & New York: Routledge, 'The Actor's Dramaturgy' (26–29), and Barba, E. (1997) 'An Amulet Made of Memory: The significance of exercises in the actor's dramaturgy' *TDR*, Vol. 41, No. 4 (128, 129–130).

Anne Bogart and Tina Landau: Bogart, A. & Landau, T. (2005) *The Viewpoints Book*, New York: Theatre Communications Group, 'Viewpoints and Composition: What Are They?' (7–13).

Bertolt Brecht: Willett, J. (ed.) (1978) *Brecht on Theatre: The Development of an Aesthetic*, London: Methuen, 'Short Description of a new technique in acting which produces an alienation effect' (136–140).

Michael Chekhov: Chekhov, M. (2002) *To The Actor*, London & New York: Routledge, extract from 'Character and Characterization' (77–81).

Dario Fo: Fo, D. (1991) *The Tricks of the Trade*, London: Methuen (35–36, 36–37).

Jacques Lecoq: Lecoq, J. (2000) *The Moving Body*, London: Methuen, extracts (60–62, 64–65).

Sanford Meisner: Meisner, S. & Longwell, D. (1987) *Sanford Meisner on Acting*, New York: Vintage (34, 36–37).

Odin: Christoffersen, E. E. (1993) *The Actor's Way*, London & New York: Routledge (124–125).

Open Theatre: Pasolli, R. (1972) *A book on the Open Theatre*, New York: Avon (20–22).

Konstantin Stanislavsky: Stanislavski, K. (2008) *An Actor's Work*, London & New York: Routledge, extracts from 'The Supertask, Throughline' (307–309, 316–317, 318–319).

Peter Brook: Brook, P. (1993) *There Are No Secrets: Thoughts on Acting and Theatre*, London: Methuen, 'The Slyness of Boredom' (76) and Brook, P. (1993) *Platform Papers: 6. Peter Brook*, London: National Theatre, extracts (6–7, 10).

Joseph Chaikin: Chaikin, J. (1991) *The Presence of the Actor*, New York: Theatre Communications Group (21–23, 59–60, 65–67).

Jacques Copeau: Rudlin, J. & Paul, N. (eds.) (1990) *Copeau: Texts on Theatre*, London & New York: Routledge, 'Towards a New Concept of Theatrical Interpretation' (10–12).

Philippe Gaulier: Gaulier, P. (2006) *The Tormentor: le jeu, light, theatre*, Paris: Filmiko, 'Truth kills the joy of imagining' (193–195).

Keith Johnstone: Johnstone, K. (1981) *Impro: Improvisation and the Theatre*, London & New York: Methuen, 'Spontaneity' (81–82, 87–88, 92–93, 100).

Jacques Lecoq: Lecoq, J. (2006) *Theatre of Movement and Gesture*, London & New York: Routledge (69, 72–73, 76–78).

Joan Littlewood: 'Working with Joan: Theatre Workshop actors talking to Tom Milne and Clive Goodwin' in Marowitz, C. & Trussler, S. (eds.) (1967) *Theatre at Work: Playwrights and Productions in the Modern British Theatre*, London: Methuen (114, 115, 116–117, 119, 121, 122).

Ariane Mnouchkine: extracts from: Féral, J., Mnouchkine, A. & Husemoller, A. (1989) 'Building up the Muscle: An Interview with Ariane Mnouchkine', *TDR*, Vol. 33, No. 4 (Winter, 1989) (91, 93–94); from Féral, J. (1989) 'Mnouchkine's Workshop at the Soleil: A lesson in theatre', *TDR*, Vol. 33, No. 4 (Winter, 1989) (85–87); and, from Pavis, P. (ed.) (1996) *The Intercultural Performance Reader*, London & New York: Routledge (95).

Wlodzimierz Staniewski: Staniewski, W. with Hodge, A. (2004) *Hidden Territories: the theatre of gardzienice*, London & New York: Routledge, 'Actors and acting' (92–97, 101).

Ruth Zaporah: Zaporah, R. (1995) *Action Theater: The improvisation of presence*, Berkeley, Ca.: North Atlantic Books (4–5, 10–11, 18–20, 29–30, 41, 191).

Yoshi Oida: Oida, Y. & Marshall, L. (1997) *The Invisible Actor*, London: Methuen (124–125).

Contributors

Mark Evans is Professor of Theatre Training and Education and Associate Dean (Student Experience) in the School of Art and Design at Coventry University. He has published books and articles on movement, theatre training, performance and creative entrepreneurship education. His most recent publications include *Jacques Copeau* (Routledge, 2006), *Movement Training for the Modern Actor* (Routledge, 2009), *Making Theatre Work* (PALATINE, 2010) and a chapter on the French ensemble tradition in *Encountering Ensemble* (Methuen, 2013). He has published journal articles on Jacques Lecoq's pedagogy, the politics of movement training, and on somatic practices and movement. He is an Associate Editor of the *Theatre Dance and Performance Training* journal, and was guest editor of the Sports Special Issue (2012). He is currently writing a new book for Palgrave Macmillan entitled *Performance, Movement and the Body* and co-editing *The Routledge Companion to Jacques Lecoq*.

Dick McCaw was co-founder of the Actors Touring Company in 1978, and of the Medieval Players in 1981. Between 1993 and 2001 he was Director of the International Workshop Festival for whom he curated 9 festivals featuring major figures in the performing arts (documentations of some of the workshops can be accessed through the Exeter Digital Archive). Since 2002 he has been an independent researcher and senior lecturer at Royal Holloway, University of London. He has edited two books, *With an Eye for Movement* (on Warren Lamb's development of Rudolph Laban's movement theories) for Brechin Books (2005) and *The Laban Sourcebook* for Routledge (2011) and is now working on a book on Mikhail Bakhtin and Russian Theatre. He is a qualified Feldenkrais practitioner.

Bella Merlin is an internationally acclaimed actor, writer and actor trainer. Her acting appearances include seasons at the Colorado Shakespeare Festival, the National Theatre with Max Stafford-Clark's Out of Joint company, roles in theatre, film and television throughout the UK, and the US premiere of her one-person play, *Tilly No-Body: Catastrophes of Love*. She has written chapters and articles on acting processes, fact-based drama, playing Shakespeare, women/autobiography/performance, and Stanislavsky's final legacy, Active Analysis. She is the author of *The Complete Stanislavsky Toolkit* (Nick Hern Books, 2007), *Acting: The Basics* (Routledge, 2009), *With the Rogue's Company: Henry IV at the National Theatre* (Oberon/National Theatre, 2005), *Konstantin Stanislavsky* (Routledge Performance Practitioners, 2003) and *Beyond Stanislavsky: The Psycho-Physical Approach to Actor Training* (Nick Hern Books, 2001). She co-edited Michael Chekhov's autobiography *The Path of the Actor* with Andrei Kirillov, and is a contributor to the *Cambridge World Encyclopedia of Stage Actors and Acting*. She is Professor of Acting and Directing at the University of California, Riverside, and is currently writing a new book for Nick Hern Books entitled *Facing the Fear: An Actor's Guide to Overcoming Stage Fright*.

Jonathan Pitches is Professor of Theatre and Performance in the School of Performance and Cultural Industries (PCI). He is Leader of the Practitioner Processes Research group in the School and the Faculty Lead for Blended Learning. He has published a number of books on performer training: *Vsevolod Meyerhold* (2003), *Science and the Stanislavsky Tradition of Acting* (2006/9) and, as contributing sole editor, *Russians in Britain* (2012). Other publications include a major co-edited text-book on Performance Studies, *Performance Perspectives: a critical introduction* (Palgrave 2011), combining practitioners' and artists' voices with academic commentary. He specializes in the study of performer training regimes and their transmission across borders and has wider interests in intercultural performance, digital reflection and blended learning, and embodied practices and archival reconstructions. He is co-founder and co-editor of the Routledge journal *Theatre, Dance and Performance Training* and is currently working on two new books: a world-wide analysis of Stanislavsky's impact on training, *Stanislavsky in the World* (with Dr Stefan Aquilina) and a monograph on *Theatre, Performance and Mountains*.

Ian Watson is Professor of Theatre and Chair of the Department of Arts, Culture and Media at Rutgers University, Newark. He is the author of *Towards a Third Theatre: Eugenio Barba and the Odin Teatret* (Routledge, 1995, 1993) and *Negotiating Cultures: Eugenio Barba and the Intercultural Debate* (Manchester University Press, 2002). He edited *Performer Training Across Cultures* (Harwood/Routledge, 2001). He has contributed chapters to over a dozen books, including most recently *Collective Creation in Modern Performance* (Palgrave/Macmillan, 2013), *Im Modus der Gabe: In the Mode of Giving* (Kerber Verlag, 2011), *Twentieth Century Actor Training* (Routledge, 2010), *Scholarly Acts: A Practical Guide to Performance Research* (Palgrave/ Macmillan, 2009), and is a contributor to the *Oxford Encyclopedia of Theatre and Performance*. He has also published numerous articles in professional journals such as *Theatre, Dance and Performer Training; New Theatre Quarterly; About Performance*; and *The Drama Review*.

Introduction

Mark Evans, Coventry University, UK

WHY AN ACTOR TRAINING READER?

A **READER**, by its very nature, can never give more than a snapshot of the practitioners that provide its contents. Furthermore, although the texts are for the most part in the practitioners' own words, they have been chosen by someone else. Thus, they are presented to us partially, at a distance, and from one particular viewpoint. Some may argue that this is a weakness, but it is also a strength. Looking from a distance, we become less aware of the individual and more aware of the crowd. In the same way, this book invites you to pull back from a close-up view of actor training and to consider a wider view.

This book is intended to act amongst other things as a companion volume to Alison Hodge's excellent collection, *Actor Training* (Hodge 2010). *The Actor Training Reader* attempts to gather writings from as many of the practitioners included in Hodge's book as possible, filling out their ideas in their own words. It also provides an opportunity to include extracts by other practitioners for whom Hodge was not able to find space. Most, but not all of these extracts are in the voice of the original practitioner. Sometimes this is because of the difficulty of locating an extract; Joan Littlewood, for instance, wrote very little about her own training practices, however her practice comes through very clearly in the voices of those she worked with. In other instances interviews have better captured the ways in which the practitioner's work relates to the practice of training actors (e.g. Mnouchkine and Feldenkrais). Christoffersen's extract, though not strictly by a practitioner, is included for the clarity of its exposition of Odin Teatret's dramaturgy of the actor. Some of the practitioners included were not directly involved in the training of actors, however all of them have deeply influenced actor training theory and practice. Unfortunately we were not able to include extracts for some of the practitioners featured by Hodge (e.g. Lee Strasberg and Monika Pagneux); either permissions were not available or relevant material simply did not exist. No significance should be placed on the length of the extracts selected – the intention throughout has been to include only so much as captures the key ideas and conveys them convincingly. For some practitioners this is achieved in a few paragraphs, for others more detail is required. Every reader will be able to identify texts they consider should not have been omitted; it will be left to future editors to compile collections that might focus on voice, movement, intercultural training, and training for other performance forms than acting.

This Reader, as with Hodge's book, starts from an acknowledged bias towards Western theatre practice. This is not to deny the importance of global actor training regimes and systems in the twentieth and early twenty-first century[1]; it is simply an acknowledgement of the significant amount of important and influential writing undertaken in the field of Western actor training over the last hundred or so years. Some extracts from non-Western practitioners have been included (such as those by Yoshi Oida and Tadashi Suzuki, both of whom have collaborated with Western practitioners – Oida with Brook and Suzuki with Bogart), and elsewhere, other extracts by or about leading practitioners suggest the influence and impact of non-Western practices (e.g. Ariane Mnouchkine).

A Reader such as this is situated within a wider tradition of edited collections on acting. Just as the radical development of actor training really began in earnest during the first three decades in the twentieth century, so we can map a contemporaneous increase in actor training texts that sought to record and promote the various theories and practices that emerged at this time. Writing about actor training is of course just one form of documentation. This Reader does not attempt to capture non-textual modes of dissemination, but it should be noted that across the last hundred years or so practitioners have increasingly made use of drawings, photographs, diagrams, films, videos, motion capture, digital archiving and audio recordings. Even if this book restricts its remit to the written word, we can still find a fascinating diversity of styles within the texts included: from Stanislavsky's[2] autobiographical accounts in *My Life in Art* and his semi-fictionalized account of his actor training in *The Actor's Work*, to the polemical statements of Brecht; from the poetic incantations of Artaud to the anthropological reflections of Barba.

The emergence of a diversity of approaches to acting at the start of the century created an environment in which each practitioner needed to identify themselves as the sole authority on their own practice in order to maintain their pre-eminence in the field. Nonetheless, the diversity of approaches also meant that there was perceived value in books that collected a range of writings in a convenient fashion for the interested reader. If we review such edited collections, we can perceive how they reveal the interests and fascinations of their time. Cole and Chinoy's comprehensive collection of writings on acting (1970, but first published in 1949) presents a selection from early Greek performance through to American, Russian and European theatre of the 1970s. Their chronological presentation encourages the reader to perceive acting as a practice evolving over time, progressing inevitably towards the present and connected by recurrent themes. Senelick (2008) collects writings on acting from the Theatre Arts Magazine (the earliest from 1916 and the latest from 1963). His extracts offer a snapshot of thinking about acting and actor training over the middle part of the century, including reflections on the British and American traditions, Stanislavsky's legacy and the role of the actor. For a sense of how actor training sits within a wider context, it is worth turning to Drain (1995), Zarrilli (1995), or Brayshaw and Witts (2013). Drain, like Brayshaw and Witts, offers texts that address theatre and performance in general, with some reference to acting and only limited reference to actor training. Zarrilli gathers writings that cover a wide range of approaches to acting, including the non-European, and includes some practitioners' texts as well as several essays with a more critical or academic focus. Finally some other books worth mentioning are Cole (1955), Munk (1967) and Bartow (2006), although all three texts limit their focus to the Stanislavsky tradition of actor training and its development in America. Cole collects a range of texts on Stanislavsky's practices, Munk offers writings that track the development of Stanislavsky's ideas in America into what became known as 'The Method', and Bartow selects essays that outline the American tradition from Strasberg through to Viewpoints[3]. These, though limited in scope, provide further reading around some important areas of practice. What this current volume offers is a continuous focus on actor training across the American, Russian and European traditions. It aims to span the twentieth century and to capture key practice and ideas, wherever possible in the words of the practitioners themselves.

THE STRUCTURE OF THE BOOK

Seeing so many practitioners gathered in this way enables the reader to broaden their perspective and review the relationships between different practitioners and their ideas. To this end, this Reader also includes four essays by leading academics in the field of actor training. Each essay introduces a selection of extracts chosen for their relevance to four central themes: Purpose, Technique, Composition and Character, and Presence.

The section on Purpose opens with an essay by Ian Watson in which he explores the tension between the expansive and the specialized in training, and between serving particular circumstances and serving an ideal. He discusses the notion of the full training cycle, examining the sense in which training can be understood as overlapping components, each of which might come into play at different times and for different purposes. In the essay that introduces the next section, Jonathan Pitches examines how technique might be considered as either 'full' or 'empty' and how such terms relate to notions of external and internal technique and the implied Cartesian dualism[4]. He also considers the ways in which the techniques of the different practitioners might be organized: what connects them, what separates them, and the different forms of transmission that have constructed and continue to construct their histories and their legacies. The focus of Bella Merlin's essay is on the ways that different actor trainers and acting theorists approach the problem of constructing character and the theatrical event. Drawing on her experience as a professional actor as well as an academic, she brings a particular perspective to her essay, sifting the words of the practitioners for their value against the challenges facing the contemporary actor. Finally Dick McCaw considers how different approaches to actor training have attempted to deal with the complex problem of the actor's presence – what is it that makes an actor more or less watchable, and whether/ how it can be taught. McCaw also takes the notions of fullness and emptiness and examines what they might mean in relation to the actor's presence. McCaw's essay continues with a discussion of the importance of playfulness, joy and fun within acting, and the ways in which rhythm becomes a playground for the actor's imagination.

Overall, what comes through strongly in each of the essays is a sense of the commitment, responsibility, social and cultural awareness, depth of understanding and attention, and also the attunement to others that is required in order to be an actor. At the same time the essays give an idea of the arc of training across an actor's development, of the inter-relationships and differences between regimes, and of the historical and socio-cultural contexts that give each training method meaning.

The four sections and the essays that accompany them aim to make interesting and provocative reading. Whether teacher or student, actor or audience, the reader might also consider creating their own journey through the extracts, relevant to their own experiences and interests, and composing their own essay to justify their choice. One might for instance consider any of the following general themes: politics and actor training; intercultural actor training; gender and actor training (how many extracts are by or about women practitioners, and what does that reveal?); the role of the body and/or the voice in actor training; the tension between professionalism and innovation; historical or genealogical connections; different styles of teaching and transmission; continental and sub-continental connections and differences across Europe, America, Russia and Asia; and, different approaches to writing about actor training. A few of these will be touched on below.

This Reader is intended for a varied audience – you may be a student, a teacher, a trainer, an actor, a researcher, a director, or just someone interested in theatre and the art of the actor. You will have your own idea of what you want to get from this book, of the key issues, problems and challenges facing actor training. Each of the essay authors has provided, at the end of their essay, a list of provocations intended to invite you to frame your own response in whatever form best suits you – essay, statement, perform- ance, blog or tweet. Teachers might use these as the starting point for essay questions for their students, or as the stimulus for a practical exploration in class. Students might use them to pin down what it is they themselves are struggling with in their own learning about acting. For the reader with a general interest in acting the questions might take them on to other texts and different books on actors and acting. The provoca- tions, often framed as questions, are an invitation to begin on your own unique journey. To assist this process, profiles of each practitioner are appended at the end of relevant chapters. The profiles also list suggested additional writing by the practitioner, followed by a short list of key critical writing on their work.

What follows is an overview of the development of actor training during the twentieth century viewed in the light of a number of additional themes.

HISTORY AND ACTOR TRAINING

At the end of the nineteenth century, actor training across Europe was largely a matter of apprenticeship, family tradition and learning on the job. A few private schools existed, along with a limited number of national conservatoires, all of which tended to teach students how to replicate conventional interpretations of canonical plays, alongside basic principles of elocution, deportment, social dance and stage combat. The private schools were often family businesses, run by former actors or actresses, as indeed were many of the companies that those leaving the Schools joined.

Early innovations in the first decades of the twentieth century need to be viewed in the light of the immense social upheaval caused by events such as the First World War and the Russian Revolution. These events generated vigorous artistic responses, and galvanized a generation of theatre makers into a rejection of what had gone before and a desire to re-examine the fundamental principles of their practice. At the same time, advances in the scientific understanding of the body, of the mind and emotions, of movement and efficiency, inevitably influenced thinking about the kind of skills required to act and to perform, and how they should be taught. For most of the nineteenth century, the actor had been seen as a figure of moderately low social standing, at best an artisan at worst an amoral vagabond or glorified prostitute. The drive by the acting

profession to achieve a respectable professional status required the creation of systematic regimes of professional training and of a sense of the social and moral purpose of
theatre and acting. The writings of Stanislavsky need to be seen in this light. The work
of Strasberg, Chekhov and Vakhtangov picks up on this journey, building a coherent
argument for the actor's artistry and integrity. As the century progressed, new ideas for
the nature and purpose of theatre emerged out of a desire to move beyond rejuvenating
the old theatre and towards creating a new one. Copeau, Meyerhold, Artaud and Brecht
all seek to describe a vision of how theatre can build from its historical roots towards
new forms better fitted for the opportunities and trials of modern society. During the
1920s and the 1930s there was a strong movement towards collaboration and many of
the leading practitioners met during this period and planned for international collaboration. After the Second World War, the Cold War meant that differences between
Russian and American interpretations of Stanislavsky's work became increasingly
polarized and Western understanding of the work of some Russian practitioners (such
as Meyerhold) was very limited. In Communist Poland, Grotowski's work in the 1960s
can be seen as a rigorous extension of Stanislavsky's system into an intense and physical expression of the actor's conception of their role. In America, Stella Adler and
Sanford Meisner continued the work on psychological realism that had begun with the
Group Theatre. Post World War Two, influences from Asia began to have more and
more impact, both in America and Europe – evidenced in the work of Suzuki, Oida and
Mnouchkine. At the same time, conceptions of the embodied nature of human existence
became increasingly influential. Consider, for instance, the work of Laban and
Feldenkrais, both of whom have deeply effected the ways that actors' bodies are trained
for performance. The various historical lines of connection had, by the end of the
century, become diverse, distinct and multiple; their influence increasingly overlapping
and responding to local social, cultural and political agendas and needs. Although the
work of Boal, Gardzienice and Littlewood has been put to use in different ways in many
different places, there is still a strong sense in which we understand their work as
rooted in the conditions of its origins – and none the less important for that. Likewise
the actor's understanding of their training as preparation for a social and political role
as much as a professional one has varied according to their understanding of their
historical and economic context.

The extracts in this book are not presented chronologically, nor do they directly
address historical themes, but they should not be seen as ahistorical. A challenge for
the reader might be to consider which non-theatrical texts one might place alongside
each extract in this book in order to best represent its social, cultural and political
context. Where might one include William James on psychology[5], or Frederick
Winslow Taylor on efficiency[6]? What examples of popular culture might one include?
What works on education, on science, on women's history, or on the migration of
cultural practice? For further information on the social, scientific, political and
cultural history of acting and actor training, consult Evans (2009), Pitches (2009),
Roach (1993) and Sanderson (1984).

THE BODY

> The essential thing is that everything must come from and through the
> body. First and foremost, there must be a physical reaction to everything
> that affects us.
>
> (Grotowski 1969: 204)

Even on an initial or cursory reading of the extracts, it is clear that one significant feature of actor training in the twentieth century is the emphasis on the actor's physical training, on the relationship between the body[7] and the process of acting. As Michel Saint-Denis puts it, for the twentieth century actor, 'Acting is Action' (Saint-Denis 1982: 149). Throughout the twentieth century practitioners struggled with the desire to find a 'meeting point between the internal and the external' something that is viewed as 'one of the essential secrets of acting' (Saint-Denis 1982: 175). As concepts of the relationship between the mind and the body evolved over the century, and as practitioners became increasingly suspicious of dualistic approaches to understanding the human subject, there is a growing sense among several key actor trainers (for example Stanislavsky and Meyerhold) that, in Saint-Denis' words, 'If one does not feel anything, it often helps to *do* something concrete, something physical; then the feeling comes' (Saint-Denis 1982: 175). Perhaps this changing emphasis also relates to the development of new spaces for performance – spaces that gave greater emphasis to movement and to the expressive plasticity of the actor's body[8].

Voice, which had traditionally been prioritized as a separate and dominant discipline and as a discipline closely associated with text, found itself more and more strongly associated with movement, the body and somatic practice. This change is poetically encapsulated by Artaud's announcement that, 'an actor delves down into his personality by the whetted edge of his breathing' (Artaud 1970: 91), a statement that announces the voice as intimately linked with the actor's sense of self and their physical presence. By the 1960s, influential trainers such as Kristin Linklater (voice) and Patricia Arnold (movement) at London Academy of Music and Drama (LAMDA) were exploring how movement and voice could work together. Michel Saint-Denis, whose ideas were hugely influential in the development of several leading international acting conservatoires, declared not long after, that:

> It is an accepted idea that speech is the beginning, that it is, in fact, the everything of acting, the only way to convey meaning, emotion and character. This is to ignore completely the richness of the body's physical expression and the fact that this physical expression can often convey much more than speech.
>
> (Saint-Denis 1982: 146)

The body both energizes and regulates the actor's emotions, rather than the other way round. Indeed, for Ruth Zaporah, emotions are not simply psychological, but 'are configurations of energy brought on by a certain environment. [. . .] We are not them nor they us' (Zaporah 1995: 142). The increasingly holistic understanding of the nature of acting that emerged over the twentieth century can also be examined for its historical relationship to the politics of the body, a key legacy of post-Second World War feminism. If a stronger sense of our embodiment has professional benefits as well as political significance, to what extent are these effects contradictory or in tension with each other?

AVAILABILITY AND IMMEDIACY

The emphasis on the body effectively created the need for the twentieth century student actor to be 'in a state of constant physical *availability* from which he [sic] can spring into action at any moment' (Saint-Denis 1982: 151). This heightened state of readiness and engagement mirrors the cultural and industrial imperatives of the twentieth century – the increasing pace of change and the requirement for efficiency and flexibility as the cornerstones of modern professionalism. Readiness implies an immediacy, a determination for a reality that is rooted in the here and now. As Grotowski (1969: 212) declares, for the twentieth century actor theatre is an encounter, a point at which the actor is challenged to enter into a profound and direct communication with themselves and with the audience. Many of the practitioners included in this Reader sought or continue to seek answers as to how the actor can achieve such relationships, especially given the industrial contexts within which they work and the commercial nature of so many professional theatre events. In so far as these authors seek to change theatre through their practice and what they offer the student actor, they demand full engagement: 'If you start on something, you must be fully engaged in it [. . .] it is better not to think but to act, to take risks' (Grotowski 1969: 204).

In order to achieve the physical engagement and immediacy that these kinds of changes necessitate, a new approach to the work of the actor is required. Improvisation develops the ability of the actor to be 'in the moment' within performance and to respond with great flexibility to a variety of contexts; it also refines their sensitivity to the other actors, to the characters and narrative drive of the situation, and to the stage environment (set, costumes and lighting). It takes them into the psychological condition of the character, where, 'You can see where you've been, but you can't see where you're going' (Zaporah 1995: 54). Although improvisation had, of course, been part of the actor's repertoire over the centuries, before the twentieth century it had not been systematized as part of a method of training, a way of making theatre, and even in some instances an approach to living.

At the start of the century, actor trainers developed sets of principles and techniques for improvisation. In some instances, students were even required to wear particular types of clothing for these sessions: 'For classes in Improvisation the student is clothed as in movement class: the legs, shoulders, arms and neck as bare as possible' (Saint-Denis 1982: 150), thus making the systematization visible and formally acknowledged, and also removing the student even further from the conditions of their typical future employment. In this sense, flexibility, availability and improvisation all relate to a notion of neutrality, of the actor/student as a *tabula rasa*, upon which the playwright, teacher or director will inscribe meaning. Can you read within the extracts where a practitioner is exhorting the student/actor to erase his or herself within a role and where the student/actor is invited to resist such implied instrumentalism?

SYSTEMS, METHODS AND MANIFESTOS

The twentieth century was in many senses a century of methods and manifestos. Practitioners became increasingly concerned with the problem of constructing a reliable and repeatable system for actor training – a system that enables the student/ actor to nourish their spontaneity, playfulness and flexibility and to increase their awareness of the principles underlying the practice. However, for some practitioners these projects were misleading, misplaced and impossible to achieve. Typically they believed that acting simply could not be taught systematically. Edward Gordon Craig, for instance, stated that:

These systems and their misleading textbooks are drawn up to rid the
actor of 'artificiality' (something so akin to art that to destroy it is very
dangerous) and to create in him that feeling which a born-actor is never
without, and which cannot be pumped into anyone.

(Craig in Walton 1983: 90)

For Craig, 'None but born actors should be trained to act' (Craig in Walton 1983: 89).
Although an old idea, there are echoes of this attitude throughout the century. Even a
theatre radical such as Joseph Chaikin stated that, 'There is no way to develop talent,
only to invite it to be released' (1991: 154). However, many would argue that systems
of training can nurture, direct and support talent, even if they cannot create it.

In defence of a systematic approach, Stanislavsky declares that:

Inner creative work demands even greater order, organization and discipline. The mind is subtle, complex and extremely delicate. We must work
in strict obedience to the laws of the human mind.

(2008: 554)

Michael Chekhov, in his advice to the professional actor, asserts that, '*every* art, even
the actor's, must have its principles and aspirations, and its professional techniques'
(2002: 154). For him, 'The art of acting can grow and develop only if it is based
upon an *objective* method with fundamental principles' (2002: 155). Chekhov goes
on to suggest that this discipline eventually becomes synonymous with a way of
thinking: 'The method, when understood and applied, will inculcate in the actor a
most gratifying habit of professional *thinking*, whether he is evaluating the creative
work of his colleagues or his own' (Chekhov 2002: 157). The heart of such a system
then is the discipline and coherence it requires in its execution; as Stanislavsky
puts it, 'If there were no Throughaction, all the Bits and Tasks in the play, all
the Given Circumstances, communication, Adaptions, moments of truth and belief,
etc. would vegetate separately from one another, with no hope of coming alive'
(2008: 312).

Some systems and methods of actor training are about making conventional
theatre practices more effective, despite the skepticism implicit in Craig's pronounce-
ment; others aim to train a new kind of actor for a new kind of theatre. For Meyerhold,
for instance:

an acting school must exist *independently* and must not teach the current
style of acting. It must be organized so that a new theatre arises out of it,
so that there is only one possible path leading from it: if the pupils do not
go into the new theatre which they have created for themselves, they go
nowhere.

(Meyerhold in Braun 1969: 46)

The desire to change, to revolutionize, and to reject what had gone before, was part
of a wider modernist project, linked back to the Enlightenment and its themes
of change, progress and systematic improvement. The continuing radical, liberal
spirit of the Enlightenment is evidenced in Keith Johnstone's belief that: 'if we [do]
the opposite of what our own teachers did we'd be on the right track' (1981: 105).
The desire to innovate however creates a tension between what we understand by
education and by training. Many students have sought and continue to seek training

as an actor in order simply to become employable within the wider theatre and performance industry. In this context they are understandably content to follow closely the instructions of a trainer and to adhere to industry expectations. Other students take the risk of opting for a training, or perhaps rather an education, that does not claim to prepare them for the industry as it currently exists. Where would you position your own experience and ambitions? Remember of course, that most of those included in this collection, including those whose ideas and practices are now considered canonical, achieved their success and status precisely because they rejected convention and set out to create what, at that time, amounted to a new form of theatre and performance.

By the start of the twenty-first century, theories (both radical and conventional) have multiplied to the point where it seems difficult to conceive of new approaches to actor training, or to know which practices to follow. A book such as this one marks the very moment towards which Ariane Mnouchkine seems to be indicating when she suggests that everything important has already been worked out:

> you do not invent theories of acting anymore. The problem is that theories exist but they have been buried at the same rate as they have been pronounced. Let the young students read Zeami, Artaud, Copeau, Dullin, Jouvet, also Brecht . . . Everything is there. And let them do theatre. We do not need to say more.
>
> (Mnouchkine in Féral 1989: 97)

It is hard for the student actor to know what methods to study, what theories to adhere to; each vociferously stakes its claims to coherence, distinctiveness and exclusivity, and yet the student is aware of the contingent nature of any one approach. Is the only solution, as Jonathan Pitches suggests in his essay, to 'pick and mix' from the methods and systems available, constructing a hybrid approach that responds to the needs of the individual? If so, on what basis does the student make their choice? And how is the student to foresee which approach will bring them whatever personal, social or professional success they might dream of? The geographical and cultural boundaries that made transmission of methods harder in the past have been eroded by modern technologies so that the student may feel increasingly able to select, mix and mingle approaches according to need, to context, or to predilection. In such a scenario, the role of the teacher changes from the instructor to the guide, who, 'looks for the right steps for each student, and when the student is about to make his discovery, [disappears]' (Chaikin 1991: 154). The student becomes an autodidact. The reader might consider: how and to what extent might a book such as this function as a handbook for the student/actor to create his or her own method of acting? What is the effect of adopting someone else's system rather than creating one's own?

POLITICS OF SEEING AND DOING

At the heart of each method, and therefore often embedded in its conception, is a new way of seeing the world, a new way of understanding how and why people behave in the way that they do. Each generation seeks to clear away the preconceptions that have accumulated in the act of observing the world. Dario Fo exhorts the actor that, 'It is important to begin from reality and not from the conventions of reality'

(Fo 1991: 144); even though Fo accepts that a completely objective position is not possible, he still knows the importance of striving to see with fresh eyes. Many of the practitioners included in this book emphasize the importance of training the actor to look anew at the world they live in and at the theatre practice that surrounds them. Of course, looking without purpose is not seeing: for Brecht this distinction is paramount, and hence, for him:

> Observation is a major part of acting. The actor observes his fellow-men (*sic*) with all his nerves and muscles in an act of imitation which is at the same time a process of the mind. For pure imitation would only bring out what had been observed; and that is not enough, because the original says what it has to say with too subdued a voice. To achieve a character rather than a caricature, the actor looks at people as though they were playing him their actions, in other words as though they were advising him to give their actions careful consideration.
>
> (Brecht in Willetts 1978: 196)

For Brecht, acting is about demonstrating a knowledge 'of human relations, of human behaviour, of human capacities' (Brecht in Willetts 1978: 26). And in that context, training then becomes about more than technique, it must also be about historical, social and political knowledge and understanding. The purpose of technique is to reveal the outcome of observation and experience. The challenge for the actor is to resist the desire to please the audience and to focus instead on how to show them the world in ways they have not experienced before.

The student actor learns to refine their awareness, seeking not only to recognize forms of human behaviour but also to investigate and reveal their social, historical and political significance. For Dario Fo, this means understanding that 'the style of gesture of every people derives from its relationship with the need to survive' (1991: 29), so that the very ways that gesture is used reflect the social, historical and cultural conditions of the person doing the gesturing. At the same time, as an embodied art form, the student actor also learns that observing is an embodied process that situates the actor in a particular relation to their own body, to other bodies and to those bodies' modes of engagement with the world.

The constant renewal of actor training practice requires that we repeatedly look again at the world from new and different perspectives that are better attuned to the challenges of the world we live in. Consider whose perspectives might be missing from the extracts in this book – does it matter, for instance, that most extracts are written by or about white, able-bodied, middle-aged, men? In what ways does the actual style of writing for each extract, as much as the content, reveal a different way of understanding the world? How do these extracts reflect the politics of actor training – who has access, where does power lie in the classroom, what ideological assumptions are implicit in the training?

TEAMWORK, DISCIPLINE AND PLEASURE

> Every member of the team must feel that he is a "cog" in a large, complex machine, and be clearly aware of the danger to the whole show if he doesn't do what he should, or if he departs from established procedure.
>
> (Stanislavski 2008: 554)

Regardless of the intended purpose of the training, all the practitioners included in this Reader stress the importance of teamwork, responsibility and discipline. For many of them, their training practice came out of the context of ensemble work in the making of theatre performance[9]. In this context, the process of making a performance is not simply a physical discipline, nor just a mental one; it is a social and political activity.

If the internal rigour of a system is about justifying one's actions and words on stage, then the external rigour is about a professional attitude and a responsible approach to working with others. It is a sense of this external discipline that informs Stanislavsky's famous declaration that, 'there are no small roles, only small actors' (2008: 573), and his assertion that, 'People who love themselves in art, not the art in themselves, should [. . .] be fired' (2008: 573). Aside from rejecting egotistical acting, such an attitude is also about achieving a form of authenticity in performance, 'it is valuable to learn how to analyse, constantly, with rigour and imagination, the situations and impact of every performance. It is essential to stop actors from merely repeating the lines or gestures they have acquired' (Fo 1991: 60).

Despite training being so strongly associated with the acquisition and refinement of technique, it is also true for many practitioners that acting can and should be energizing, joyous, and fulfilling. Training can sometimes seem to be drudgery, leading the student either nowhere or backwards, as they feel themselves getting worse before they get better. It can also be psychologically testing; becoming aware of one's own personal traits as a performer, learning to unmake and remake oneself around fictional identities sometimes quite alien to one's own, can be an emotionally challenging process. However, Michael Chekhov reminds us that alongside the struggle and turmoil, 'acting should be a joyous art and never enforced labor' (2002: 153). Despite the fact that getting up on stage for many people would be immensely stressful, actors find ways of dealing with that stress and training can even enable and allow them to find enjoyment in the activity of acting. Acting may in this sense be as joyous as bungee jumping – terrifying to consider, but exhilarating once you commit to it and safe once you understand what you need to do and how your training supports you.

For Kristin Linklater, the presence of the actor and the joy and excitement of full engagement in the theatrical process is part of what sets theatre apart from other entertainment media:

> Today's actors, if they are to compete for audiences with the technological powers of film, electronically souped-up music and television, must generate within themselves an electric presence that transcends technological excitement.
>
> (Linklater 1976: 210)

Ultimately, and not despite of but in addition to rigour and discipline, we perhaps have to recognize that pleasure and enjoyment has its own valuable effect on the actor's training and on their technique and performance:

> I decided I wouldn't think about whether I was good or bad, I would simply try to enjoy myself on stage. Every day, in a sense egotistically, I tried to find the pleasure in my performance. And people suddenly said that I was much better than before.
>
> (Oida 1997: 121)

So, those of us interested in actor training might want to ask: What value does pleasure in acting and actor training have? Can pleasure and discipline go hand in hand, or is part of actor training learning to deal with difficulty, setback and even failure?

NEW DEVELOPMENTS – WHERE NEXT?

As the novelist William Gibson reputedly once remarked, 'the future is already here – it's just not very evenly distributed'[10]. Somewhere out there are the practitioners of the future, those whose words may fill a future volume such as this. If we could guess at what those words might be about, at what themes they would cover, what would we suggest? Here are some ideas; you might consider what texts might fill out such a selection of topics, or you might want to play with some ideas of your own:

- Training for performance within digital environments – film, television and online.
- The impact of neuroscience on actor training.
- Training for immersive and interdisciplinary theatre performance.
- The impact of non-traditional training practices – for example parkour, Gabrielle Roth's Five Rhythms, Tanya Gerstle's Pulse, capoeira, and circus skills.
- Training for acting in applied contexts (within the community, in commercial contexts, as part of therapeutic practice).
- Training and cultural crossover – transgendered performance, acting and disability, ethnic casting policies and actor training.
- Training and inter-culturalism – how to recognize the increasing cultural diversity of performers, theatre makers and audiences.
- Training and globalization – how to train for a global performance economy and in response to global challenges to the nature of theatre and performance.

Notes

1 Key examples of this influence include: the Beijing Opera artist Mei Lanfang and Bertolt Brecht (Brecht in Willetts 1978: 91–99); the impact of Yoga on the work of Grotowski (Kapsali 2010); Balinese theatre practice and Antonin Artaud (Artaud 1970: 36–49); and, the relationship between African and Asian theatre and the work of Peter Brook (Williams 1988).
2 There are various spellings of his name (Constantin or Konstantin; Stanislavski or Stanislavsky), all used by a variety of different authors. For this essay, I am using the spelling that is currently the most accepted version. Where texts are cited I have however retained the spelling used in that text for ease of reference, even if it differs from the spelling adopted in this introduction.
3 Viewpoints is a compositional technique for movement and gesture first developed by choreographer Mary Overlie and adapted for use in the theatre by Anne Bogart and Tina Landau.
4 The idea put forward by the French philosopher René Descartes (1596–1650), that there is a separation between mind and body, which in his view are not and cannot be viewed as identical.
5 See James (1890).

6   See Taylor (1911).
7   The term body is used in a general sense here, and in relation to actor training it is intended to include voice and movement.
8   For example, Copeau's Théâtre du Vieux-Colombier in Paris and Meyerhold's constructivist sets for productions such as *The Magnanimous Cuckold*.
9   For a detailed discussion of ensemble theatre making see Britton (2013).
10   *The Economist*, 11 October 2001.

Bibliography

Artaud, A. (1970) *The Theatre and its Double*, London: Calder and Boyars.
Bartow, A. (ed.) (2006) *Training of the American Actor*, New York: Theatre Communications Group.
Braun, E. (ed.) (1969) *Meyerhold on Theatre*, London: Methuen.
Brayshaw, T. and Witts, N. (eds) (2013) *The Twentieth Century Performance Reader*, London & New York: Routledge.
Britton, J. (ed.) (2013) *Encountering Ensemble*, London: Bloomsbury/Methuen.
Chaikin, J. (1991) *The Presence of the Actor*, New York: Theatre Communications Group.
Chekhov, M. (2002) *To the Actor*, London & New York: Routledge.
Cole, T. (ed.) (1955) *Acting: A Handbook of the Stanislavski Method*, New York: Crown Publishers.
Cole, T. and Chinoy, H. K. (eds) (1970) *Actors on Acting: The Theories, Techniques, and Practices of the World's Great Actors, Told in Their Own Words*, New York: Three Rivers Press.
Drain, R. (ed.) (1995) *Twentieth Century Theatre: A Sourcebook*, London & New York: Routledge.
Evans, M. (2009) *Movement Training for the Modern Actor*, London & New York: Routledge.
Féral, J. (1989) 'Building Up The Muscle: An Interview with Ariane Mnouchkine', *Tulane Drama Review*, Vol. 33. No. 4, pp. 88–97.
Fo, D. (1991) *The Tricks of the Trade*, London: Methuen.
Grotowski, J. (1969) *Towards a Poor Theatre*, London: Methuen.
Hodge, A. (ed.) (2010) *Actor Training*, 2nd edition, London & New York: Routledge.
James, W. (1890) *The Principles of Psychology, Vols. 1 and 2.*, New York: Dover Publications.
Johnstone, K. (1981) *Impro: Improvisation and the Theatre*, London: Methuen.
Kapsali, M. (2010) '"I don't attack it but it's not for actors": the use of yoga by Jerzy Grotowski', *Theatre, Dance and Performance Training Journal* Vol. 1, Issue 2, pp. 185–198.
Linklater, K. (1976) *Freeing the Natural Voice*, New York & Hollywood: Drama Publishers.
McCaw, D. (ed.) (2011) *The Laban Sourcebook*, London & New York: Routledge.
Munk, E. (ed.) (1967) *Stanislavski and America: "The Method" and Its Influence on the American Theatre*, Greenwich, Conn.: Fawcett Premier.
Oida, Y. (1997) *The Invisible Actor*, London: Methuen.
Pitches, J. (2009) *Science and the Stanislavsky Tradition of Acting*, London & New York: Routledge.
Roach, J. (1993) *The Player's Passion: Studies in the Science of Acting*, Ann Arbor, Mich.: University of Michigan Press.
Saint-Denis, M. (1982) *Training for the Theatre: Premises and Promises*, New York: Theatre Arts Books.
Sanderson, M. (1984) *From Irving to Olivier: A Social History of the Acting Profession*, Basingstoke: Palgrave Macmillan.
Senelick, L. (ed.) (2008) *Theatre Arts on Acting*, London & New York: Routledge.
Stanislavski, C. (1980) *My Life in Art*, London: Eyre Methuen.
Stanislavski, K. (2008) *An Actor's Work*, London & New York: Routledge.
Taylor, F. W. (1911) *The Principles of Scientific Management*, London & New York: Harper and Brothers.
Walton, J. Michael (1983) *Craig on Theatre*, London: Methuen.

Willetts, J. (ed.) (1978) *Brecht on Theatre: The Development of an Aesthetic*, London: Methuen.

Williams, D. (ed.) (1988) *Peter Brook: A Theatrical Casebook*, London: Methuen.

Zaporah, R. (1995) *Action Theater: The Improvisation of Presence*, Berkeley, Ca.: North Atlantic Books.

Zarrilli, P. (ed.) (1995) *Acting (Re)Considered: Theories and Practices*, London & New York: Routledge.

PART I

Prologue

Chapter 1

Jacques Copeau

AN APPEAL TO THE YOUNG

FINAL ADVICE TO THE YOUNG

YOU ARE ADDRESSED ON all sides; you are beseeched, flattered, solicited, bribed, molested and exhorted, perhaps more than you are guided.

I see many of you suffering from not knowing where to begin, how to find a balance, or what way to start working. Students complain that they receive only vague instructions and lack the basics. And their teachers, their elders and their leaders are sorry to find only an inconsistent clay to mould, minds which are not sufficiently docile.

How I should like to help you! How I should like to find the words to answer your questions, to enlighten your minds and to warm your hearts!

I think you are placed between two dangers: the one of blindly and radically repudiating what was said and done before you, and the other of awaiting future salvation from some other effort than the one you will be able to make on your own. Contempt and disgust for old disciplines is no less perilous than hesitation and laziness in forming new ones.

I am neither a sociologist nor a qualified moralist. I am only a sincere worker, a friendly adviser who does not claim to give advice except from his own personal experience. For this reason, I can tell you two things. The first is that no great change is valid, no great renewal is durable, until it is linked to a living tradition, a profound native spirit.

The second is that, in order to bear fruit that is neither artificial nor ephemeral, a renewal of this kind must begin with the human being. Without falling back, without egoism, with as much modesty as ardour, it is primarily with yourselves that you should begin, with lucidity, simplicity, seriousness, application and courage. Try to be men, whatever your desires and aspirations, the career you choose to follow, or the technique you intend to master. Do not let yourselves get dried up, nor debauched, but apply yourselves with a will to making a beautiful, solid, happy, courageous and adaptable human harmony prevail in your character. You see, my friends, it is especially and uniquely important, in the midst of such confusion, to sign a pact with your soul, and to hold firmly to it. Do not smile too much at the gravity of my words. Everything today is of an exceptional and implacable gravity. You have no choice. Each one of you must, in your secret soul, be a hero. . . and a saint for yourself.

You are probably saying that this takes us a long way from theatre and devotion to theatre. Far from theatre perhaps, but not from the devotion I think is needed, and will be for a long time yet, if we intend to make a new spirit prevail. My language has hardly changed in thirty-one years, and has often been ridiculed. Indeed, I have been able to observe too often that theatrical mores have not changed very much. Even today I see theatre threatened by the same evils, the same abuses and the same treacheries it suffered from when I declared war on them a quarter of a century ago. We still find arrogant stars, sordid intrigues and base literature in the theatre, and I am afraid there always will be. Thus, it is another reason for increasing the numbers of its defenders and for closing ranks; another reason for trying to purify it, even if, and especially if, we do not flatter ourselves that we completely succeed.

Let us make an effort to acquire the craft and not let ourselves be devoured by it. Actors, authors, critics, public: let us prepare a phalanx of energetic theatre people with a healthy and elevated taste, full of fervour, gaiety and severity. [. . .]

Therefore, respect for work, assiduousness and diligence, punctuality at rehearsals, attention to minute details in preparation; in short, respect for the public for whom the work is being done. Faith in art, in work, in the public, and, above all, faith in the young.

[From 'Dévotion à l'Art Dramatique', lecture at the Théâtre Récamier, Paris, 16 May 1944, published in *Registres I*, pp. 108–10]

JACQUES COPEAU (1879–1949)

Copeau was a French theatre director and pedagogue. He founded the Théâtre du Vieux-Colombier in Paris in 1913, later creating an innovative theatre school alongside the company. In 1924 he disbanded the company and retreated to Burgundy with a troupe of colleagues and students (Les Copiaus) where he experimented in devised, improvised and community theatre. His work strongly influenced the development of actor training, ensemble theatre and mime during the twentieth century.

See also: **Jacques Lecoq, Philippe Gaulier, Ariane Mnouchkine.**

SUGGESTED FURTHER READING

Rudlin, J. and Paul, N. (eds.) (1990) *Copeau: Texts on Theatre*, London & New York: Routledge.

Evans, M. (2006) *Jacques Copeau*, London & New York: Routledge.
Rudlin, J. (1986) *Jacques Copeau*, Cambridge: Cambridge University Press.
Rudlin, J. (2010) 'Jacques Copeau: The quest for sincerity', in Hodge, A. (ed.) (2010) *Actor Training*, London & New York: Routledge.

Konstantin Stanislavsky

THE BEGINNINGS OF MY SYSTEM

DURING ONE PERFORMANCE IN which I was repeating a rôle I had played many times, suddenly, without any apparent cause, I perceived the inner meaning of the truth long known to me that creativeness on the stage demands first of all a special condition, which, for want of a better term, I will call the creative mood. Of course I knew this before, but only intellectually. From that evening on this simple truth entered into all my being, and I grew to perceive it not only with my soul, but with my body also. For an actor, to perceive is to feel. For this reason I can say that it was on that evening that I "first perceived a truth long known to me". I understood that to the genius on the stage this condition almost always comes of itself, in all its fullness and richness. Less talented people receive it less often, on Sundays only, so to say. Those who are even less talented receive it even less often, every twelfth holiday, as it were. Mediocrities are visited by it only on very rare occasions, on leap years, on the twenty-ninth of February. Nevertheless, all men of the stage, from the genius to the mediocrity, are able to receive the creative mood, but it is not given them to control it with their own will. They receive it together with inspiration in the form of a heavenly gift.

Not pretending at all to be a god and to hand out heavenly gifts, I nevertheless put the following question to myself:

"Are there no technical means for the creation of the creative mood, so that inspiration may appear oftener than is its wont?" This does not mean that I was going to create inspiration by artificial means. That would be impossible. What I wanted to learn was how to create a favorable condition for the appearance of inspiration by means of the will, that condition in the presence of which inspiration was most likely to descend into the actor's soul. As I learned afterward, this creative mood is that spiritual and physical mood during which it is easiest for inspiration to be born.

KONSTANTIN STANISLAVSKI (1863–1938)

Stanislavski's involvement in theatre began in his family's amateur dramatic circle. In 1881 he went to Moscow to study acting and over the next decade became increasingly curious about the nature of great acting. Influenced by developments in naturalistic theatre production, he eventually realized the need to devise a system through which the actor could achieve a consistent level of truth and believability in performance. He co-founded the Moscow Art Theatre in 1898, producing memorable productions of the plays of Anton Chekhov. His ideas on acting have been published widely and have been hugely influential.

See also: **Vsevolod Meyerhold, Yevgeny Vakhtangov, Michael Chekhov, Jerzy Grotowski.**

SUGGESTED FURTHER READING

Stanislavski, K. (2009) *An Actor's Work,* trans. J. Benedetti, London & New York: Routledge.
Stanislavski, K. (2009) *An Actor's Work on a Role,* trans. J. Benedetti, London & New York: Routledge.

Carnicke, S. (2008) *Stanislavsky in Focus,* London & New York: Routledge.
Carnicke, S. (2010) 'Stanislavsky's System: Pathways for the actor', in Hodge, A. (2010) *Actor Training,* London & New York: Routledge.
Merlin, B. (2003) *Konstantin Stanislavsky,* London & New York: Routledge.

PART II

Purpose

Introduction to Part II: The Purpose of Actor Training

Ian Watson, Rutgers University, USA

WHY DO ACTORS TRAIN? Or, put another way that is more in keeping with this section of extracts, what is the purpose of actor training?

If one accepts the Oxford English Dictionary (OED) definition of purpose, which is, "the reason for which something is done," the answer would appear to be simple.

The purpose of training is to learn a set of skills (i.e., a technique) that the actor can apply in both preparing a production and performing it for an audience.

But simplicity avoids the distraction of considered scrutiny.

Even attempts to get at the core of training and/or technique for the actor in a few words by some of those who have devoted a large portion of their professional lives to mastering, applying, and in most cases teaching a technique they have developed to others suggests something more is at play. Joe Chaikin, for example, defines technique as "a means to free the artist," (1984: 5) while the Atlantic Theatre School views the purpose of training as a means of finding "a way to live truthfully under the imaginary circumstances of the play" (1986: 5); for Vazkressia Vicharova, "training . . . is about being ready for the moment of transformation" (2012: 396), but for Jerzy Grotowski it is to realize what he termed "the holy actor" (1968: 33–39); while for the great master, Konstantin Stanislavski, technique is a means of retaining a "creative state of mind" during performance (1967: 426).

As open to interpretation as these thumbnail sketches of training are, the differences each from the others hint at a more nuanced relationship between training and purpose than suggested by the simplistic definition above. A hint confirmed by a little further examination.

For example, is the purpose of training at Eugenio Barba's Odin Teatret in rural western Denmark the same as that of the training one receives at the Stella Adler Studio in New York? Is the purpose of a Boal-based training the same as that at the École Internationale de Théâtre Jacques Lecoq?

The fact is that the notion of shared purpose in training lies in generalities, in remaining with the largest of subset categories: theatre and training. The devil, however, is in the details. As soon as one moves from theatre to ask, "What type of theatre?" purpose spawns cousins. Even a casual acquaintance with Barba, Adler,

Augusto Boal and Lecoq reveals difference, a difference bound up with the unique theatrical vision of each of these masters.

The training developed by all four of them focuses on the performer's expressive instrument (embodiment, voice, links between interiority and expression, intention, action etc.), but they do so in very different ways. Barba's training is shaped largely by two factors: the tension between the actors' need to create the raw material of a production through a lengthy rehearsal process and a performance aesthetic that emphasizes a somatic rather than semantic relationship with the audience, and a process that is unconcerned with the psychology of character or preparing an actor to transform a play script into a mise-en-scène; alternatively, the psychology of character and the semantic is the very genesis of an Adler training, which is predicated upon developing an actor's ability to transform a writer's words into living matter; for Boal, training is rooted in his notion of theatre as a tool of social justice in which interactive and participatory techniques examine forms of social oppression and offer alternative strategies to generate change; meanwhile, a Lecoq training is largely movement-based with an emphasis on mime, clowning, interactive improvisation and an emphasis on each performer developing his own creativity rather than on a prescribed method or system that is passed on from teacher to pupil.[1]

The connections between a particular training regimen and purpose are largely shaped by function and the efficacious because training is a utilitarian enterprise directed at providing the actor with the means to create and perform; if it does not, she may well abandon it for failing the litmus test of efficacy.

Implicit in this relationship between the utilitarian and efficacy is that no single training method is encyclopedic. Of course training systems may be adapted to a range of performance genres and visions of what theatre should be – many large professional acting schools are predicated upon this premise; but no single training is necessarily the best preparation for all possible types of theatre. Chaikin and his colleagues who formed the Open Theatre in New York in the early 1960s, for example, developed a form of training in order to explore the non-realistic theatre that interested them because they regarded the realism-oriented training that dominated American theatre at the time inadequate to realize nebulous ambitions that eventually became productions such as *The Serpent* and *Terminal*. Likewise, Grotowski's training/research aimed at forming the holy actor may not be the best preparation for playing a Shakespeare comedy, while a Lecoq training may lend itself more readily to aspects of *Waiting for Godot* than a Horton Foote domestic drama.

This tension between the expansive and specialized in training is further complicated by the English language. This is because training is a somewhat amorphous term (at least in English), it can refer to a single class or workshop; it can equally be applied to a series of the same. It can encompass specific, singular skills, such as the voice, a particular movement skill, or improvisation techniques. It is equally applied to a skill-encompassing, curriculum form of study that takes place over an extended period of time, such as those offered in conservatories like RADA in the UK or the Juilliard School in New York.

That said, the limits of any one form of actor training highlights the fact that purpose all too often serves circumstances rather than the ideal; this is primarily because there are numerous, substantially different forms of training available to actors and because of the capricious nature of a profession in which independent ethos-driven troupes struggle to survive while the repertory company is rare. The consequence is that most actors are hired by the production based on their reputation, relationship with those responsible for casting, or success at an audition – with little more than a passing thought given to their training.

Freelance professional or longtime company member aside, the relationship between one's training and purpose might be better understood by examining two areas that are fundamental to an actor's training history: the full training cycle and the tension between art and craft in both the cycle and the empty spaces it prepares one to inhabit.

THE FULL TRAINING CYCLE

The full training cycle encompasses a performer's professional career and in its fullest iteration (which not all actors are exposed to) contains at least five overlapping components: foundational training; experiential training; production-specific training; vocational training; and the training of others.

Foundational training is the actor's initial training, though it is often difficult to define where it begins and ends in an actor's professional career. In a common North American model it can begin in high school then continue on to an undergraduate experience followed by a graduate school conservatory training; it can also be the product of a private studio, such as those founded by Uta Hagen (HB Studio) and Sanford Meisner (The Neighborhood Playhouse); it can take the form of an apprenticeship-type experience, as at Odin Teatret; or numerous other related iterations. This aspect of training generally has a relatively clear purpose that is shaped by the vision of theatre or educational thrust underlying it. The Actors' Studio in New York, for example, prepares one best for a script-driven realism rooted in the psycho-emotional emphasis of the Method, developed by the studio's iconic leader for many years, Lee Strasberg; whereas, the Acting Program at the Juilliard School Drama Division continues (despite numerous changes over the years) to reflect the broader training philosophy of one of its founders, the French-born director, teacher and actor Michel Saint-Denis, that encompasses the skills needed to inhabit various theatrical styles ranging from the classics, to realism, the absurd, and beyond.[2]

Experiential training is even less clearly delineated than its foundational counterpart because it concerns the accumulated knowledge an actor gleans from rehearsing and performing productions for an audience and it can encompass an entire professional career. It is a form of "on the job" training in which the actor learns how to apply and adapt her foundational knowledge in the rehearsal room and in front of an audience; it informs how to create and shape works, how to relate to other actors on stage, communicate with an audience, timing, staging etc. Like most other components of the training cycle, it is difficult to identify when it begins or ends in a particular actor's career, most especially because at least part of this stage of the training cycle is absorbed and applied tacitly rather than as an explicitly conscious process.

Purpose is often less clear in experiential training than in its foundational counterpart. This is because unless an actor is involved for a very long period with a theatre troupe predicated upon a clear and consistent understanding of its theatrical ethos (Kneehigh, Odin Teatret or The Wooster Group, for example), the peripatetic nature of the acting profession makes it likely that he will be engaged in an array of theatrical works that are quite different (realistic, absurdist, comedy, Greek tragedy etc.) and which offer a range of theatrical experiences rather than one shaped by a singular vision of theatre. Thus, for many actors, experiential training is more about adapting their foundational knowledge and their gradual accretion of work experiences than on applying their foundational knowledge in a form of theatre that has shaped that training.

Production-specific training, as it implies, is training that is bound-up with a particular production. The boxing training undertaken by members of Frantic Assembly for their 2010 co-production with the National Theatre of Scotland, *Beautiful Burnout,* by Bryony Lavery that involved performers first learning how to box and then adapting that training into a workshop/rehearsals process leading to the mise-en-scène is one such example (see Evans 2012 for a description of this process). Production-specific training has been a staple at Odin Teatrėt from at least the early 1970s when during rehearsals for the company's 1972 production *Min Fars Hus,* the actors learned to play instruments (the accordion and clarinet) for the production and explored ways to use the instruments as expressive props, and continues to the current day as the longtime members of the company have abandoned the daily training, which was a common practice for many years, and now only develop new training that is linked to a specific upcoming production (Ledger 2012: 63).

Purpose would seem to be transparent in the case of production-specific training because there is a clear link between the learning and its function; this form of training is only introduced during a fixed rehearsal cycle and is designed to inform the creation and performance of a singular production. But, as the history of Odin Teatret, one of the rare theatre troupes whose training history has been well documented for almost all of its fifty years, demonstrates, the explicitly delineated purpose in this form of training can have implications that inform purpose long after the production that generated it is over.

The Odin actress Roberta Carreri, for instance, explored the multiple ways a deck chair could be used as a seat, as a prop, as a partner, as a means of generating action etc., during rehearsals for her 1987 solo production *Judith.* At that time most Odin actors continued with daily training and I witnessed one such session, which I have written about elsewhere (Watson 1993), in which Carreri continued to explore the deck chair as partner and as a generator of action after rehearsals for *Judith* were complete. The activity hardly seemed to be training in the conventional sense and I addressed this in an interview with Carreri following the session. She explained that she was exploring an Odin acting principle of body segmentation in the exercise. She was, in other words, building upon what she had explored/learned in her production specific training to continue the broader remit of her training going forward.

For Carreri, training is a gradual accretion of embodied (often tacit) learning that informs rehearsals and performance rather than a means of acquiring a learned fixed "toolkit of techniques" that are applied from one production to the next. As she put it herself in an interview about the intercultural influences on her training:

> I began elaborating my own training. My elaborations were inspired by other cultures. First. . . . I met the Brazilian masters, the Candomblé dancers I told you about. Then I met the eastern masters [Nihon Buyo and Balinese Dance-drama especially]. . . . These meetings helped me develop my own training. But, the training is one thing, the work on performance is something else. Training allows me to develop my physical intelligence, my body memory. When I make an improvisation I don't think about looking Japanese or looking Balinese or anything; that is out of my mind. Yet it is in my body. This means that when I do something, whether I recognize it or not, it has to do with my training and what

inspired the training. . . . I will not take the outside elements, what is visible; I will not walk like a Balinese in the improvisation. Everything I have learned is chewed and digested, it has gone into my blood – my body through experience, and it comes out like Roberta.

(in Watson 2002: 84)

This reflection would suggest that the full gamut of the training cycle has potential consequences beyond any component's immediate impetus; one may well have a singular purpose for studying Candomblé (to include a sequence of it in a production, for example), but the embodied learning involved can have a lifetime of implications.

Vocational training refers to the professional workshops and master classes many actors avail themselves of during their working careers. The legendary master scene classes at the Actors Studio in which seasoned professionals sometimes explore new work which is critiqued by senior teachers and other members of the studio is a historically renowned example of such training; other instances include any one of the myriad short-term workshops available to professionals and neophytes alike in various specific techniques such as Viewpoints and Suzuki training, mask work, clowning, and vocal workshops by the likes of Kristin Linklater and Roy Hart trained teachers.

The distinction between production-specific and vocational training is, like so many of the stages in an entire training cycle, sometimes difficult to tease apart. It is not unheard of for vocational training to be part of the rehearsal process for a specific production, as was the boxing training done prior to the formal rehearsals that drew extensively upon the earlier training in the Beautiful Burnout production touched on above, for instance; and the voice work done with a dialect coach or fencing workshops with an experienced teacher during rehearsals for particular productions are other instances that blur the lines between the two.

That said, much like production-specific training, vocational training hints at a link to purpose because these post-foundational training workshops and master classes are invariably undertaken to compliment one's training and professional experience. Unlike production-specific training, however, the purpose is often less immediately pragmatic since, despite the fact that it is often skill specific, vocational training invariably informs the spectral arc of one's training rather than a specific production. But, this is a shift in emphasis rather than a clear distinction between production-specific and vocational training since, as Carreri made clear earlier, even if it is a secondary outcome, production-specific training also informs/contributes to the entirety of the performing body.

The final component of the training cycle, teaching others, is hardly one all actors embrace; but some do, and at least some of these insist that doing so informs their understanding of their own training. One of Odin Teatret's founding actors, Torgeir Wethal, touches on this in discussing his first teaching experiences following the company's move from Norway to Denmark in the early 1960s, "These times of the first teaching are always important, they are when you realize your own experience. You start to understand what you are doing . . . I learned more than we taught. We all did" (in Watson 1993: 46); Carreri, who joined the company nearly 10 years after Wethal, echoes the importance of teaching to her training:

In the autumn of 1974, after only six months with the group, Eugenio Barba asked me to lead the training with objects for the ten participants of the International Brigade [a six month workshop mounted by the Odin in the mid-1970s]. This task was of utmost importance in my formation. In order to be able to transmit my experience in a clear and efficient way, I was obliged to formulate it first for myself. Teaching allowed me to take possession of my knowledge. This understanding was to accompany me throughout the course of my professional life.

(Carreri 2014: 20)

Teaching provided the opportunity for Wethal and Carreri to take ownership of their training; and for Carreri, at least, offered a lifetime of perspective – which, since Odin actors developed their own training as of the early 1970s, hints at a consideration of purpose in choosing one's training trajectory.

Art, craft and purpose

Scholar-theatre artists such as Herbert Blau, Richard Schechner and Phillip Zarrilli have noted that actor training is often caught up in the dilemma of Cartesian dualism (Zarrilli 1995: 10–16); this is due in no small part to acting being an embodied practice, which may appear to call for little else than preparing the body to be an articulate instrument of expression. But closer examination reveals the demands it places on more cognitive skills – such as a trained imagination, certain analytic abilities, an empathetic understanding of social situation, and the ability to link the psycho-emotional to physical expression.

The reality is that actor training is not simply a mastering of physical skills. It rather engages the mind-body constellation in significant ways because of the demands it places on combining the physical and the mental in both the full training cycle and in its application of that training for the stage.

This form of what scientists and philosophers term embodied cognition has implications for understanding the spectrum of purpose in actor training (that is a recognition of the role the body plays in understanding, learning, and thinking).

Elsewhere I have explored the differences between education and training (Watson 2014). To summarize, education implies a holistic trajectory that at the very least can encompass things such as one's entire schooling and higher learning cycle as well as one's socio-cultural development from childhood to maturity.

Training, meanwhile, which the OED defines as "sustained instruction and practice (given or received) in an art, profession, occupation, or procedure, with a view to proficiency in it," is a subset of education that is concerned with the acquisition of a limited, related set of skills.

Where education tends to the global, training is specific; where the former prepares one for life, the latter has a vocational and/or craft bent that focuses on mastering and applying a specific set of skills.

Despite the embodied cognition involved, these skills highlight the body-centric in actor training because, even though training encompasses psycho-physical and psycho-vocal components, the body is both the actor's medium as well as her message.

This is a duality that demands the articulate and focuses its training accordingly.

That said, the education-training binary can be misleading. We may well understand the conceptual difference between a practice that bears the hallmarks of the vocational and one that suggests an entire acculturation, but teasing them apart is often far from simple. Training in many of the arts, for example, tends to the expansive. A young actor training at the Stella Adler Acting Studio, at the Central

School of Speech and Drama in London, or with the Odin Teatret is learning specific skills (acting technique, voice, movement, improvisation etc.,) in order to be proficient in her chosen profession. The focus is on mastering what many characterize as a craft; but the craft portends to a wider world, a broader spectrum of experience, learning and education.

This portent touches on the differences between the actor as craftsperson and the actor as artist. The likes of Stanislavsky, Adler, the author(s) of the Natyashastra, Zeami, Grotowski, Barba and numerous others view(ed) acting as an art; by which they mean it has the potential to convey and/or tap into our common humanity. In other words, the great actor engages craft to become something more than a mere display of mastered skills.

The performer's ability to become the agent of "something more" than an embodied competence moves her from the realm of training to the wider world of the accultured global that is formed in large part by the broader compass of education and the fusing of the Cartesian binary rather than the narrower physical skill-focused mandate of training.

As Boal puts it in an excerpt included in the section below:

> The actor works with human beings, and therefore works with herself, on the infinite process of discovering the human. In this way alone can she justify her art. The other would be the sort of craftsmanship which, though perfectly commendable, is not art. Craftsmanship reproduces pre-existing models; art discovers essence.
>
> (Boal 1995: 37)

But, how one discovers and conveys essence to an audience or where the shift from craft to art happens in the larger scheme of things is difficult to pin down; this is because it is the product of so many variables, not least of which is the intangible connection between the moment-to-moment particulars of a performance and the individual spectator's idiosyncratic personal history and experience of the production. One may well recognize when he witnesses the move from craft to art, yet explaining the "what and how" of the experience in a meaningful way is something altogether different.

The fundamental question does not lie with the spectator, however. It is for the actor to consider when she steps into the training studio on the first day of class: what is the purpose of the journey I begin today? Is it to simply reproduce the actor's craft or is it to strive for something greater, something rooted in an educational paradigm that moves expression from the corporeal to the soul?

Many of those who wrote the following excerpts endorsed the more ambitious path and I would encourage any reader seriously interested in acting to read these authors' works in full to better understand the nature of purpose in an actor's training.

The excerpts

The following excerpts confirm that purpose in relation to training is a nuanced term shaped by the vision of theatre that generates it and, as one might expect from what are mostly iconic figures in the field, a valence that favors art over craft.

Though each of the authors has his own (for they are all men) take on purpose and none discusses training in light of its cycle, there are several common themes running through the selections. The most common is that the ultimate purpose of training is to go beyond craft to discover the art of acting.

Another theme is that the purpose of training is to gain a mastery of a learned technique that can then be applied in rehearsals and performance.

Some offer that purpose is rooted in the personal, arguing that since each person is different, an actor should develop a personalized variation of one or more particular technique(s).

While the entirety of the excerpts and the stature of the authors confirm that, just as there is no single purpose involved in training, there is no universal acting system – there are multiple techniques, and purpose lies in the hands of the would-be actor-artist.

Through a comparison with dancers who continue to train throughout their professional careers, Mike Alfreds focuses his attention on the experiential and vocational phases of actor training. He argues that, since acting calls for a more comprehensive technique than dance (which demands a daily training), it likewise should encompass a daily regimen. Thus for Alfreds, one purpose of actor training is to continually exercise the physical, the vocal and the imaginative capacity to translate words and/or images into a cohesive embodied presence in order to optimize the actor's expressive and interpretive instrument throughout his career.

Eugenio Barba casts purpose in starkly ethical terms in his 'Letter to Actor D.,' as he chastises the recipient of his letter for a lack of commitment to everything s/he does in the theatre. Drawing upon religious (Christian) metaphors, Barba makes the case that one purpose of his actor-centered theatre (and by inference the entire training cycle underlying it) is to generate actions "powered by the flame hidden in red-hot iron, the voice in the burning bush;" then, and only then, will one's actions "live on in the senses and the memory of the spectator." For Barba, acting brooks no compromise and the purpose of every element in the training cycle is to infuse performance with the power and conviction of a deeply held faith.

In an elegant marriage of art and social action, Augusto Boal argues that the purpose of training, as well as theatre in general, is to challenge both the conscious and unconscious coercion of social inculturation. This challenge is realized through a process that gradually shifts an actor from the limitations of craft, which can at best only reproduce "pre-existing models," to the realm of art, which as Boal's puts it "discovers essence" through an "infinite process of discovering the human." For Boal, this process appears to emphasize the foundational and experiential periods of the training cycle because these are where the greatest emphasis is placed on moving from novice to competent. However, since the potential for growth and change is latent in all aspects of the cycle, the production specific, vocational, and training of other elements could also conceivably play a role in the shift from craft to art and the escape from incultured servitude.

Mel Gordon writes in his introduction to Michael Chekhov's *On the Technique of Acting* that Chekhov "was one of the most extraordinary actors and teachers of the twentieth century" (1991: ix). Unfortunately, like all great stage actors, little remains of his acting career, save descriptions and a few Hollywood films. Luckily, that is not the case with his understanding of the actor's craft and how to transform it into art. We have his books, most especially *On the Technique of Acting*, which is an insightful examination of the actor's craft through the lens of a specific technique. The concise yet comprehensive sweep of this volume, from its introductory exercises through to its closing chapter that provides an overview of the entire rehearsal process, touches on all stages of the training cycle – the most potent exemplar of which is Chekhov's own life. As one might expect from an expansive theatre mind like his, Chekhov's excerpt here does not limit itself to a single purpose when it comes to training. It rather comprehends multiple, related, purposes. One is to realize the innate technique of those "born as actors;" another is to provide a method that encompasses bodily expression and psychology; while a third is to train both the body and emotions while putting intellect at the service of both.

In an audacious challenge to actor training (and theatre as a whole), Gordon Craig denies any purpose to actor training as he banishes the actor from the stage altogether. For Craig, the actor is someone incapable of a genuine act of creation who should be replaced by an inanimate Über-marionette.

In what seems almost addressed to Craig, Jerzy Grotowski views the ideal performer as decidedly human; he is, in fact, a person of privilege because he is uniquely qualified to engage knowledge through action. It is as if the borders between the purposes of training and performing are intentionally blurred for Grotowski since the aim of both is to engage one's personal process as a means of accessing the essentially human. In terms of the training cycle, it is worth noting that this extract was written during a time when Grotowski's interest was in researching performance without regard to presentations before an audience. In fact, few people outside of those working with him even witnessed what he was doing. It was a period in his life when he worked with two basic constituencies: master performers from various performance traditions deeply embedded in their specific cultures; and young, committed youth who realized much of Grotowski's experimentation. It is debatable if one can even talk of an actor training cycle with regards to Grotowski's post-theatre phase, however, both the master performers and the young people were exposed to training, either prior to working with Grotowski (mostly the master performers) or underwent a training of sorts during their time with him (mainly the young people). Thus for the former, the training cycle was decidedly at the latter end of its cycle (especially since anecdotal evidence suggests that part of Grotowski's research included the master teachers working with and teaching the young people) while for the young people it was much closer to the early days of its history of foundational and experiential learning.

Interestingly, Jacques Lecoq is the only author in this section on purpose who is primarily recognized as a teacher of performers. As such, his focus is on the foundational and experiential facets of training, and he addresses the notion of purpose through the lens of what he hoped to achieve in his teaching. For him, this included preparing the performer to create through a genuine ability to play, steering clear of linking theatre to therapy, developing the skill to observe life in meticulous detail as a basis for improvising with insight, and in a rather expansive ambition that even he questions, to equip one for life.

Yoshi Oida's contribution is essentially a summary and commentary on the chronology of the actor's journey from its beginning (ideally at the age of six) through to old age in the treatises by the great Noh master from Japan's Middle Ages, Zeami. In the spirit of Zeami, whose writings include numerous comparisons between young performers and their older, master counterparts (much of which draws upon Zeami's observations of his own father's growth as a performer), Oida's concern embraces the entire training cycle, by implication if not explicitly. This embrace is echoed in what Oida identifies as the essential purpose of training conveyed in Zeami's writings, namely that contrary to the primacy of mastering skills as one might expect, the deep purpose is to do what Oida characterizes as "going beyond technique."

For Konstantin Stanislavsky the summary purpose of training is for the actor to be able to generate and retain the "creative state," both in rehearsals and during performance. In the style of his famous nod to the fictional in much of his theatre writings, here he explores the conditions that are necessary for generating this creative state during rehearsals. In doing so he makes the point alluded to in Barba's earlier extract, that training includes learning the need "to develop the right *artistic ethics and discipline*," not simply during performance, but in every aspect of the work from the entire training cycle through rehearsals as well as during performance; this, for Stanislavsky, is the only way to transform craft into genius.

PROVOCATIONS

1 What do you understand as the difference between craft and art in relation to acting?
2 Is any one phase in the training cycle more important than another; if so, why?
3 Is the ideal technique strictly prescriptive or is it rather a personal variation of one or more techniques that is individual for each actor?
4 Can an acting technique rooted in an aesthetic actually challenge one's social inculturation, as Augusto Boal suggests?
5 What does Yoshi Oida's notion of "going beyond technique" mean in practical terms for an actor?

Notes

1 These brief descriptions are but the tip of a large iceberg, as this and other related volumes attest (see for example, Hodge, 2010; Bartow, 2006; Watson, 2001).
2 See Scheeder and Strasberg in Bartow, 2006, pp. 3–27 for a brief but informative overview of the Actor's Studio history, Strasberg's contribution, and The Method; See Saint-Denis, 1960, pp. 90–110 for an insight into the founding principle of the Drama Division of the Juilliard School that were rooted in Saint-Denis' earlier experience of establishing the Old Vic School in London; see the Juilliard's Drama Division's website for information on its current program: http://www.juilliard.edu/degrees-programs/drama

Bibliography

Atlantic Theatre School (1986) *A Practical Handbook for the Actor* (authored by Melissa Bruder, Lee Michael Cohn, Madeleine Olnek, Nathaniel Pollack, Robert Previto, Scott Zigler), New York: Vintage Books.
Bartow, A. (ed.) (2006) *Training of the American Actor*, New York: Theatre Communications Group.
Carreri, R. (2014) *On Training: Traces of an Odin Actress*. Trans. and ed. F. Camilleri, London & New York: Routledge.
Chaikin, J. (1984) *The Presence of the Actor*, New York: Atheneum.
Evans, M. (2012) "Interview with Frantic Assembly: *Beautiful Burnout* and Training the Performer," *Theatre, Dance and Performance Training*, Vol. 3(2), pp. 256–268.
Gordon, M. (1991) "Introduction," in *On the Technique of Acting* by Michael Chekhov, New York: Harper.

Grotowski, J. (1968) *Towards a Poor Theatre*, New York: Touchstone Books.

Hodge, A. (ed.) (2010) *Actor Training*, (Second Edition), London & New York: Routledge.

Ledger, A. J. (2012) *Odin Teatret: Theatre in a New Century*, London: Palgrave Macmillan.

Saint-Denis, M. (1960) *The Rediscovery of Style*, New York: Theatre Arts Books.

Scheeder, L. (2006) "Strasberg's Method and the Ascendancy of American Acting," in *Training of the American Actor*, edited by Arthur Bartow, New York: Theatre Communications Group.

Stanislavski, C. (1967) *My Life in Art*, (translated by Elizabeth Reynolds Hapgood), Harmondsworth, England: Penguin.

Strasberg, A. (2006) "Lee Strasberg Technique," in *Training of the American Actor*, edited by Arthur Bartow, New York: Theatre Communications Group.

Vicharova, V. (2012) "Answer the Questions: What is the best advice you would give to someone about training?" *Theatre, Dance and Performance Training*, 3:3 (October), 395–396.

Watson, I. (1993) *Towards a Third Theatre*, London & New York: Routledge.

Watson, I. (ed.) (2001) *Performer Training: Developments Across Cultures*, London & New York: Harwood/Routledge.

Watson, I. (2002) *Negotiating Cultures: Eugenio Barba and the Intercultural Debate*, Manchester and New York: Manchester University Press.

Watson, I. (2014) "The Weave of Cultural Production, Education, and Training in the Work of the Borderland Organization (Pogranicze Organizacja)," *Theatre, Dance and Performer Training*, 5:3 (October), 304–320.

Zarrilli, P. (ed.) (1995) *Acting (Re)Considered*, London & New York: Routledge.

Chapter 3

Mike Alfreds

DIFFERENT EVERY NIGHT

OTHER PERFORMERS – SINGERS, dancers and musicians – know they cannot sing, dance or play an instrument without intense and specialised training. Indeed, their lives are accompanied by continuous coaching, study and exercise. (Dancers know that if they don't take a daily class, their muscles will seize up.) Whatever their natural talent, it needs skills and structures to release its potential. Actors know little of such rigour. A human being's potential is inexhaustible, but most actors seem to settle for a sort of competence. Their potential remains largely unchallenged. Indeed, most casting directors and many directors, too, abet this; they want actors for exactly what they've done before and exactly as they are. They like the security of a known product. For them, actors are a commodity like soap powder, the more predictable the better, and the less they confuse their possible employers with options and choices, the better. The profession is ecologically wasteful, destructive. It uses up its most valuable resource (actors), but does nothing to nurture or replenish what it devours. It's an unspoken assumption that there will always be a constant flow of fresh actors coming on stream. But, like cod or oil, the source may one day dry up; people who might have the urge to act may realize what a mug's game it is for the majority of the profession and curb their impulses. Some of the larger theatre organisations talk about furthering the actors' training, but make little more than perfunctory gestures in that direction. Nobody gives a damn about an actor's growth. So actors have to take the fate of their development into their own hands.

This contrast in attitude to training lies largely in the perceived demands of different performance skills. Anyone can see that to sing, dance or play an instrument requires exceptional abilities well beyond the norms of everyday life. It's given to relatively few, say, to dance Petipa, sing Wagner or play Liszt. You have to master incredibly demanding techniques and then keep on top of them for the rest of your career. And, to a certain degree, you cannot cheat. At very least, you have to be seen to get on point or heard to hit that note right in its centre. On the other hand, all that actors are seen to do, mostly, is talk and walk about, displaying attitudes and emotions common to us all. In theory, anyone can do what actors do. This in a way is true: part of an actor's job *is* to reveal what is common to us all. However, they should do so in a way that is heightened, selected and resonant. The Victorian actor, William Macready, unexpectedly, has something to say on the subject:

> One of the disadvantages incident to the pursuit of the theatrical act is the supposed facility of its attainment, nor is it less cheapened in public estimation by the general assumption of the ability to criticise it. How frequent, to questions of opinion on other arts, are the evasive answers, 'I am no judge of poetry'; 'I have never studied pictures'; 'I do not know much about sculpture.' Yet the person confessedly ignorant on these subjects, would be at no fault in pronouncing a decisive judgement on 'the youngest of the sister arts where all their beauty blends!' [i.e. acting!] ... It surely needs something like an education for such an art and yet that appearance of mere volition and perfect ease, which cost the accomplished artist so much time and toil to acquire, evidently leads to a different conclusion with many, or amateur acting would be in less vogue.

Employable dancers nowadays must have a practical knowledge of many disciplines – classical ballet, Graham, jazz, tap, Laban, acrobatics, for starters ... Can actors similarly offer their directors competence in, say, Stanislavsky's physical actions, Michael Chekhov's psychological gestures, Laban's efforts, Meyerhold's biomechanics, Grotowski's cat, Meisner's repetitions and Boal's forum techniques ...? (And would many directors know to ask for any of these?) The irony is that by comparison, actors, who work with their entire being – body, voice, emotion, will and interpretative skill, *whose job, I believe, is ultimately the most demanding* – hardly train at all. This may account for the rapturous and endless applause that greets dance and opera performances and rarely finds its way to straight theatre. Possibly I idealise the rigour of other disciplines, from where I stand, that particular grass often looks greener.

*   *   *

It's a sort of miracle that productions ever come to fruition, let alone achieve any degree of excellence. You could describe many rehearsal experiences as a group of people who have probably never before worked together, cooped up for far too brief a period in a frequently disagreeable, dark, dirty and noisy space, without a shared language or shared vision of what they believe theatre to be, in order to create something as profound and complex and intimate as a performance. Some people stagger through rehearsals by an arbitrary and inconsistent mixture of moment-to-moment decisions ('Wouldn't it be good if . . .', '. . . fun if . . .', 'Here, why don't we . . .', 'How about if you . . .') or of superstitious routines that, with some actors, pass for technique ('I always take a long walk in the park', 'I have to know my moves before I learn my lines', 'I can't work without the real props', 'I find the character when I get the right shoes'). These are really nothing more than habits of limited usefulness that have grown into delusional crutches.

No, acting is not an exact science, but if other professions proceeded with the same lack of a shared language, knowledge and rigour, buildings would crash, bridges collapse and patients die on operating tables as a matter of daily routine. Actors are physical, emotional, mental – and, if you like, even spiritual – athletes; they should treat themselves as such and those that work with them should treat them with appropriate care, expectations and demands. Acting at its best is an act of bravery. Nothing lies between actors and their audiences' observation of every aspect of their physicality, taste, sensibility and intelligence. To face such scrutiny, the actor needs to be master of many skills.

Acting is hard. That some actors seem to compound this fact with the determination not to continue to develop their skills seems a form of complacency, if not insanity. Or fear – fear of having to learn things that might disturb their sense of themselves and how they already function. True, it must be painful to face the fact that for many years you could have been going about your work in a far more creative and productive way than you actually do. It can be more comfortable to avoid this sort of realization. This is not dissimilar to the sort of trauma a lot of acting students go through in their first year of study, when they're forced to realize that acting has nothing to do with their fantasies of what it might be – showing off (those inclined to comedy), going on an emotional binge (those inclined to tragedy) and having lots of fun, money and fame.

MIKE ALFREDS (1934–)

Alfreds trained in the USA and Israel. He was the founding director of Shared Experience, one of the most successful touring companies in the UK. His work with Shared Experience explored storytelling and performance. He is renowned for his work as a director and teacher and has worked with many leading actors at the National Theatre and with Cambridge Theatre Company, later renamed Method and Madness.

See also: **Konstantin Stanislavky.**

SUGGESTED FURTHER READING

Alfreds, M. (1979) *A Shared Experience*: *The Actor as Story-teller*, Dartington: Theatre Papers.
Alfreds, M. (2007) *Different Every Night: Freeing the Actor*, London: Nick Hern Books.
Alfreds, M. (2013) *Then What Happens: Storytelling and Adapting for the Theatre*, London: Nick Hern Books.

Chapter 4

Eugenio Barba

LETTER TO ACTOR D.

This letter was written by Eugenio Barba to one of the actors of the Odin in 1967. It has often appeared in books and magazines in different parts of the world, either to illustrate the Odin's vision of theatre or to present, in more general terms, its attitude towards a new actor. It was first published in the book **Synspunkter om kunst** (Copenhagen, 1968).

I HAVE OFTEN BEEN struck by a lack of seriousness in your work. This is not the same as a lack of concentration or good will. It is the expression of two attitudes.

First of all, it seems as if your actions are not driven by any inner conviction or irresistible need which leaves its mark on your exercises, improvisations and performance. You may be concentrated in your work, without sparing your energies, your gestures may be technically correct and precise, but your actions remain empty. I don't believe in what you are doing. Your body clearly says: "I have been told to do this". But your nerves, your brain, your spine, are not committed, and with this skin-deep commitment you want to make me believe that what you are doing is vital to you. You do not sense the importance of that which you want to share with the spectators. How then can you expect the spectator to be gripped by your actions? How can you, with this attitude, uphold the understanding of the theater as a place where social inhibitions and conventions are annihilated to make way for an open-hearted and absolute communication? You represent the community within this space, with the humiliations you have undergone, the degradation which has closed you up, your cynicism as self-defence, and your optimism as the essence of irresponsibility. All this, together with your guilt, your need to love, the longing for a lost paradise hidden in the past, close to the person who could make you forget fear. Everybody present with you in this space will be shaken if you succeed in rediscovering these sources, this common ground of human experience, the hidden fatherland. This is the bond that unites you to the others, a treasure that lies buried deep within all of us, never unearthed, because it is our only comfort, and because it hurts when we touch it.

The second attitude I see in you is your embarrassment in considering the seriousness of your work. You feel the need to laugh, to sneer, and come with humorous comments about what you and your colleagues are doing. It is as if you want to flee from the responsibility that you feel is inherent in your craft, which consists in establishing communication with human beings and in assuming the responsibility for what you are revealing. You are frightened by seriousness, the knowledge that you are on the fringes of the permissible. You are frightened that everything you do is synonymous with tediousness, fanaticism, or over-specialization. But in a world where people around us either no longer believe in anything, or only pretend to believe in order to be left in peace, he who digs deep within himself to reach a clarity about his own situation, his absence of ideals, his need for spiritual life, will always be called fanatic or naive. In a world with cheating as a norm, he who seeks his own truth is taken for a fraud, a hypocrite. I wonder if you realize that all you create, everything liberated and given form by your work is also a part of life and deserves care and respect. Your actions before the community of the spectators should be powered by the flame hidden in the red-hot iron, the voice in the burning bush. Only then will your actions live on in the senses and the memory of the spectator, fermenting into unforeseeable consequences.

We know that when Dullin lay on his deathbed, his face deformed itself into all the important roles he had played: Smerdiakov, Volpone, Richard III. It was not just the man Dullin who was dying but also the actor, as well as the many stages of his working life.

If I ask you why you became an actor, you will reply: "To fulfil myself, to express myself". But what does this mean? Who has fulfilled himself? Was it Manager Hansen who lived a quiet life, respectable and without problems, never tormented by answerless questions, or the romantic Gauguin, who broke with all of the social norms and finished his life in miserable poverty and degradation in a Polynesian village, convinced that he had found the lost freedom, Noa-Noa? In an epoch where belief in God is diagnosed as a neurosis, we lack the scales to weigh our life and tell us whether we have been fulfilled or not. No matter which personal and hidden motives have led you to the theater, once you are within, you must find a meaning which, stretching beyond your own person, confronts you socially with others.

It is only within the catacombs that we can prepare a new life. It is here that one can seek spiritual commitment without fear of confrontation with questions that will bring about a new morality. This presupposes courage: the majority of people has no need of us. Your work is a sort of social meditation upon yourself, your human condition and the events that touch you to the quick through the experiences of our age. In such a precarious theater which shocks the normal psychic well-being, every performance can be your last. You should consider it as such, the final possibility of reaching out to others, crying out your last word, your testament, the reckoning of your actions.

If being an actor can mean all this to you, then a new theater will be born. A new approach to the literary tradition will spring forth, a new technique and a new relationship between you and the people who come to see you each evening because they need you.

EUGENIO BARBA (1936–)

Born in Italy, Barba worked for a period with Grotowski before founding Odin Teatret, based in Holstebro, Denmark. He is internationally recognized for his work with Odin and with the International School of Theatre Anthropology. His work has influenced theatre dramaturgy, pedagogy and performance internationally for at least four decades.

See also: **Jerzy Grotowski.**

SUGGESTED FURTHER READING

Barba, E. (1986) *Beyond the Floating Islands*, New York: Performing Arts Journal Publications.
Barba, E. (1995) *The Paper Canoe*, London & New York: Routledge.

Turner, J. (2004) *Eugenio Barba*, London & New York: Routledge.
Watson, I. (1995) *Towards a Third Theatre*, London & New York: Routledge.

Chapter 5

Augusto Boal

WHAT IS THE ACTOR?

THE HUMAN BEING IS – to a limited extent and with a large margin of error – a knowable entity; we know more about its body than its psyche. We know a certain amount about some elements of the workings of its psyche, those that relate to consciousness. And we have some hypotheses, some conjectures about those that do not.

We can compare the unconscious to a pressure-cooker. All manner of demons bubble away inside it: all the saints, all the vices, all the virtues, everything that, not being act, exists in potential. Each of us has, within him, everything that all other men, all other women have; Eros and Thanatos. We have loyalty and treachery, courage and cowardice, bravery and fear. We desire life and death, for ourselves and for others. We have the whole gamut, in pure potentiality, boiling away, in a hermetically sealed pan. We have within us such a wealth of possibilities! And we know so very little of it, so little about what we have, and almost nothing about what we are!

All possibilities being within us, it is impossible for us to manifest this potential in its totality. Within us, we have everything, we are a *person*. But this *person* is so rich and so powerful, so intense, with such a multiplicity of forms and faces, that we are constrained to reduce it. This suppression of our freedom of expression and action results from two causes: external, social coercion and/or internal, ethical choice. Fear and morality. I do or do not do thousands of things, I behave or do not behave in thousands of different ways because I am constrained by social factors, which force me to be this or stop me from being that.

This assortment of factors includes police and family, universities and churches, judges and advertisers. They tell us what is permitted and what is forbidden. And, for the most part, we accept it. Or equally, we define ourselves and oblige ourselves to be what we are, to do what we do, not to do what we think is wrong. There is one external morality, conditioned by the outside world, and another internal morality conditioned by habit. Both forces, a welter of obligations and interdictions, constrain us. We always remain the *person* we are, but we only transform a tiny portion of our potentiality into *acts*. I shall call this reduction *personality*.

We all have a *personality*, which is a reduction forced out of our *person*. The latter boils on in the saucepan; the former escapes through the safety valve. And, in this fashion, we scrape along perfectly well. Because we pretend to be only that part of ourselves which is excusable; the rest we keep carefully hidden. However, both our demons and our saints remain alive, very much alive, at boiling point, and they may declare their presence by means of symptoms, ulcers, rashes or other, even worse, manifestations. Nevertheless, to all appearances we are healthy smiling people.

Now let us take an actor, the very incarnation of smiling sanity. Suppose all her material problems are solved, she has long contracts, large salaries; she has simple and normal preoccupations. Suppose, then, that we are talking about someone 'normal', that is, according to the socially accepted norms defining 'normal' people.

This normal actor pursues a strange and perilous occupation: she interprets parts in plays, characters, dramatis personae. Where can she go to find them?

And, before we go any further, who are they, these people we call 'characters'? Let's be frank: from a medical point of view, they are all neurotics, psychotics, para-noiacs, melancholics, schizophrenics: in short, sick people! As literature, sure, they are enthralling; but in reality, they would be in urgent need of medical attention. Characters in plays are sick people: this generalisation we can make without fear of error. And it is for this single reason that we go to the theatre. I have seen *Hamlet* dozens of times, I love the play and its eponymous protagonist, but I am not sure if I would want to invite him round to dinner every Saturday, along with other friends, to spend the evening chatting about being or not being.

Take the following scenario. Who would want to go out to go and see a piece of theatre like this? A young man and a young woman, both good-looking and in good health, in love with each other, watch their children getting ready for school, where they are by far the best pupils. They accompany them to the school gate. Then they cross a flower-filled garden under the admiring and sympathetic gaze of their friendly neighbours, when, all of a sudden – here comes the postman! Hold onto your hats . . . he is the bearer of glad tidings – both mothers-in-law are in perfect health, and they are on a cruise around the Greek islands, and the weather is good. . . .

Who would happily sit through such a play? No one! Not even Doris Day would perform in such a play. The only audience in such a theatre would be flies. The thing that prompts us to go to the theatre is conflict, combat; we want to see mad people and fanatics, thieves and murderers. And, I accept, a smattering of good souls, just enough to set off the evil in all its glory. We hunger for the strange, the abnormal.

And so our actor – of sound mind – must play a sick character. Where then can she go to seek such a character? Not into her personality, which is, as we know, exempt from evil, but into her person, deep within, right inside, in the pressure-cooker, the place where the demons dwell at boiling point. And the actor, having patiently tamed her wildcats long ago, is once again obliged to go and waken them. That is why the profession of actor is so unhealthy and so dangerous. I swear, actors should be entitled to the same danger money allowances as miners seeking out coal or tin in the depth of mines, or astronauts who have to fly to vertiginous and infinite heights. Actors search the depths of the soul and the infinity of the metaphysical.[1] Bless them!

Actors taunt the lion with a blade of grass.[2] Their *personalities*, a picture of health and sanity, go looking in their *persons* for sick people and demons – the dramatis personae or *personnages* (French) – in the hope that, once the curtain has fallen, they will be able to get them back into their cages. And, in the best of hypotheses, they succeed in doing this. They always try, and when they succeed, they enjoy a catharsis. But sometimes – and it is tragic when it happens! – once awoken, Iago and Tartuffe, having discovered the bright limelights, also want to know the light of day, and refuse to return to the darkness of that Pandora's box which each of us is. There are actors who become ill. Our profession is truly unhealthy!

But whether dangerous or not, it is there, in the depths of the person, that the actor is obliged to seek out her characters. Otherwise, she would be a mere conjurer or jongleur, playing with her characters, but with no proximity to them; a puppet-master controlling her puppets, at a safe distance. Or, at its most extreme, a manipulator of mannequins, whose contact with her characters is hardly skin-deep. No. The actor does not work with mannequins, marionettes, balls or rods. The actor works with human beings, and therefore works with herself, on the infinite process of discovering the human. In this way alone can she justify her art. The other would be the sort of craftsmanship which, though perfectly commendable, is not art. Craftsmanship reproduces pre-existing models; art discovers essences.

Sarah Bernhardt, speaking of her creative process, wrote:

> Little by little, I used to identify with my character. I used to dress her with great care and leave my Sarah Bernhardt in a corner of the dressing room: I made her into a spectator of my new 'self'; and I went on stage ready to suffer, cry, laugh, love, unaware of what the 'I' of my 'other self' was doing up in my dressing room.[3]

To sum up, the healthy personality of the actor searches out, in the richness of her person, her characters or *personnages*, beings less healthy than herself, sick people.

Thus, within the limits of the scene and the moment, the free exercise of all asocial tendencies, unacceptable desires, forbidden behaviours and unhealthy feelings is allowed. On stage, all is permissible, nothing is forbidden. The demons and saints which inhabit the person of the actor are completely free to blossom, to experience the orgasm of the show, to pass from potential into act. In a mimetic and emphatic fashion, the same thing happens with the analogous demons and saints which are awakened in the hearts of the spectators. Always in the hope that, after it is all over, they will be tired out and will go back to sleep. In the hope that, in this holy and diabolic ball, the saints and demons of actors and audience will return, exhausted, to the unconscious darkness of the person, restoring the health and equilibrium of the personalities, which will then be able, without fear, to reintegrate their lives into society. In the hope that after the carnivalesque paroxysms of theatre will come once again the Ash Wednesday of a new day's work.

These new techniques, such as The Cop in the Head and Rainbow of Desire, as with the Theatre of the Oppressed as a whole, advance the hypothesis that the same path can be travelled, in an inverse manner, with different, even opposite, objectives.

To be an actor is dangerous, yes, but why? Because the catharsis that one seeks is not inevitable. For all the security his profession gives him, for all the protection offered by the rituals of theatre, for all the established theories about what is fiction and what is reality, none of this can prevent the possibility that one day these aroused personalities (characters, *personnages*) may refuse to go quietly back to sleep, these lions may refuse to return to their cages in the zoo of our souls.

If that is the case, we can envisage the contrary hypothesis: a sick personality can, in theory, try to awaken healthy *personnages*, this time not with the goal of dispatching them back into oblivion but in the hope of mixing them into his personality. I am afraid, but inside me there also lives the courageous man; if I can wake him up, perhaps I could keep him awake.

Who is the 'I'? The person, the personality or the *personnage*? It is very easy for us to decide – in fatalistic fashion – that we are the way we are, full stop, end of story. But we can also imagine – in a more creative fashion – that the playing cards can be re-dealt.

In this dance of potentialities, different powers take the floor at different times – potential can become act, occupy the spotlight and then glide back to the sidelines, powers grow and diminish, move in to the foreground and then shrink into the background again – everything is mutable. Our personality is what it is, but it is also what it is becoming. If we are fatalists, then there is nothing to be done; but if we are not, we can try.

In this book I give some examples of this. Without dogmatism. Without triumphalism. Without wishful thinking. To tell the truth, without being absolutely sure. But with enormous hope. A well-founded hope: if the actor can become a sick person, the sick person can in turn become a healthy actor.

Notes

1   Theatre is the fire which makes the pressure-cooker explode and release the angels and devils dwelling inside it.
2   Brazilian expression meaning 'to tempt fate'.
3   Sarah Bernhardt, *The Art of Theatre*, p.204.

AUGUSTO BOAL (1931–2009)

Originally a student of chemical engineering in Rio de Janeiro, Boal also studied theatre in New York. On his return to Brazil, he adapted the ideas he had studied in New York (e.g. Brecht and Stanislavski) to the relevant social and political conditions. His ideas for theatre practice, strongly influenced by the radical educationalist Paulo Freire, led to his political exile from Brazil from 1971 to 1986. His method seeks to lead to the creation of 'spect-actors', where the audience become critical and active participants.

See also: **Bertolt Brecht, Dario Fo.**

SUGGESTED FURTHER READING

Boal, A. (1979) *Theatre of the Oppressed,* London: Pluto Press.
Boal, A. (2002) *Games for Actors and Non-Actors,* 2nd edition, London & New York: Routledge.

Babbage, F. (2004) *Augusto Boal,* London & New York: Routledge.
Cohen-Cruz, J. & Schutzman, M. (eds.) (2005) *A Boal Companion: Dialogues on Theatre and Cultural Politics,* London & New York: Routledge.

Chapter 6

Michael Chekhov

LESSONS FOR THE PROFESSIONAL ACTOR

THE ACTOR'S BODY AS AN INSTRUMENT

I USE THIS SAME body for everything in my daily life, I use my voice for everything, for quarreling, for making love, for expressing my indifference. It is strange to realize that I have nothing more to show to the audience than myself. I found it difficult to find a justification for using the most abused thing in my life, my body, as something which I have to show every evening as a new thing, interesting, attractive. My own body, my own emotions, my own voice . . . I have nothing except myself.

Then I understood that if it is so that the actor cannot have a musical instrument or a brush, or paint, then he must have a special kind of technique which he must find inside himself. If we find this technique, or at least the approach to this hidden, mysterious thing sitting in ourselves, then maybe we shall get to the point where we shall hope to have a technique.

After many years of trying to find this technique I found that everything we need in order to develop such a technique is already there in us, if we are born as actors. That means that we have only to find out which sides of our own nature have to be stressed, underlined, exercised, and the whole technique will be there. Because while we act, good or bad, we are using our own nature but in a very chaotic way, in such a way that one part of our nature is disturbing the other part and the third part comes in between, and something else falls down upon us, etc. But the elements are there, the thing is how to anatomize our own nature—to find what is a, b, c, and d, and then when "a" is well-shaped and "b" is well-shaped, we can let these letters come intuitively together and create words which will mean something and will not be so chaotic.

I have found three things—when I say "found," I mean I have been attentive to certain points and they have become obvious; I have invented nothing—the three realms which have, first of all, to be distinguished: 1) our bodies 2) our voices 3) our emotions. At first I thought that we must keep each one of them apart and try to develop them as if in different rooms. But I found that when we start to develop the body, for instance, we find a very interesting thing. Trying to make exercises with our bodies only, in a purely physical way, we find gradually that we are already in the other room where our emotions are. So that our body becomes, later on, nothing other than our psychology incorporated in our whole body—hands, fingers, eyes, etc.

THE ACTOR'S PSYCHOLOGY

Thus, the body becomes part of our psychology, which is a very interesting experience and a very surprising one. Suddenly we feel that this same body which we use the whole day through for going here and there, this body is a different one when we are on the stage, because there it becomes, as it were, my condensed, crystallized psychology. If I have something inside me, it becomes my hand, my arm, my cheek, my eye, etc.

Then we go into the other room, where pure psychology is—nothing to do with the body, only ideas, feelings, will, impulse, etc.,—and we try to develop them as purely psychological things. Suddenly we discover that it is our body also. If I am unhappy, it is my body, my face, my arms, my hands, every part of me becomes unhappy if I have trained my body sufficiently, but it is possible only if my psychology has been developed separately from the beginning.

THE INTELLECT

Then they, the body and the psychology, find each other somewhere in the subconscious regions of our creative soul, and when they meet each other, we find the following thing: that all that we have to do on the stage is to find out gradually that when the developed psychology and the developed body find each other and join together in our subconscious life, then we have to exclude one disturbing element in our profession. It is our dry intellect which tries to interfere with our emotions, with our body, with our art. Intellect in the sense of dry thinking. Perhaps you will help me find the right term because actually "intellect" is a very high term. But by intellect, we mean a cold, dry, analytical approach to things which cannot be approached in this way. This is the only difficulty we must exclude.

We have to rely on the training of our bodies on the one hand, and the training of our emotions on the other, and on excluding this intellect for the time being. This does not mean that one has to become a fool—but to rely upon our emotions, on our bodies, and not to rely upon this clear, cold thinking, this "murderer," which sits in our head. Later on it will become very useful when it sees that it cannot kill the body or the emotions, because it is in the actor's power. I can become gay and laugh, or sorry and thoughtful as I wish because I have trained myself.

Then the intellect becomes very useful because it makes clear for me everything in my profession—starting with the written play and finishing with the production on the stage. Every detail becomes full of meaning, full of sense, because the intellect knows that it cannot do anything but serve me. But to start by making agreements with the intellect, to fawn before it, to obey it, then we are lost. When the intellect is allowed to become the master, it becomes a fool, an evil fool and a merciless one. Everything which the intellect can make clear it makes obscure if it knows, "I am the only master." Then we are lost.

DEVELOPING THE ACTOR'S NATURE

Now, the last thing for today. The way to develop our own nature takes time. We have to use a certain amount of time and effort for training ourselves, but after this period of training which may be a long one, we will find it a real economy of time. Sometimes this period of training is mistaken in our profession for a loss of time, when we have to produce plays in four weeks. We think that if this training takes years there must be something wrong. The wrong is only if we think the period of training is an eternal one. No. It is a long one, but when it is accomplished it is such an economy of time. When you can laugh, cry, sing, be happy at once—when you have trained your imagination so that you can see the whole of *Othello* at once—that is real economy of time.

If we don't have to keep our hands in our pockets for the first two weeks before we overcome our sense of shame, we will realize what our hands and arms can do for us as means of expression. If we are free to move our hands and arms from our center and not from our joints and are free, then we can speak of economy of time. So really it is the greatest economy of time to spend a long period of time in training. When everything is there, after a long period of training, then I will believe that the performance can be done even in two weeks. But not now.

MICHAEL CHEKHOV (1891–1955)

Michael Chekhov was the nephew of the playwright Anton Chekhov, and was considered by his teacher, Stanislavsky, to be one of his most gifted students. He eventually split from Stanislavsky to set up his own studio. From 1936 to 1939 he ran a theatre school at Dartington Hall in Devon. He later moved to America, where he ran a theatre school and appeared in several Hollywood films. His approach is more intuitive than that of Stanislavsky, and places more emphasis on the imagination.

See also: **Konstantin Stanislavski.**

SUGGESTED FURTHER READING

Chekhov, M. (1985) *Lessons for the Professional Actor*, New York: Performing Arts Journal.
Chekhov, M. (2002) *To The Actor*, London & New York: Routledge.

Chamberlain, F. (2004) *Michael Chekhov*, London & New York: Routledge.
Petit, L. (2009) *The Michael Chekhov Handbook*, London & New York: Routledge.

Chapter 7

Edward Gordon Craig

ACTORS AND ACTING

... **THE BODY OF MAN** ... is by *nature* utterly useless as a material for an art. I am fully aware of the sweeping character of this statement; and as it concerns men and women who are alive, and who as a class are ever to be loved, more must be said lest I give unintentional offence. I know perfectly well that what I have said here is not yet going to create an exodus of all the actors from all the theatres in the world, driving them into sad monasteries where they will laugh out the rest of their lives, with the Art of the Theatre as the main topic for amusing conversation. As I have written elsewhere, the theatre will continue its growth and actors will continue for some years to hinder its development. But I see a loophole by which in time the actors can escape from the bondage they are in. They must create for themselves a new form of acting, consisting for the main part of symbolical gesture. Today they *impersonate* and interpret; tomorrow they must *represent* and interpret; and the third day they must create. By this means style may return. Today the actor impersonates a certain being. He cries to the audience: 'Watch me; I am now pretending to be so and so, and I am now pretending to do so and so;' and then he proceeds to *imitate* as exactly as possibly, that which he has announced he will *indicate*. For instance, he is Romeo. He tells the audience that he is in love, and he proceeds to show it, by kissing Juliet. This, it is claimed, is a work of art: it is claimed for this that it is an intelligent way of suggesting thought. Why – why, that is just as if a painter were to draw upon the wall a picture of an animal with long ears and then write under it 'This is a donkey.' The long ears made it plain enough, one would think, without the inscription, and any child of ten does as much. The difference between the child of ten and the artist is that the artist is he who by drawing certain signs and shapes creates the impression of a donkey: and the greater artist is he who creates the impression of the whole genus of donkey, the *spirit* of the thing.

The actor looks upon life as a photo-machine looks upon life; and he attempts to make a picture to rival a photograph. He never dreams of his art as being an art such for instance as music. He tries to reproduce Nature; he seldom thinks to invent with the aid of Nature, and he never dreams of *creating*. As I have said, the best he can do when he wants to catch and convey the poetry of a kiss, the heat of a fight, or the calm of death, is to copy slavishly, photographically – he kisses – he fights – he lies back and mimics death – and, when you think of it, is not all this dreadfully stupid? Is it not a poor art and a poor cleverness, which cannot convey the spirit and essence of an idea to an audience, but he can only show an artless copy, a facsimile of the thing itself? This is to be an imitator, not an artist. This is to claim kinship with the ventriloquist.

There is a stage expression of the actor 'getting under the skin of the part'. A better one would be getting 'out of the skin of the part altogether'. 'What, then,' cries the red-blooded and flashing actor, 'is there to be no flesh and blood in this same art of the theatre of yours? No life?' It depends what you call life, signor, when you use the word in relation with the idea of art. The painter means something rather different to actuality when he speaks of life in his art, and the other artists generally mean something essentially spiritual; it is only the actor, the ventriloquist, or the animal-stuffer who, when they speak of putting life into their work, mean some actual and lifelike reproduction, something blatant in its appeal, that it is for this reason I say that it would be better if the actor should get out of the skin of the part altogether. If there is any actor who is reading this, is there not some way by which I can make him realise the preposterous absurdity of this delusion of his, this belief that he should aim to make an actual copy, a reproduction?

'. . . I am not sure I do not wish that photography had been discovered before painting, so that we of this generation might have had the intense joy of advancing, showing that photography was pretty well in its way, but there was something better!' 'Do you hold that our work is on a level with photography?' 'No, indeed, it is not half as exact. It is less of an art even than photography. . . .'

Eleanora Duse has said: 'To save the theatre, the theatre must be destroyed, the actors and actresses must all die of the plague. They poison the air, they make art impossible.'

We may believe her. . . . The actor must go, and in his place comes the inanimate figure – the Über-marionette we may call him, until he has won for himself a better name. Much has been written about the puppet, or marionette. There are some excellent volumes upon him, and he has also inspired several works of art. Today in his least happy period many people come to regard him as rather a superior doll – and to think he has developed from the doll. This is incorrect. He is a descendant of the stone images of the old temples – he is today a rather degenerate form of a god. Always the close friend of children, he still knows how to select and attract his devotees.

When any one designs a puppet on paper, he draws a stiff and comic-looking thing. Such an one has not even perceived what is contained in the idea which we now call the marionette. He mistakes gravity of face and calmness of body for blank stupidity and angular deformity. Yet even modern puppets are extraordinary things. The applause may thunder or dribble, their hearts beat no faster, no slower, their signals do not grow hurried or confused; and, though drenched in a torrent of bouquets and love, the face of the leading lady remains as solemn, as beautiful and as remote as ever. There is something more than a flash of genius in the marionette, and there is something in him more than the flashiness of displayed personality. The marionette appears to me to be the last echo of some noble and beautiful art of a past civilisation. But as with all art which has passed into fat or vulgar hands, the puppet has become a reproach. All puppets are now but low comedians.

They imitate the comedians of the larger and fuller blooded stage. They enter only to fall on their back. They drink only to reel, and make love only to raise a laugh. They have forgotten the counsel of their mother the Sphinx. Their bodies have lost grave grace, they have become stiff. Their eyes have lost that infinite subtlety of seeming to see; now they only stare. They display and jingle their wires and are cock-sure in their wooden wisdom. They have failed to remember that their art should carry on it the same stamp of reserve that we see at times on the work of other artists, and that the highest art is that which conceals the craft and forgets the craftsman. . . .

May we not look forward with hope to that day which shall bring back to us once more the figure, or symbolic creature, made also by the cunning of the artist, so that we can gain once more the 'noble artificiality' which the old writer speaks of? Then shall we no longer be under the cruel influence of the emotional confessions of weakness which are nightly witnessed by the people and which in their turn create in the beholders the very weaknesses which are exhibited. To that end we must study to remake these images – no longer content with a puppet, we must create an Über-marionette. The Über-marionette will not compete with life – rather will it go beyond it. Its ideal will not be the flesh and blood but rather the body in trance – it will aim to clothe itself with a death-like beauty while exhaling a living spirit. Several times in the course of this essay has a word or two about Death found its way on to the paper – called there by the incessant clamouring of 'Life! Life! Life!' which the realists keep up. And this might be easily mistaken for an affectation, especially by those who have no sympathy or delight in the power and the mysterious joyousness which is in all passionless works of art. . . .

To speak of a puppet with most men and women is to cause them to giggle. They think at once of the wires; they think of the stiff hands and the jerky movements; they tell me it is 'a funny little doll'. But let me tell them a few things about these puppets. Let me again repeat that they are the descendants of a great and noble family of images, images which were indeed made 'in the likeness of God'; and that many centuries ago these figures had a rhythmical movement and not a jerky one; had no need for wires to support them, nor did they speak through the nose of the hidden manipulator. . . . I pray earnestly for the return of the image – the Über-marionette to the theatre; and when he comes again and is but seen, he will be loved so well that once more will it be possible for the people to return to their ancient joy in cere-monies – once more will Creation be celebrated – homage rendered to existence – and divine and happy intercession made to Death.

EDWARD GORDON CRAIG (1872–1966)

The son of the actress Dame Ellen Terry, Craig worked as an actor initially and then later as a designer. He designed productions for Max Reinhardt, Eleonora Duse and Stanislavsky amongst others. He was notorious for his proposal that the actor should be more like a marionette, and can be seen as an early advocate of what would now be understood as director's theatre. His writings were very influential, including his journal *The Mask* (1908–1929). He briefly ran his own theatre school in Rome just before the First World War.

See also: **Konstantin Stanislavsky.**

SUGGESTED FURTHER READING

Craig, E. G. (2009) *On the Art of the Theatre,* London & New York: Routledge.

Innes, C. (1998) *Edward Gordon Craig: A vision of the theatre,* Amsterdam: Harwood Academic Press.
Walton, J. M. (ed.) (1983) *Craig on Theatre,* London: Methuen.

Chapter 8

Jerzy Grotowski

PERFORMER

PERFORMER, WITH A CAPITAL letter, is a man of action. He is not somebody
who plays another. He is a doer, a priest, a warrior: he is outside aesthetic genres.
Ritual is performance, an accomplished action, an act. Degenerated ritual is a show.
I don't look to discover something new but something forgotten. Something so old
that all distinctions between aesthetic genres are no longer of use.

   I am a *teacher of Performer* (I speak in the singular: *of Performer*). A teacher – as in the
crafts – is someone through whom the teaching is passing; the teaching should be
received, but the manner for the apprentice to rediscover it can only be personal. And
how does the teacher himself come to know the teaching? By initiation, or by theft.
Performer is a state of being. A man of knowledge, we can speak of him in reference to
Castaneda's novels, if we like romanticisms. I prefer to think of Pierre de Combas. Or
even of this Don Juan whom Nietzsche described: a rebel face to whom knowledge
stands as duty; even if others don't curse him, he feels to be a changeling, an outsider.
In Hindu tradition they speak of *vratias* (the rebel hordes). *Vratia* is someone who is
on the way to conquer knowledge. A man of knowledge [*czlowiek poznania*] has at his
disposal *the doing* and not ideas or theories. The true teacher – what does he do for
the apprentice? He says: *do it*. The apprentice fights to understand, to reduce the
unknown to the known, to avoid doing. By the very fact that he wants to understand,
he resists. He can understand only after he *does* it. He *does* it or not. Knowledge is a
matter of doing.

DANGER AND CHANCE

When I use the term: warrior, maybe you will refer it to Castaneda, but all scriptures
speak of the warrior. You can find him in the Hindu tradition as well as in the African
one. He is somebody who is conscious of his own mortality. If it's necessary to
confront corpses, he confronts them, but if it's not necessary to kill, he doesn't kill.
Among the Indians of the New World it was said that between two battles, *the warrior
has a tender heart, like a young girl*. To conquer knowledge he fights, because the pulsation

of life becomes stronger and more articulated in moments of great intensity, of danger. Danger and chance go together. One has no class if not face to the danger. In a time of challenge appears the rhythmization of human impulses. Ritual is a time of great intensity; provoked intensity; life then becomes rhythm. *Performer* knows to link body impulses to the song. (The stream of life should be articulated in forms.) The witnesses then enter into states of intensity because, so to say, they feel presence. And this is thanks to *Performer*, who is a bridge between the witness and this something. In this sense, *Performer* is *pontifex*, maker of bridges.

Essence: etymologically, it's a question of being, of be-ing. Essence interests me because nothing in it is sociological. It is what you did not receive from others, what did not come from outside, what is not learned. For example, conscience is something which belongs to essence; it is different from the moral code which belongs to society. If you break the moral code you feel guilty, and it is society which speaks in you. But if you do an act against conscience, you feel remorse – this is between you and yourself, and not between you and society. Because almost everything we possess is sociological, essence seems to be a little thing, but it is ours. In the seventies, in Sudan, there were still young warriors in the villages Kau. For the warrior with organicity in full, the body and essence can enter into osmosis: it seems impossible to dissociate them. But it is not a permanent state; it lasts not long. In Zeami's words, it's the *flower of youth*. However, with age, it's possible to pass from the *body-and-essence* to the *body of essence*. And that in outcome of difficult evolution, personal transmutation, which is in some way the task of everyone. The key question is: What is your process? Are you faithful to it or do you fight against your process? The process is something like the destiny of each one, his own destiny, which develops inside time (or which just unfolds – and that is all). So: *What is the quality of submission* to your own destiny? One can catch the process if what one does is in keeping with himself, if he *doesn't hate what he does*. The process is linked to essence and virtually leads to the *body of essence*. When the warrior is in the short period of osmosis *body-and-essence*, he should catch his process. Adjusted to process, the body becomes non-resistant, nearly transparent. Everything is in lightness, in evidence. With *Performer*, performing can become near process.

THE I–I

It can be read in ancient texts: *We are two. The bird who picks and the bird who looks on. The one will die, the one will live.* Busy with picking, drunk with life inside time, we forgot to *make live* the part in us which looks on. So, there is the danger to exist only inside time, and in no way outside time. To feel looked upon by this other part of yourself (the part which is as if outside time) gives another dimension. There is an I–I. The second I is quasi virtual; it is not – in you – the look of the others, nor any judgment; it's like an immobile look: a silent presence, like the sun which illuminates the things – and that's all. The process can be accomplished only in the context of this still presence. I–I: in experience, the couple doesn't appear as separate, but as full, unique.

In the way of *Performer* – he perceives essence during its osmosis with the body, and then works the process; he develops the I–I. The looking presence of the teacher can sometimes function as a mirror of the connection I–I (this junction is not yet traced). When the channel I–I is traced, the teacher can disappear and *Performer* continue toward the *body of essence*; that which can be – for someone – as if seen in the photo of Gurdjieff, old, sitting on a bench in Paris. From the photo of the young warrior of Kau to that of Gurdjieff is the passage from the *body-and-essence* to the *body of essence*.

I–I does not mean to be cut in two but to be double. The question is to be passive in action and active in seeing (reversing the habit). Passive; to be receptive. Active: to be present. To nourish the life of the I–I, *Performer* must develop not an organism-mass, an organism of muscles, athletic, but an organism-channel through which the energies circulate, the energies transform, the subtle is touched.

Performer should ground his work in a precise structure – making efforts, because persistence and respect for details are the rigor which allow to become present the I–I. The things to be done must be precise. *Don't improvise, please!* It is necessary to find the actions, simple, yet taking care that they are mastered and that they endure. If not, they will not be simple, but banal.

WHAT I RECALL

One access to the creative way consists of discovering in yourself an ancient corporality to which you are bound by a strong ancestral relation. So you are neither in the character nor in the non-character. Starting from details you can discover in you somebody other – your grandfather, your mother. A photo, a memory of wrinkles, the distant echo of a color of the voice enable to reconstruct a corporality. First, the corporality of somebody known, and then more and more distant, the corporality of the unknown one, the ancestor. Is it literally the same? Maybe not literally – but yet as it might have been. You can arrive very far back, as if your memory awakes. That is a phenomenon of reminiscence, as if you recall *Performer* of the primal ritual. Each time I discover something, I have the feeling it is what I recall. Discoveries are behind us and we must journey back to reach them. With the breakthrough – as in the return of an exile – can one touch something which is no longer linked to beginnings but – if I dare say – *to the beginning*? I believe so. Is essence the hidden background of the memory? I don't know at all. When I work near essence, I have the impression that memory actualizes. When essence is activated, it is as if strong potentialities are activated. The reminiscence is perhaps one of these potentialities.

Translated by Thomas Richards
© 1990 Jerzy Grotowski

JERZY GROTOWSKI (1933–1999)

Grotowski studied acting in Krakow and then in Moscow, and saw himself as drawing on the tradition from Stanislavsky. In 1958 he became director of the Theatre of 13 Rows in Opole, Poland. This was eventually to become the Teatr Laboratorium, and was eventually located in Wroclaw. Key productions that helped to define his concept of 'poor theatre' include: *Akropolis, Doctor Faustus* and *The Constant Prince*. His later work included a phase which focused on paratheatrical activity, a period of anthropological performance research, a period of research on the impact of ritual and song on performance (Objective Drama), and his final project, Art as Vehicle.

See also: **Eugenio Barba, Wlodzimierz Staniewski, Peter Brook.**

SUGGESTED FURTHER READING

Grotowski, J. (1969) *Towards a Poor Theatre*, London: Methuen.
Schechner, R. & Woolford, L. (eds.) (1997) *The Grotowski Sourcebook*, London & New York: Routledge.

Kumiega, J. (1985) *The Theatre of Grotowski*, London: Methuen.
Slowiak, J. & Cuesta, J. (2007) *Jerzy Grotowski*, London & New York: Routledge.

Chapter 9

Jacques Lecoq

TOWARDS A YOUNG THEATRE
OF NEW WORK

THE AIM OF THE school is to produce a young theatre of new work, generating performance languages which emphasise the physical playing of the actor.
Creative work is constantly stimulated, largely through *improvisation*, which is also the
first approach to playwriting. The school's sights are set on art theatre, but theatre
education is broader than the theatre itself. In fact my work has always nurtured a
dual aim: one part of my interest is focussed on theatre, the other on life. I have
always tried to educate people to be at ease in both. My hope, perhaps utopian, is for
my students to be consummate livers of life and complete artists on stage. Moreover,
it is not just a matter of training actors, but of educating theatre artists of all kinds:
authors, directors, scenographers as well as actors.

One of the school's unique features is to provide as broad and as durable a
foundation as possible, since we know that each student will go on to make his own
journey using the foundations we provide. Students we train acquire an understanding of acting and develop their imaginations. This allows them either to invent
their own theatre or to interpret written texts, if they so desire, but in new ways.
Interpretation is the extension of an act of creation.

Improvisation is at the heart of the educational process and is sometimes confused
with expression. Yet a person expressing himself is not necessarily being creative.
The ideal, of course, would be for creation and expression to go hand in hand, in
perfect harmony. Unfortunately many people enjoy expressing themselves, 'letting it
all hang out', and forgetting that they must not be the only ones to get pleasure from
it: spectators must receive pleasure, too. There are many teachers who confuse these
two points of view.

The difference between the act of expression and the act of creation is this: in the
act of expression one plays for oneself alone rather than for any spectators. I always
look for an actor who 'shines', who develops a space around himself in which the
spectators are also present. Many absorb this space into themselves, excluding spectators, and the experience becomes too private. If students feel better after doing the
course, that is a bonus, but my aim is not to provide therapy through theatre. In any

process of creation the object made no longer belongs to the creator. The aim of this act of creation is to bear fruit which then separates from the tree.

In my method of teaching I have always given priority to the external world over inner experience. In our work the search for self-enlightenment and for spiritual bliss has little attraction. The ego is superfluous. It is more important to observe how beings and objects move, and how they find a reflection in us. We must give priority to the horizontal and the vertical, to whatever exists outside ourselves, however intangible. People discover themselves in relation to their grasp of the external world, and if the student has special qualities, these will show up in the reflection. I do not search for deep sources of creativity in psychological memories whose 'cry of life mingles with the cry of illusion'. I prefer to see more distance between the actor's own ego and the character performed. This allows the performer to play even better. Actors usually perform badly in plays whose concerns are too close to their own. They adopt a sort of blank voice because they retain part of the text for themselves without being able to hand it on to the public. Neither belief nor identification is enough – one must be able genuinely to play.

My first response to any performer's improvisation or exercise is to make observations, which are not to be confused with opinions. When a car tyre bursts, that's not an opinion, it's a fact. I observe. Opinions can only be formulated afterwards, based on this observation of reality. Observations are made by the teacher surrounded by students. While I am observing, I sense the students anticipating what I shall say. My job is to articulate the observation, but it must be shared by all. There is not much point, after seeing an improvisation, in a teacher saying: 'that gave me pleasure', or 'I liked that a lot.' Different people will like different things. But for an observation to be made one must pay close attention to the living process, while trying to be as objective as possible.

The critical comments one makes about the work do not attempt to distinguish the good from the bad, but rather to separate what is accurate and true from what is too long or too brief, what is interesting from what is not. This might appear pretentious but the only thing which interests us is what is accurate and true: an artistic angle, an emotion, a colour combination. All these aesthetic elements can be found in any durable work of art, independent of its historical dimension. They can be sensed by anyone and an audience always knows perfectly well when something is accurate and true. They may not know why, but it is up to us to know, because we are, after all, specialists.

My comments are always related to the movement I see. Why did that bit of movement fade? Why did we feel that another bit would go on forever? These are simple observations, placed at the service of a living structure. Now every living structure emerges from movement which rises and falls and has its own rhythm. This organic process can be found at work in every improvisation. In this sense, the school could also be seen as providing an education in seeing. Anyone can suggest a theme for an improvisation; it is far more difficult to comment on it afterwards. Rather than handing on a set body of knowledge, it is a question of reaching a common understanding. Master and student must both reach an enhanced level of insight. The master articulates for his students something which he would never have been able to formulate without them, permitting the students, through their commitment and curiosity, to assist at the birth of new insights.

Of course students also need to have their own point of view. In their work they must have ideas and opinions. But if these ideas are not grounded in reality, what use are they? The same phenomenon can be found in painting: Corot, Cézanne or Soutine were able to paint all kinds of trees, to transfigure them or to capture a particular facet, an unusual light for example, but if 'The Tree' had not been there in the painting, nothing would have happened. We always return to the observation of nature and to human realities. I have a strong belief in permanency, in the 'Tree of trees', the 'Mask of masks', the balance that sums up perfect harmony. I realise that this tendency of mine may become an obstacle, but it is one that is necessary. Starting from an accepted reference point, which is neutral, the students discover their own point of view. Of course there is no such thing as absolute and universal neutrality, it is merely a temptation. This is why error is interesting. There can be no absolute without error. I am fascinated by the difference between the geographic pole and the magnetic pole. The north pole does not quite coincide with true north. There is a small angle of difference, and it is lucky that this angle exists. Error is not just acceptable, it is necessary for the continuation of life, provided it is not too great. A large error is a catastrophe, a small error is essential for enhancing existence. Without error, there is no movement. Death follows.

JACQUES LECOQ (1921–1999)

Originally trained in sports, Lecoq became involved in theatre during the Second World War. He worked with Jean Dasté, Copeau's son-in-law, before moving to Italy where he worked with Dario Fo and explored the techniques of Commedia dell'Arte. He returned to Paris in 1956 to found his own international theatre school, which is still operating. Former students include: Geoffrey Rush, Julie Taymor, Simon McBurney, Steven Berkoff, Luc Bondy and Ariane Mnouchkine.

See also: **Jacques Copeau, Dario Fo, Philippe Gaulier, Ariane Mnouchkine.**

SUGGESTED FURTHER READING

Lecoq, J. (2000) *The Moving Body*, London: Methuen.
Lecoq, J. (2006) *Theatre of Movement and Gesture*, ed. D. Bradby, London & New York: Routledge.

Murray, S. (2003) *Jacques Lecoq*, London & New York: Routledge.
Murray, S. (2010) '*Jacques Lecoq*, Monika Pagneux and Philippe Gaulier: Training for play, lightness and disobedience', in Hodge, A. (ed.) (2010) *Actor Training*, London & New York: Routledge.

Chapter 10

Yoshi Oida

LEARNING

IN JAPAN THERE IS a saying that it is better to spend three years looking for a good teacher than to occupy the same period of time doing exercises with someone inferior.

You have to train in order to develop, but you can't study with just anyone. You need to find the right teacher. It doesn't really matter which style or technique you learn. In fact, you could train in disciplines as different as aikido, judo, ballet, or mime, and gain equal benefit. This is because you are learning something beyond technique. When you study with your master, the skills are only the language of understanding, not the purpose. Because you are learning something beyond technique, the subject is less important.

In the martial arts, the stated purpose of training is 'freedom'. Nonetheless, this doesn't mean that the martial arts are automatically the best way to learn 'how to find freedom'. In fact, any physical training system can work. All of them are designed to help you experience how the body and the voice function, which in turn enables you to find freedom through physical activity.

Of course, psychoanalysis or intellectual clarity also help you to become free in your thinking. Movement is not the only way to become mentally free.

According to Zeami, it is useful to commence training in singing and dance at the age of seven (in the Western system of counting age, this would be six years), since at that age children are not self-conscious. They have no ambition, and no clearly defined sense of exhibitionism or 'being successful'. They do not feel pressurised and so when they perform something interesting emerges. A certain beauty.

Zeami called this quality hana, the 'flower' of a performer, and included the sense of 'charm' and 'novelty' in its meaning. This 'charm' is not the same charm that we see in daily life, which is a type of social ease. Nor does it mean physical beauty. It refers specifically to a particular quality of the performer on stage. L.M.

Zeami noted how this *hana* changes as the performer moves through the different stages of his or her career. He says that children have a 'natural flower' that makes almost anything they do interesting to watch, and that it continues up until the age of sixteen or seventeen.

There is an old actor's saying that, 'You should never perform with animals and children, because they will always upstage you.' They are certainly fascinating to watch, but why is our eye caught and held by them? It is a bit of a mystery.

Zeami noted that during the early teens, a performer can probably demonstrate a certain level of technical mastery (if he or she has commenced training at five or six), and this, combined with their natural 'flower', enables them to be quite watchable. As a young actor, your 'charm' disguises weak points in the performance. Nonetheless, you must be careful not to take it too seriously if someone exclaims at the beauty of your acting, since all young actors have this 'charm'. You must not be seduced into believing that you are God's gift to the theatre. Instead, you need to really concentrate on developing your technique: how to strengthen and extend the voice, how to use the body, since the charm you have depended on for so long is about to vanish.

When you reach the age of sixteen or so, you hit a difficult period theatrically. Visually and vocally you appear to be an adult: your body has altered and your voice has either changed or is in the process of changing. Similarly, your thinking patterns are more adult. Consequently, the audience will perceive you as an adult and judge your work accordingly. They will expect to see a polished performance, and you are not technically capable of delivering it. You have lost the 'flower' of childhood, but have not yet fully mastered your craft as a professional. It is a very awkward period, and the most useful thing to do at this point is simply to concentrate on your training. If you find yourself performing badly, don't worry too much, just keep on working.

This difficult period comes to an end around twenty-three or twenty-four, when you enter the most important stage of your professional life. By now your body has virtually finished growing and changing, and you are able to 'digest' physically whatever you have learnt. Your training and your physical development have come together, like a fruit that has ripened. At that age, if you perform in a young role, such as Romeo or Juliet, many people will be impressed and believe you to be a very good actor. It is true that you will look better and perhaps more convincing in that role compared to an older actor, but you shouldn't get too carried away by this success. It is merely a kind of coincidence: being in the right role at the right time. It isn't a measure of skilled acting. When people say that you are good at that age, it is possibly true that you have talent, but you must learn to look at it objectively. If you get carried away with the idea that you are a theatrical genius, you will lose whatever talent you have. You have to look at what you have done objectively, rather than subjectively. If you do so, you will quickly understand how your early success is a kind of coincidence, and that there is no guarantee that it will remain or continue.

Zeami considered the age of thirty-three or thirty-four to be the richest period in an actor's life. You can see the results of all your training, and if you have attained a certain standard or recognition in your work, it will be permanent. It is equally true that if you are still working as a second-rank actor at this age, it is unlikely to change in the future. At twenty-four anything is possible: you can suddenly transform from a mediocre to an excellent actor; but after thirty-four miracles rarely happen. You must be very honest with yourself and objectively analyse your abilities. In addition, if you haven't achieved technical mastery of your art at that age, you have a problem. In about ten years your physical skills will start to decline (around the age of forty-five), so if you haven't got your technique firmly under your belt by thirty-five you will have very little to work with. If, at thirty-five, you are able to 'charm' the audience, this is the real flower of your art. Not the flower of youth or coincidence, but the genuine article.

However, if you cannot find this 'charm' by the age of thirty-five, you should consider your future very carefully. Either you will have to concentrate on your work with twice as much effort, or you should give up. Apart from anything else, you have to realistically examine where and how you can be cast in order to continue working in theatre.

Zeami noted that around forty-three or forty-four you hit another change. Your physical beauty is starting to decline, and your body's energy begins to run out. While you can do extravagant, extraordinary feats of skill at the age of thirty-four with relative ease, you can't do the same actions in the same way at the age of forty-four. This doesn't mean that you have nothing to offer the audience. Instead of demonstrating your technical prowess, you focus on exactly what you are saying or doing. You reduce the outside expression but retain the integrity of your actions. You are no longer dependent on physical beauty, but the audience still senses something delicate and moving that comes from inside. This again is a 'real flower' of the actor's art. Zeami also commented that at this age it is important to analyse carefully what you can and can't do. And to start teaching. This combination of self-analysis and the nourishing of younger actors (and the inevitable dialogue that occurs between these two activities) will keep you developing as a performer right into your old age.

After the age of fifty, Zeami felt that it was almost impossible for an actor to physically reproduce what he had done in the past. At this age, the ability to hold the audience's attention cannot depend on exterior skills. Instead you must base your performance on something which is interior: the 'invisible' part of acting. If this exists, the audience's attention will remain focused on your performance. If an actor has learned real, true acting over all the years prior to the fifties, then even if the tree is old, a bit bent and gnarled, it will still be able to produce a flower. This will not be an extravagant 'charm', but rather a deep and enduring beauty. In an older actor who is truly skilled, the voice might be weak, the body unable to sustain strong activity, yet there will be something interesting, compelling, charming and moving about their work. In this case the acting is almost entirely 'interior'.

But in order to produce a beautiful flower, you have to know what the seed consists of. I believe that the beautiful 'flower' emerges from the opening of the heart. A beautiful 'flower' depends on how you move your inner being. You must discover how this operates, since the quality of your acting reflects this. Even if your body is withered and old, something very beautiful and clear can emerge, if you have maintained a strong and open heart. This goes beyond technique.

Zeami offers three concepts to define the actor's craft. He describes these elements as 'skin', 'flesh' and 'bone'. The skin is the exterior beauty of the actor, the flesh is the beauty that comes through training, and bone is the essential nature of the person, a kind of spiritual beauty. Certain actors are born with an innate quality, which is the skeleton of their craft. Then training provides the flesh, and what finally appears on the outside, to an audience, is the skin.

Another way of describing this is 'looking', 'hearing', and 'feeling'. The audience looks at the actor; the beauty you see is 'skin'. Then the musicality of the performance, the timing, and harmony of expression that you hear is the 'flesh'. Finally, the actor's performance moves you on a deep, almost metaphysical level: you feel something very profound. This is the 'bone' of the artist's craft. On the stage is the beauty of the body, the beauty of the performance, and the beauty of the mind that has created the performance. To be a good actor, each of these elements needs to be maintained at the highest level.

When I talk about the 'beauty', I do not mean 'prettiness' or fashionable beauty. If your spirit ('bone') is beautiful, this is what will appear on the surface.

YOSHI OIDA (1933–)

After training in traditional Japanese theatre, Oida moved to Europe in 1968 to join Peter Brook's international troupe. He has worked extensively with Brook as part of the International Center for Theater Research (C.I.R.T.), performing in *Les Ik, The Conference of the Birds, the Mahabharata* and *The Tempest*, amongst others. He continues to act and direct around the world.

See also: **Peter Brook.**

SUGGESTED FURTHER READING

Oida, Y. (1992) *The Actor Adrift*, London: Methuen.
Oida, Y. (1998) *The Invisible Actor*, London: Methuen.
Oida, Y. (2002) *An Actor's Tricks*, London: Methuen.

Chapter 11

Konstantin Stanislavsky

AN ACTOR'S WORK

CLASS TOOK PLACE in one of the green rooms.

The students had asked to meet long before the rehearsal began. We were afraid we would disgrace ourselves on our first appearance, so we asked Rakhmanov to tell us how we were to behave.

To our amazement and delight Tortsov came to the meeting.

We heard he had been deeply touched by our serious approach to our first appearance.

'You'll know what you have to do and how you have to behave if you think about teamwork,' he told us.

'We all create together, we help each other, we depend on each other. We are all guided by one person, the director.

'Teamwork is pleasant and fruitful if it is properly organized, because then we help each other.

'But without proper order, creative teamwork is torture. People mill about and get in each other's way. Clearly, everyone must, therefore, establish and maintain discipline.'

'How do we do that?'

'First, get to the theatre half or a quarter of an hour before rehearsal starts to assemble all the elements of your creative state.

'If one person is late there's a muddle. If everyone is just a little late then working time is lost in waiting. That leads to a bad atmosphere in which no one can work.

'If, on the other hand, people take their responsibilities to each other seriously and come to rehearsal prepared, that creates a happy atmosphere which encourages you. Then work goes well, because we are all helping each other.

'Imagine for a moment that you've come to the theatre to play a leading role. The show begins in half an hour. You're late because you've had a few minor personal worries and annoyances. Your apartment is in a mess. You've been burgled. The thief took your coat and a new suit. You're also upset because when you got to your dressing room you noticed that the key to the desk where you keep your money is still at home. What if they steal your money, too? You have to pay the rent tomorrow.

You can't put it off as you don't get on with your landlady. And then there's a letter from home. Your father's ill and that upsets you. First, because you love him and second, because if anything happens to him you'll be without financial support. And wages at the theatre are low.

'But, worst of all, is the attitude of the other actors and the management towards you. They laugh at everything you do. They spring surprises on you during the show. They deliberately leave out a key line or suddenly change the moves, or whisper something insulting or disagreeable in mid-action. And you're a shy man, so you get into a muddle. That's what they want, they think it's a laugh. They concoct all sorts of silly tricks because they're bored or for the fun of it.

'Let's explore the Given Circumstances I've just outlined a little further and decide, is it easy to prepare the creative state in these conditions?

'We all recognize, of course, how difficult this is, especially in the short space of time you have before curtain up. With any luck you'll be able to make up and dress.

'But don't worry about that,' Tortsov assured us. 'Our hands automatically put on our wig, make-up and spirit-gum. We don't even know we're doing it. At all events you manage to run onstage at the last minute. The curtain has gone up before you can catch your breath. But your tongue reels off scene one out of habit. Then, once you've got your breath, you can think about "the creative state". You think I'm joking, that I'm being ironic?

'No. Unfortunately we have to admit that this abnormal attitude to our artistic responsibilities occurs all too frequently,' Tortsov concluded.

After a short pause he turned to us again.

'Now,' he said, 'I'll paint another picture.

'Your private life is the same as before – you have problems at home, your father's ill, etc. But there's something quite different in store for you at the theatre. All the members of the artistic family understand and believe what is stated in My Life in Art, that we actors are lucky people because out of all the immeasurable space in the world fate has given us a few square yards in which to build a beautiful artistic life of our own, where we live creatively, and make our dreams flesh by working with others. We are constantly in contact with writers of genius like Shakespeare, Pushkin, Gogol, Molière and others.

'Isn't that enough to create a beautiful little corner for us here on earth?

'But it is even more important, in practical terms, to live in an atmosphere which is conducive to your creative state.'

'It's clear which version we prefer. What's not so clear is how to do it.'

'Very simple,' Tortsov responded. 'If you protect your theatre against "all pollution", you will automatically establish a good atmosphere, which is favourable to the creative state.

'Here's a piece of practical advice. My Life in Art tells us we shouldn't come to the theatre with muddy feet. Clean off the dust and dirt outside, leave your galoshes, your petty cares, squabbles and irritations, which complicate your life and distract you from your art, at the stage door.

'Clean up before you come to the theatre. And once inside, don't spit in corners. Most actors, however, bring all the dirt of their daily lives into the theatre – gossip, intrigue, tittle-tattle, slander, envy, petty vanity. The result is not a temple of art but a spittoon, a rubbish heap, a cesspit.'

'That's inevitable, it's human – success, fame, competition, envy,' said Grisha in defence of the theatre.

'You must rip it all out by the roots!' Tortsov insisted, even more vehemently.

'Is that possible?' Grisha persisted.

'All right. Let's admit you can't get rid of all the dirt in life. But you can, of course, stop thinking about it for a while and turn to something more appealing. You just have to want it deliberately enough and hard enough.'

'An easy thing to say,' said Grisha doubtfully.

'If that's beyond you,' said Tortsov still trying to convince him, 'keep your own dirt at home and don't spoil other people's mood.'

'That's harder still. We all want to get things off our chest,' our argumentative friend persisted.

'I don't understand why Russians think it's their privilege to make a song and dance about their domestic problems and ruin the atmosphere with their whining,' said Tortsov in amazement. 'In all other civilized countries that is considered unseemly, a sign of bad breeding. But we see it as a sign of our profound, sensitive, "Russian soul". How cheap!' said Tortsov, genuinely indignant. 'No, no and no again! We must understand once and for all that washing your dirty linen in public is vulgar, that it reveals a lack of self-control and respect for other people, that it's a bad habit,' said Tortsov hotly. 'We must stop indulging in this self-pity and self-denigration. When you're with other people you must smile, like the Americans. They don't like frowning faces. Weep and wail at home, but when you're with others be warm; happy and pleasant. You must discipline yourselves to do this,' Tortsov insisted.

'We'd be happy to, but how?' the students wondered.

'Think more about other people and less about yourselves. Be concerned for everybody else's mood, everybody else's work and less for your own, then things will go right,' Tortsov advised.

'If all three hundred members of a theatre team brought positive feelings to their work it would cure anybody, even in the blackest mood.

'Which is better, to rummage around in your minds and go over all your grievances, or let the combined strength of three hundred other people help you stop indulging in self-pity and get on with the things you love?

'Who is more free, people who are constantly defending themselves from attack, or people who forget about themselves and are concerned with other people's freedom? If we all behaved this way, in the final analysis, the whole of mankind would defend my freedom.'

'How so?' Vanya asked, puzzled.

'What's so difficult to understand?' asked an astonished Tortsov. 'If ninety-nine people out of a hundred were concerned with their common, that is, my freedom, life would be wonderful for them and me. But if these ninety-nine people are only thinking about their own freedom, and oppress people because of it, and me with them, then I have to fight all the other ninety-nine single-handed to defend my own freedom. Their concern for their own freedom is an unwitting attack on mine. It's the same in the theatre. Not only you, but all the other members of our theatrical family should be able to live happily inside the building. We would create an atmosphere that would overcome bad moods and make you forget your grievances. Then you could work.

'We term this preparation for work, this positive mental disposition, the pre-work state. That is the state in which you should always arrive at the theatre.

'As you can see, we need order, discipline, ethics and the rest not only for the overall structure of our affairs but above all for the artistic goal of our creative work.

'The first condition for creating this pre-work state is expressed in the saying, *love the art in yourself, not yourself in art.* So let your major concern be the well-being of your art.

'Most actors seem to think you only have to work in rehearsal and that you can relax at home.

'That's not the way it is at all. All you learn from rehearsal is what you have to work on at home.

'That's why I mistrust actors who talk a lot in rehearsal. They're convinced they can remember everything without taking notes and planning their work at home.

'Really?! I know perfectly well you can't remember everything, first because the director discusses so many major and minor details, no one could retain them, second because we're not dealing with established facts, but, in most rehearsals, exploring impressions in our Emotion Memory. If you want to understand and recall them, you have to find the right words, expressions, examples, the right written or other kinds of lures so you can evoke and then fix the feeling in question. You must think about it a long time at home before drawing it out of yourself. That's an enormous undertaking and demands great concentration, not only at home but when getting the director's notes.

'We directors know better than most what value to place on an unattentive actor's opinions. We have to remind them of the same note over and over again.

'This attitude towards teamwork is a great obstacle to the common effort. Seven people can't wait for one. So, you have to develop the right *artistic ethics and discipline.*

'That obliges actors to prepare properly for each rehearsal at home. It should be considered shameful and a outrage to the entire cast if the director has to repeat something he has already explained. You mustn't forget the director's notes. You may not be able to take them all in at once, you may have to go back to him to study them further but they shouldn't go in one ear and out the other. That's a crime against everyone working in the theatre.

'So, you must develop an ability to work independently at home, if you want to avoid that. That's not easy, and you must learn to do it properly while you are here at school. I can talk about it slowly and in detail here and now, but I can't turn a rehearsal into a class. The theatre places much more rigorous demands on you than the school. Remember that and prepare for it.'

See pp. 5–6.

PART III

Technique

Introduction to Part III: Technique – Training the Actor's Body and Voice

Jonathan Pitches, University of Leeds, UK

EMPTY (AND FULL) TECHNIQUE

QUESTIONS OF TECHNIQUE in twentieth century actor training are not as cut and dried as the pragmatism of the word implies. Whilst all the practitioners represented in this section recognize the importance of 'good technique' in maintaining a rigorous and responsive acting profession, the term is nevertheless haunted by a concern that proficient technicality is only the first step towards that goal. This ambivalence is reflected in different ways in the practitioner voices featured here. For Vsevolod Meyerhold, for instance, technique is viewed as a necessary foundation for the work of the actor, set in productive tension with the more chaotic forces of creativity. He equates the set of techniques that make up his training in biomechanics with the technical studies or 'études' of a pianist. Indeed, he used the same word for his own acting exercises. Thus in his formulation: 'technique arms the imagination' – and mastering technique is the only way to master art (Schmidt 1996: 41). His roll call of ideal performers personifies this celebration of what he calls 'technical mastery': Duse, Bernhardt, Grasso, Chaliapin and Coquelin (1969: 199). Dario Fo, on the other hand, is far more cautious about the virtues of explicit technique. For him, demonstration of technique is tantamount to creative vacuity, a problem caused, not solved, by the training institution:

> There are very important drama schools which train you in gesture. I know them and have given lessons at them. And what I have noticed is that the young people there have taken on only the *technique* of a given exercise. In the end they are just like empty eggshells. I ask you!
> (Fo & Rame 1983: 23, emphasis in original)

Never frightened to go against the grain, it is hardly surprising that Fo was critical of institutionalized training, but that aside, his observation raises important questions for this essay: if technique can be disappointingly 'empty', what is a *full* technique and how might it be achieved?

This conundrum has been occupying Phillip Zarrilli for nearly four decades (since at least 1976) and his writings on psycho-physicality signify a shift in the way the debate between external technique and the actor's inner processes is expressed. Describing the gradual impact on himself of his training in India in the 1970s, specifically in kalarippayattu and kathakali, he records a change in his experience on stage:

> I was moving from a concern with the physical, external form to aware-
> ness of the subtler internal (psycho-) dimension of how to fully embody an
> action. My body and mind were beginning to become one *in practice*.
> (Zarrilli 2009: 24, emphasis in original)

Zarrilli coins the term 'bodymind' (ibid) for this phenomenon, a neologism designed to conflate the distinction between inner and outer work and an attempt to eliminate what is frequently referred to as a Cartesian divide or dualism. Like Fo, he is concerned with metaphors of emptiness and fullness and sees the integration of the physical and psychological as a pre-requisite for a dynamic creative practice. Such a concern is a running theme in the writings in this section but it is worthy of note that the *expression* of these ideas changes as we move through the last century and into this one. Vakhtangov, writing in 1918, clearly divides inner creative processes (both conscious and unconscious) from what he terms the Organic Outer Technique (Vakhtangov in Malaev-Babel 2011: 120), echoing much of the Russian psycho-physical tradition of training begun by his teacher and mentor Stanislavsky. Zarrilli, almost a century later, is consciously shifting the agenda away from such brute distinctions of body and mind, even if he is searching for a cognate organicity. In fact, all the practitioners represented here struggle with this fundamental problem: how to express a holistic view of the performer's task, valuing the rigour and craft associated with physical technique, whilst celebrating the ineffable spark of inspiration.

PRINCIPLES OF TAXONOMY: ORGANISING THE PRACTITIONERS

Before proceeding to a consideration of how this core theme of psycho-physicality relates to the other themes in this section, let us pause and consider the practitioners themselves and, specifically, how we might organise them – a complex and political task in itself. The passage above already assumes some knowledge of existing principles of organisation for training regimes that perhaps need making explicit. I have referenced the Russian tradition, without explaining that different countries come with varied histories and lineages and fascinating connections between practitioners passing on ideas within a culture. I have suggested that thinking chronologically might raise an awareness of *changes* in perception and expression that operate across these geographies – from inner-versus-outer to the idea of 'bodymind'. I have also implied that practitioners have their own reference points (Meyerhold's wish-list of ideal performers, for example) and this, itself, raises interesting questions of how practitioners borrow ideas and practices from other traditions as well as from their own. This latter phenomenon might be simply expressed as the difference between horizontal (synchronic) and vertical (diachronic) transmission.

In addition to these points is the important consideration of gender, too often overlooked in writings on training and on practitioners. There are thirteen practitioners describing their understanding of technique in this section and only one of them is female, Kristin Linklater. This fact accurately expresses the depressing balance of power in actor training over the last century – Alison Hodge's first edition of *Twentieth Century Actor Training* (2000), featured only two women out of fourteen practitioners, for instance. But it does not represent the current state of actor training criticism. The second edition of Hodge's book (2010) included six female actor trainers – Monika Pagneux, Stella Adler, Anne Bogart, Joan Littlewood, Maria Knebel and Ariane Mnouchkine – and we might immediately add to that list recent documentation of the training practices of: Lorna Marshall, Katie Mitchell, Mary Overlie, Litz Pisk, Uta Hagen, Viola Spolin, Joanna Merlin, Rena Mirecka, Cicely Berry, Niamh Dowling, Pina Bausch, Anna Halprin, Dorinda Hulton, Patsy Rodenberg and Alison Hodge herself[1]. Second, third and fourth editions of this Reader will no doubt capture this shift.

So, to return to the question of organisation, I would like to suggest three complementary taxonomies for this section: i) grouping by historical context, ii) by tradition (geographically and culturally) and, iii) by the system-individual dialectic suggested by Ian Watson in *Performer Training: Developments across Cultures* (2001). Watson argues that:

> [The] expansion of interest in training has led to a shift in concern that in some ways rejects the very notion of systematized training ... Experimentalists like Grotowski and Barba especially ... have moved away from the idea of developing a system of training consisting of skill development and perfected techniques. Their concerns are with the individual actor.
>
> (Watson, 2001: 7)

In many ways the historical context is the most straightforward, notwithstanding the problems of periodization that dog all theatre historiographies[2]. The writings here span over 90 years of theatre practice from Vakhtangov's 'On consciousness' (1917) to Zarrilli's 'Beginning with the Breath' (2009). The majority of the work was written after the Second World War but Meyerhold (1922) and Artaud (1938) offer significant additions to Vakhtangov's pre-war statements and Saint-Denis' *On Training* is a synthesis of ideas formed first with his uncle Jacques Copeau in France in the 1920s and then solidified with his founding of the London Theatre Studio and Old Vic Theatre Studio (1935 and 1947, respectively). Laban's work on *Effort* was published just after the war in 1947. The remaining examples span the 1960s (Grotowski, 1969; Feldenkrais, 1966), the 1970s (Linklater, 1976), the 1980s, (Lecoq – first published in French in 1987; Suzuki, 1986 and Barba, 1986) and finally the 1990s (Boal's *Games for Actors and Non-Actors* was first published in 1992).

Considering these practitioners in terms of the traditions they both inhabit and exemplify is more problematic but arguably still worthwhile. Indeed, the problems one encounters in attempting this kind of categorisation are instructive: no tradition is entirely sealed off from its neighbours and never more so when the focus is on embodied traditions, such as those represented here. There are three 'clear' training traditions in this section: Russian (Vakhtangov and Meyerhold), French (Artaud, Lecoq, Saint-Denis) and Polish (Grotowski and Barba[3]). It might be argued, given the work done in the UK by both Feldenkrais and Laban, more or less at the same time (i.e. the mid-late 1940s) that a British theatre tradition is also reflected in these writings, a space which Scottish-born practitioner and expert in voicing Shakespeare, Kristin Linklater, might also occupy.

That leaves the Brazilian Augusto Boal, the Japanese Tadashi Suzuki and American Phillip Zarrilli. Are these representatives of their native country's traditions too? Well, yes and no. Boal's work grew out of a very specific context of political struggle in Brazil in the 1950s and 1960s, but he was forced into exile in 1971, first in Argentina and then in Europe. Since then his work in the Theatre of the Oppressed has impacted on a truly global scale to the extent that 'there is scarcely a country it has not touched' (Babbage 2004: 30). It is misleading to say, then, that Boal's work is representative of any one tradition of training. To suggest Tadashi Suzuki's practice is exemplary of the long-standing tradition of Japanese theatre is equally problematic. As he makes clear in *The Way of Acting* below, the ancient traditions of Noh and Kabuki are central to his understanding of training and specifically in the celebration of the actor's feet as 'the basis of a stage performance' (Suzuki 1986: 6). But European Classical Ballet and the ancient Greek theatre are also fundamental reference points for the Suzuki Company of Toga, and famously the training forms 'half' of the international, cultural collaboration project, SITI Theatre Company, alongside fellow co-founder, Anne Bogart and her Viewpoints training[4]. Again, there is much more to Suzuki training than its claim to a place in the lineage of classical Japanese theatre, rich though that tradition is. For Zarrilli, the training is consciously hybridized as suggested above. An American practitioner, who has worked for many years in the British Higher Education system, Zarrilli draws on yoga, kalarippayattu and taiquiquan practices, equipping his actors with skills for contemporary theatre: a process he likens to 'transposition' rather than 'synthesis':

> When the contemporary actor trains in non-Western psycho-physical disciplines there is a necessary process of transposing the underlying psycho-dynamic elements and principles into a new key.
>
> (Zarrilli 2009: 82)

Zarrilli is clear in *Psychophysical Acting* that even the so-called vertical, indigenous practices of South Asia (such as kathakali) are undergoing significant change. What was once training in a fixed repertoire of physical and dramaturgical conventions, passed on from master to student over several years is now responding to rapid globalization, recognizing that 'young people do not have the time to devote hours to a traditional training' (2009: 81). Viewed from the point of view of tradition, then, the collection of practitioners represented here exemplifies many of the realities of cultural transmission – it is complex, non-linear, porous and consciously or unconsciously eclectic.

Finally, it might be possible to organise the readings in this section in terms of Watson's deceptively simple model of system-versus-individual. In doing so we can test his argument that the last century witnessed a move from big picture, grandiose, systems thinking – the grand narratives of modernist actor training – to a far more localized and specialized focus on individual actors. This suggestion echoes another much-debated cultural shift in the twentieth century – from modernism to post-modernism – and develops a healthy line of skepticism about training practices that claim some kind of universal applicability and, by extension, cultural dominance. Such claims might have been defensible in a context of national revisioning – in early Soviet times for instance – but are much less sustainable in a world of global mobility and technological connectivity.

Perhaps unsurprisingly the Russian tradition of training is one which is clearly underpinned by a systematizing urge – not just because Vakhtangov's teacher

Stanislavsky called his whole regime, *the* System, but also because his contemporaries were pursuing similarly utopian and all-encompassing projects. The key principles of Meyerhold's biomechanics, for instance, were expressed in the universal language of mathematics: '$N = A_1 + A_2$' (Meyerhold quoted in Braun 1969: 198) where N is the actor and $A_1 + A_2$ represent two halves of the creative process, conception and execution. Barba and Grotowski, as Watson argues, are at the other end of the spectrum, developing bespoke training approaches for each of their actors, an idea embodied in Barba's term for his actor-collaborators: 'auto-didact' or *self-*teacher. But where does one place the remaining practitioners along this continuum and does this tally with the chronology of publication dates outlined above? Again the answer is an ambivalent yes and no. Many of the practitioners here developed systems of a kind – in the form of a carefully designed training curriculum (Saint-Denis, Lecoq or, speculatively, Linklater) or in Laban's case in the form of a new notation scheme to record movement (Labanotation). Others, such as Boal, established set techniques to deliver their aims: forum theatre, invisible theatre and image theatre for instance. But the application of these techniques could never be divorced from the individual (socio-political) contexts and sites of power where Boal's ideas are applied, be that in Rio or Rochdale. One might argue that the most systematized of all the regimes represented in this section is the work of Feldenkrais, the only practitioner here whose training has a specific accreditation system and a formal qualification framework. But that would be to overlook the highly individualized approach Feldenkrais teachers adopt with their students. One of the most difficult practitioners to consider along a system-individual continuum is Antonin Artaud, perhaps an indicator in itself of his visionary iconoclasm. Even with his fascination for highly codified forms of training from South East Asia, and specifically Balinese dance, Artaud's emphasis on the *affective* possibilities of the actor and their visceral impact on the spectator must suggest that his is a theatre rooted in the individual, as he suggests in his essay below: 'the actor is a heart athlete . . . The affective area is *his own*' (1970: 88, my emphasis).

So what is there to conclude from this summary application of Watson's model to the range of practitioners in this section? Firstly, that the system-individual dialectic operates more readily *within* the practices documented here, rather than on a larger historical scale, even if the respective ends of that scale (Vakhtangov/ Stanislavsky and Barba) seem to be secure. Secondly, and more generally, that all organising principles are themselves constructs and must be treated with a healthy dose of caution – none more so than history and tradition. Such critical caution will help as we move now to identifying some more localized thematic connections.

HABIT, NEUTRALITY, MECHANICS AND ORGANICS: SOME TRAINING THEMES

The habitual in training references a number of key ideas: a daily practice, a lack of consciousness and a responsiveness resulting from intense and lengthy training processes. As such, habit is a double-edged sword in training. In many ways it is the cornerstone of technique, as the formation of habits is dependent on repetition and training is all about repetition. But several practitioners address the flipside of habit in their writings – the *unconscious*, thoughtless element of habitual movement or behavior – and identify practices designed to break habits, or at the very least defamiliarize them for an actor. For Moshe Feldenkrais the individual's habitual body (the 'self-image') is often misconstrued on a grand scale:

> Close your eyes and try to represent the width of your mouth with your index fingers. It is not unusual to discover an error of up to three hundred percent in exaggeration or underestimation.
>
> (1996: 115)

Anything more than a one hundred percent deviation between the self-image and the objective real facts is problematic for Feldenkrais because in those circumstances: 'the behavior of that part of the body is generally defective' (1996: 116). The only way to remedy this is to relinquish the habitual body attitude 'by choice', that is to divest oneself of the learnt and accustomed habits inscribed in the body by one's own unique past. In his interview with Schechner, two of the terms for this rethinking of habituated movement are laid down: i) the potential reversibility of gesture and ii), the maintenance of a state of action or readiness. These apply to all of the actor's abilities beyond just movement, including the voice, the breath, the eyes – the 'total body organism', in fact (1996: 117).

Boal raises a similar concern about habituation and repetition but his focus is on the emotional dimension of this problem. Identifying the influence of Stanislavsky, (rather than the oft-cited Brechtian inspiration for his theatre), Boal describes the challenge he faced when directing in Sao Paolo in Brazil, working with actors whose freedom to express emotions had been stymied by a history of overtly external approaches to directing. Drawing on Stanislavsky in a 'methodical study' of his works, Boal sought to undermine what he considered to be a fundamental block for Brazilian actors:

> A newly discovered emotion runs the risk of being canalised by the mechanised patterns of the actor's behaviour; the emotion may be blocked by a body already hardened by habit to a certain set of actions and reactions.
>
> (1992: 40)

Boal accepts that there are benefits to this habituation, which shields humankind from the overload of sensations we would otherwise experience on a daily basis. Our senses are protectively selective, he argues, to ensure that the complexity of each operation we undertake is not overwhelming – a process Drew Leder has articulated as the body's capacity to engineer its own absence or disappearance (Leder 1990). But such sensory deafness is not the stuff of creative practice. As Stanislavsky (2008) had recognized with his observation exercises[5], an actor needs to be dynamically sensitive to her own emotions in order that they may be communicated with freshness and surprise. Like Feldenkrais, the approach Boal advocates is one of 'detuning' so that the actor can 'relearn to perceive emotions and sensations he has lost the habit of recognising' (1992: 41).

Kristin Linklater uses another metaphor for this process, but she is demonstrably pursuing the same aim. In her 'hypothetical four year actor-training program' and in common with many conservatoire programmes, she envisions the first year as 'an undoing process [which] begins to break down physical and vocal habits' (1976: 202). Her simple formula is the principle of 'release then development', in which each individual actor is gently taught to forget any previous ways of working, to become sensitive to the 'interior world of self' (1976: 203) and then to approach making work with others in combinations of growing complexity. Her writing thus suggests a model of training based on subtraction and addition; an actor needs 'de-conditioning' (1976: 203) before reconditioning, a delicate process that can be upset by entering the industry prematurely. Whilst her focus is on physical and vocal habits and her aim is to 'free up' the voice, as the title of her book suggests, it is worth noting that critics have questioned this line of thinking, as it assumes that emptying the actor – or in other terms pursuing 'neutrality' – is achievable in the first place[6].

Jacques Lecoq's work (and also Michel Saint-Denis') operationalizes the idea of neutrality through the agency of the 'neutral mask'. But whilst the term may be part of the same questionable idea of a psycho-physical 'blank slate', in practical terms neutral mask work also reveals the individuality of the actor. Lecoq's description in *The Theatre of Movement and Gesture* draws an important distinction between the mask *as concept* and the mask *as agent*. Conceptually, Lecoq argues, 'the neutral mask is a sort of common denominator for both men and women', archetypal rather than typical in function as: 'you can't have a neutral mask called Albert who wakes up in his bed' (2006: 105). But an important part of the experience of neutral mask work is to move beyond the habits of everyday expression, to engage the body far more directly in communication and 'to discover a new freedom that is greater than the naked face' (2006: 105). That freedom can only come from what are considered to be the suppressed creative capacities of the individual actor, released, perhaps counter-intuitively, by the mask with 'no particular expression or characteristic' (2006: 105).

Pursuing this theme of neutrality further takes us to Jerzy Grotowski and his notion of *via negativa* or 'process of elimination' (1969: 101). He too sees the untrained actor as a site of negative impediments that need to be pared back in order to free the performer:

> We must find out what it is that hinders him in the way of respiration, movement and – most important of all – human contact. What resistances are there? How can they be eliminated? I want to take away, steal from the actor, all that disturbs him. That which is creative will remain with him. It is a liberation.
>
> (1969: 209)

However, it is not through the use of mask work that this liberation is discovered, but through a personalized exercise regime of auto-research, reminding us of the system-individual dialectic scrutinized above. Grotowski recognizes that there are no universals when it comes to corporeal training, only individual discoveries. The actor's task is to achieve a level of self-awareness, through personal training-as-research. Automatic repetition is to be avoided at all costs, again a common theme in this Part. Importantly, it is not the forms of the exercises themselves, but the process of what Grotowski calls *investigation* that is so valuable and here he is undoubtedly expressing the influence of Stanislavsky, whose own investigative research into the processes of acting, occupied his entire life.

The last theme to be drawn out of these writings is a two-sided one: training mechanics and training organics, a fitting concluding theme as it returns us to the bigger picture of twentieth century cultural shifts – or more accurately, tensions. I have argued elsewhere (Pitches, 2006) that there are two dominant tropes to training in the Russian tradition: a mechanistic or Newtonian strand of activity and a neo-Romantic or organic strand. The extracts below suggest that this particular modeling of the twentieth century extends beyond Russian acting.

The extent to which Meyerhold espoused industrial theories and the rhetoric of mechanics has been outlined above, through his controversial 'formula for acting'. Later in his lecture on biomechanics he claims, equally controversially, that: 'the Taylorisation of the theatre will make it possible to perform in one hour that which requires four at present' (in Braun 1969: 199). And whilst these words clearly need treating with some suspicion (his own production of *The Government Inspector* was over four hours long!), there are strong resonances between the ideas of the industrial theorist, Frederick Winslow Taylor, and the structuring and physical execution of Meyerhold's biomechanical études. A similar fascination for the scientific measurement of effort is reflected in Rudolph Laban's work, although it is fair to say that Laban's application of these ideas was far more systematic and analytical (and certainly less opportunistic). Laban's writing on effort here is directly drawn from the application of his understanding of movement principles to industry – in British factories in the late 1940s and 1950s. Laban's terminology in articulating these meeting points is indicative of the mechanistic theme:

> Man's body engine is constructed in a manner that in principle all imaginable effort-combinations can be performed with relative ease and balance.
>
> (in McCaw 2011: 224)

There are echoes here with Feldenkrais when Laban elaborates on some of the problems experienced by workers – not due to a misleading 'self-image' but to what Laban calls a 'lopsided effort-habit' (in McCaw 2011: 224), which just as significantly impedes the individual's ability to move efficiently. Laban's analysis of effort, broken down into the four measurable constituents: Time, Weight, Space and the underlying phenomenon of Flow, help him to diagnose in typically forensic terms the characteristics necessary for the realignment of effort and to recognise both physical and psychological domains.

Viewing the training process through the lens of engineering and industry offers one potent metaphor for the development of technique – indeed the dictionary definition of the term cites the meeting point between, craft, industry and dexterity: 'a particular way of carrying out an experiment, procedure, or task, esp. in a scientific discipline or a craft; a technical or scientific method . . . a skilful or efficient means of achieving a purpose'[7], reminding us of the close connections between training, making and science.

An alternative, organic perspective is even more prevalent in the writings in this section and generates similarly rich metaphors. Tadashi Suzuki's stamping practice offers one such example:

> In stamping, we come to understand that the body establishes its relation to the ground through the feet, that the ground and the body are not two separate entities. We are part of the ground. Our very beings will return to the earth when we die.
>
> (1986: 9)

Suzuki is concerned to re-engage the actor's body with the environment. Wearing footwear, whether elaborately formal or domestic, breaks the connection between the actor and the earth and shakes the foundation of her creative work. For Suzuki, the feet are a meeting point – between the past and the future, between the actor and her surroundings and between the constituents of the actor's physical expressivity – voice, rhythm, energy, gesture.

Yevgeny Vakhtangov's choice of metaphor is in very much the same vein. An actor should not submit her subconscious to training but have it *cultivated*, a subtle distinction lost on the formal training institutions:

> God only knows what goes on in theatre schools. The main mistake the schools make is that they take it upon themselves *to teach how to act*, while they should be *cultivating actors.*
>
> (in Malaev-Babel 2011: 119)

In terms starkly reminiscent of Dario Fo, quoted above, Vakhtangov is suspicious of the deadening influence formal training may have on the actor. Indeed he chose the metaphor of cultivation provocatively to underline the distinction between the heavy-handed didacticism he saw in the theatre school sector and the nurturing rhythms needed for the alternative acting pedagogy he was pursuing alongside Stanislavsky[8]. Why 'cultivation'? Because, Vakhtangov argued, the delicate relationship between the subconscious and the conscious can wither and die as easily as an untended plant.

This organic visioning of the creative processes underlying acting technique is striking in the writings in this section: Artaud's notion of the actor as 'affective organism', Zarrilli's own 'cultivated' bodymind, Michel Saint-Denis' total actor, achieving 'a chemistry that leads to vitality of speech and communication'. All these examples suggest that the practitioners are grasping for a language that expresses some of the very difficult-to-express complexities of acting. But rather than attempting to evaluate the accuracy of the metaphors themselves, it is important to reflect that these choices of allusive terminology are laden with evidence of the practitioners' own histories, traditions and cultural reference points; it is these we should concentrate on most readily.

CONCLUSION

Cautious of suggesting there is one definitive approach to understanding these fascinating source materials, I have presented a series of methods: chronological, cultural and geographical (tradition), methodological (system-individual) and finally metaphorical and thematic. I have clearly not exhausted any of these approaches and there are undoubtedly many other ways to analyze these writings on technique. I have not addressed in detail questions of psycho-physicality for instance, although all of the theatre artists represented here are concerned with the relationship between mind and body, even those who deny such distinctions. Where each of these practitioners might be located on a psycho-physical continuum is just one alternative mapping exercise. Nor have I considered the extent to which these training regimes may (or may not) be responsive to their immediate political context (a continuum of located or dislocated practice). I have only considered four of the prominent metaphors used in the writings on training but there are countless others. What would emerge from a scrutiny of the terms freedom or constraint, flow, energy, action or *reaction*? And how might these ideas be incorporated into practices undertaken today? I have only been able to sketch some of the salient moments from selected practitioners' lives – Zarrilli's epiphany of embodying action, Boal's Stanislavskian experiments in

Rio – but all of these artists enjoyed (and some are still enjoying), multi-faceted careers in actor training and theatre making, often with significant changes in their own attitudes to the idea of technique. These materials will doubtless stimulate further research journeys and curiosities.

More than anything my reading of these documents has confirmed in my mind the need for a diversity of techniques, rather than the promotion of any one Technique. This is not to say that a training in any one of the sets of ideas formulated here should be avoided; there is always the danger of dilettantism and cultural cherry-picking. But when any approach to training is raised to the status of a Technique[9], that surreptitious capitalization of the 'T' often signifies a conscious, territorial appropriation of the field, one that conveniently forgets the inevitable cross-fertilization of practices that make up all training regimes. Viewed together these thirteen essays celebrate those borrowings, appropriations and transformations either tacitly or directly – a truism that withstands, howsoever we might choose to organise them.

PROVOCATIONS

1   Technique and inspiration are incompatible bedfellows: how might actor training best ensure a happier marriage?

2   Will synchronous borrowing of ideas inevitably characterize the twenty-first century actor? And what will be the impact of such a change on the teaching and learning of technique – further dilution or greater refinement?

3   Should the development of technique through training be institutionalized or individualized?

4   Technique only creates craftspeople, it cannot create change.

Notes

1   Of course this is not meant to be in anyway comprehensive, simply a snapshot of recent publications addressing the gender imbalance in actor training documentation.

2   Thomas Postlewait is particularly lucid on this point: 'Whether we refer to large eras, such as the medieval age, or specific ones, such as the 1920s, the period concept is our way of freezing a segment of time, and giving it an identity. We must remember, though, that the concept is located within us, not within history itself. In short, it is a classification that we create and then project onto the past' (2009:157).

3   Barba is Italian and his theatre (Odin Teatret) is based in Denmark. But he visited Poland in the early 1960s where he met Grotowski and in Jane Turner's words: learnt 'what it is to create a tradition and how an actor might then go on to embody and transform that tradition' (2004: 5).

4   See http://siti.org/content/training for more details.

5   For instance in the chapter Concentration and Attention: 'I am talking about ways of giving the imagination a jolt, which would help you stir it when it is inactive. This technique arouses your powers of concentration, it leads you away from the position of coolly observing someone else's life and raises your creative temperature a degree or two (Stanislavsky 2008: 116).

6   See, for example, Mark Evans: 'the concept of the neutral body . . . has become central to much contemporary occidental actor training; however its complexity as an idea, its association with particular paradigms, and the misunderstandings the concept of

neutrality has generated . . . mean that critiquing the ''neutral'' body reveals assumptions which underpin several positions which marginalize the body' (2009: 176).

7   ''technique, n.''. OED Online. December 2013. Oxford University Press. 17 January 2014 <http://www.oed.com/view/Entry/198458?redirectedFrom=technique>.

8   For more details see Malaev-Babel's *The Vakhtangov Sourcebook*: 'Even at the most progressive Russian acting schools or conservatories of the period, students spend most of their time studying parts. The teacher, instead of providing training for specific skills and qualities essential to an actor, would see his or her duty as imposing their own way of acting particular roles on the students' (2011: 8).

9   One example of this phenomenon (evident in the contents listings, at least) is *Training of the American Actor*, edited by Arthur Bartow: 'LEE STRASBERG TECHNIQUE, STELLA ADLER TECHNIQUE, MEISNER TECHNIQUE, BEYOND MICHAEL CHEKHOV TECHNIQUE, UTA HAGEN'S TECHNIQUE' (2006: ix-x).

Bibliography

Artaud, A. (1970) *The Theatre and its Double*, trans. V. Corti. London: Calder & Boyars.

Babbage, F. (2004) *Augusto Boal*, London & New York: Routledge.

Bartow, A. (ed.) (2006) *Training of the American Actor*, New York: Theatre Communications Group.

Boal, A. (1992) *Games for Actors and Non-Actors*, London & New York: Routledge.

Braun, E. (ed.) (1969) *Meyerhold on Theatre*, London: Methuen.

Evans, M. (2009) *Movement Training for the Modern Actor*, London & New York: Routledge.

Feldenkrais, M. (1996) 'image, Movement, and Actor: Restoration of Potentially', *TDR*, 10:3,112–26.

Fo, D. and Rame, F. (1983) *Theatre Workshops at the Riverside Studios, London*, London: Red Notes.

Grotowski, J. (1969) *Towards a Poor Theatre*, London: Methuen.

Hodge, A. (ed.) (2010) *Actor Training*, 2nd edition, London & New York: Routledge.

Lecoq, J. (2006) *Theatre of Movement and Gesture*, ed. and trans. D. Bradby, London & New York: Routledge.

Leder, D. (1990) *The Absent Body*, Chicago: University of Chicago Press.

Linklater, K. (1976) *Freeing the Natural Voice*, New York: Drama Publishing.

McCaw, D. (ed.) (2011) *The Laban Sourcebook*, London & New York: Routledge.

Malaev-Babel, A. (2011) *The Vakhtangov Sourcebook*, London & New York: Routledge.

Pitches, J. (2006) *Science and the Stanislavsky Tradition of Acting*, London & New York: Routledge.

Postlewait, T. (2009) *The Cambridge Introduction to Theatre Historiography*, Cambridge: Cambridge University Press.

Schmidt, P. (1996) *Meyerhold at Work*, New York: Applause.

Stanislavsky, K. (2008) *An Actor's Work*, trans J. Benedetti, London & New York: Routledge.

Suzuki, T. (1986) *The Way of Acting: the theatre writings of Tadashi Suzuki*, New York: Theatre Communications Group.

Turner, J. (2004) *Eugenio Barba*, London & New York: Routledge.

Watson, I. (ed.) (2001) *Performer Training: developments across cultures*, London & New York: Routledge.

Zarrilli, P. (2009) *Psycho-physical Acting: An intercultural approach after Stanislavski*, London & New York: Routledge.

Chapter 12

Antonin Artaud

AN AFFECTIVE ATHLETICISM

ONE MUST GRANT the actor a kind of affective musculature matching the bodily localisation of our feelings.

An actor is like a physical athlete, with this astonishing corollary; his affective organism is similar to the athlete's, being parallel to it like a double, although they do not act on the same level.

The actor is a heart athlete.

In his case the whole man is also separated into three worlds; the affective area is his own.

It belongs to him organically.

The muscular movements of physical exertion are a likeness, a double of another exertion, located in the same points as stage acting movements.

The actor relies on the same pressure points an athlete relies on to run, in order to hurl a convulsive curse whose course is driven inward.

Similar anatomical bases can be found in all the feints in boxing, all-in-wrestling, the hundred metres, the high jump and the movements of the emotions, since they all have the same physical support points.

With this further rider that the moves are reversed and in anything to do with breathing, for instance, an actor's body relies on breathing while with a wrestler, a physical athlete, the breathing relies on his body.

The question of breathing is of prime importance; it is inversely proportional to external expression.

The more inward and restrained the expression, the more ample, concentrated and substantial breathing becomes, full of resonances.

Whereas breathing is compressed in short waves for ample, fiery externalised acting.

We can be sure that every mental movement, every feeling, every leap in human affectivity has an appropriate breath.

These breathing *tempi* have a name taught us by the Cabala, for they form the human heart and the gender of our emotional activity.

An actor is merely a crude empiricist, a practitioner guided by vague instinct.

Yet on no consideration does this mean we should teach him to rave.

What is at stake is to end this kind of wild ignorance in the midst of which all present theatre moves, as if through a haze, constantly faltering. A gifted actor instinctively knows how to tap and radiate certain powers. But he would be astonished if he were told those powers which make their own substantial journey through the senses existed, for he never realised they could actually exist.

To use his emotions in the same way as a boxer uses his muscles, he must consider a human being as a Double, like the Kha of the Egyptian mummies, like an eternal ghost radiating affective powers.

As a supple, never-ending apparition, a form aped by the true actor, imposing the forms and picture of his own sensibility on it.

Theatre has an effect on this Double, this ghostly effigy it moulds, and like all ghosts this apparition has a long memory. The heart's memory endures and an actor certainly thinks with his heart, for his heart holds sway.

This means that in theatre more than anywhere else, an actor must become conscious of the emotional world, not by attributing imaginary merits to it, but those with concrete meaning.

Whether this hypothesis is exact or not, the main thing is that it can be authenticated.

The soul can be physiologically summarised as a maze of vibrations.

This ghostly soul can be regarded as exhilarated by its own cries, otherwise what are the Hindu mantras, those consonances, those strange stresses where the soul's secret side is hounded down into its innermost lairs, to reveal its secrets publicly.

Belief in the soul's flowing substantiality is essential to the actor's craft. To know that an emotion is substantial, subject to the plastic vicissitudes of matter, gives him control over his passions, extending our sovereign command.

To arrive at the emotions through their powers instead of regarding them as pure extraction, confers a mastery on an actor equal to a true healer's.

To know there is a physical outlet for the soul permits him to journey down into that soul in a reverse direction as well as to discover existence by calculated analogies.

To understand the mystery of passionate time, a kind of musical tempo conducting its harmonic beat, is an aspect of the drama modern psychological theatre has certainly disregarded for some time.

To reforge the links, the chain of a rhythm when audiences saw their own real lives in a show. We must allow audiences to identify with the show breath by breath and beat by beat.

It is not enough for the audience to be riveted by the show's magic and this will never happen unless we know where to affect them. We have had enough of chance magic or poetry which has no skill underlying it.

In theatre, poetry and skill must be associated as one from now on.

Every emotion has an organic basis and an actor charges his emotional voltage by developing his emotions within him.

The key to throwing the audience into a magical trance is to know in advance what pressure points must be affected in the body. But theatre poetry has long become unaccustomed to this invaluable kind of skill.

To be familiar with the points of localisation in the body is to reforge the magic links.

Using breathing's hieroglyphics, I can rediscover a concept of divine theatre.

N.B. – In Europe no one knows how to scream any more, particularly actors in a trance no longer know how to cry out, since they do nothing but talk, having forgotten they have a body on stage, they have also lost the use of their throats. Abnormally shrunk, these throats are no longer organs but monstrous, talking abstractions. French actors now only know how to talk.

ANTONIN ARTAUD (1896–1948)

After prolonged sickness as a child and young man, Artaud eventually moved to Paris where he discovered his talent as a writer and his interest in avant-garde theatre. During this period he was an active member of the surrealist movement. From 1926–1928 he ran the Alfred Jarry Theatre in Paris and attracted the interest of leading literary and theatrical innovators of the time. He was later influenced by his experience of Balinese theatre. After travel to Mexico and Ireland in the early 1940s, he returned to France suffering from mental illness and was placed in an asylum. His work has been highly influential, if not often well understood.

See also: **Peter Brook, Jacques Lecoq, Jerzy Grotowski.**

SUGGESTED FURTHER READING

Artaud, A. (1970) *Theatre and its Double*, trans. V. Corti, London: Calder & Boyars.

Barber, S. (1993) *Antonin Artaud: Blows and bombs*, London: Faber & Faber.
Scheer, E. (2003) *Antonin Artaud: A critical reader*, London & New York: Routledge.

Chapter 13

Eugenio Barba

PHYSICAL TRAINING
AND VOCAL TRAINING

PHYSICAL TRAINING

DURING THE EIGHT YEARS of Odin Teatret's existence, its actors have trained regularly. Our vision of this training, its forms and aims, have undergone a continuous evolution due to experience, to the contribution of new members and to new needs which have grown up during the work.

At the beginning, the training was composed of a series of exercises taken from pantomime, ballet, gymnastics, sports – exercises which we knew or which we had reconstructed. Training was collective: everybody did the same exercises at the same tempo and in the same way.

In time, it became clear to us that rhythm varies from person to person. Some have a fast vital rhythm, others a slower one. We began to talk of organic rhythm and by this we meant variation, pulsation as with the heart. From then on the training was based on this rhythm. It became personalized, individual.

Gradually, the exercises which we developed, although remaining the same, changed their meaning. The exercise is like a gate in a slalom through which the actor guides his physical activity, thereby disciplining it.

In our theatre, training has always consisted of an encounter between discipline – that is, the exercise's set form – and the surpassing of that set form, which the exercise represents. The motivation for this surpassing is individual, varying from actor to actor, and it is this justification which determines the significance of the training.

At the present time – October 1972 – the training is based on very elementary actions – exercises which involve the whole body, making it react totally. The entire body has to think and adapt itself continually to each situation as it arises. The first example is an exercise which demands precision. You have to touch or hit your companion's chest with your foot on a precise spot just above the breastbone so that he doesn't get hurt.

(Demonstration: duel with the feet striking the chest)

This exercise serves to inspire confidence in your companion. It sounds paradoxical to awaken confidence through an action which frightens and provokes a defensive reaction. But it is a matter of having and inspiring confidence in your companion and striking him in such a way that he is able to overcome his defensive reflex. The whole body must react, adapt itself, yet work with precision and with all the senses at their sharpest.

This type of exercise demanding continual self-adaptation can vary, but always requires precision and a cool head. The actor must be carried along by his physical intelligence – it is the entire body which does the thinking and these thoughts are already actions, reactions.

Another exercise involves attempting to strike your companion's neck or ankles with a stick in order to provoke an immediate and precise reaction.

(Demonstration: duel with sticks)

This feeling of trust in your own reflexes, in your own physical intelligence and in your companion becomes apparent through physical actions. But this trust is developed further. In our theatre there are no teachers. The actors themselves have developed their training. Those who have been here longer put their experience at the disposal of the more recent arrivals. Helped by one of the older actors, the younger one begins to assimilate a particular series of exercises. When he has mastered these, he will be able to personalize them, that is, to adapt them to his own rhythm and his own justification.

First, each exercise is assimilated in a precise way.

(Demonstration: acrobatics)

Once the separate exercises are assimilated and you have mastered them completely, they can be linked, fused together in a series, like a wave of two, three, or four exercises, with a different rhythm.

The exercises have now been assimilated. Having complete mastery over them and having linked them together in little waves of three or four, you can now work with them absolutely freely according to your own rhythm.

This series of exercises is an example of physical reactions being carried to their extreme consequence. Our body really *can* fly, *can* meet the floor as if weightless, without fear. The psychological value of these exercises is enormous. They appear to be very difficult, and for someone who is confronted with them for the first time they may seem quite impossible. However, even after the first day's work, helped patiently by one of the others, you are able to do one or two of these exercises reasonably well. After a month's daily work the new member is able to do almost all of them, not perfectly perhaps, but it does not matter; he has plenty of time ahead of him. What counts is the knowledge that he *can* succeed; what seemed impossible is within his reach if he works every day.

In this lies the essential value of the training: daily self-discipline, personalization of the work, stimulation of and effect on one's companions and milieu.

Now another example of a few exercises which form the basis of the individual work of a group of actors.

(Demonstration)

Training, as we practice it in our theatre, does not teach how to be an actor, how to play a role in the Commedia dell'Arte style, or how to interpret a tragic or grotesque part. It doesn't give a sense of being able to do something, that one has acquired certain skills. Training is an encounter with the reality which one has chosen: whatever you do, do it with your whole self. For this reason we talk about training and not learning or apprenticeship. Although all our actors are formed here in our theatre, we are not a theatre school in the usual sense since there are no teachers or study program. The actors themselves devise and are responsible for their training. But in order to achieve this degree of freedom, there must be self-discipline. And this is why training is a necessity for everyone, irrespective of how long one has been working in the theatre.

Whatever you do, do it with your whole self. It sounds like – and is – a facile and rhetorical phrase. Anybody can say it. But we have only one possibility: to live it, to carry it out in our daily acts. And the training reminds us of this.

VOCAL TRAINING

The voice, in its logical and its sonorous aspect, is a material force, moving, guiding, molding, stopping. One can, in fact, talk about vocal actions which provoke an immediate reaction. Now we will demonstrate the voice as an active force.

Using a language that she has invented and which she improvises as she goes along, Iben leads two of her colleagues and tries to make them do what she wants. Her voice acts all the time; that is, it tries to persuade, beg, compel her companions to execute her wishes while at the same time her voice reacts, i.e., adapts itself to what her companions do. They have their backs to her so that they don't see her. They do nothing, play no role, only react, respond with their entire bodies to her vocal stimulus.

(Demonstration: the voice as an active force)

The voice as a physiological process engages the whole organism projecting it into space. The voice is an extension of the body and gives us the possibility of concrete intervention even at a distance. Like an invisible hand the voice extends out from our body and acts, and our entire body lives and participates in this action. The body is the visible part of the voice and one can see how and where the impulse which will become sound and speech is born. The voice is body – invisible body – operating in space. There is no separation, no duality: voice and body. There are only actions and reactions which engage our body in its entirety.

Our work has only one aim: to preserve the spontaneous organic reactions of the voice and at the same time stimulate the individual vocal fantasy of each actor.

The working situation is one in which the body and its invisible part, the voice, are constantly adapting themselves, i.e., reacting to stimuli. Here is a demonstration of how the voice reacts to stimuli.

I am going to ask Jens to hold my hand with his voice and let his speech emerge from the part of his body which is nearest my hand. Just that: hold my hand with his voice and answer the movements of my hand; in other words, react to its actions.

(Demonstration: the voice reacting to stimuli)

In the situation we have just shown, the stimulus rebounded as a vocal reaction. The body of the actor who was speaking was totally engaged. The whole body spoke, constantly adapting itself, directed towards the exterior with a very definite point of reference. The rule is this: for precise reactions the stimuli must be precise – precise in character and precisely situated in space.

I ought now to mention the spoken text. In our daily life when we talk we don't concentrate on the words, we don't interpret the words coldly. Our speech is carried on a wave, the respiratory wave, which may be long or it may be short. If the process is spontaneous, we do not think about the words. Nothing impedes us or restrains us if we have a sense of security; in other words if we are not afraid, if we are not embarrassed, if we do not have to be careful of what we say or are not speaking in a foreign language that we are not altogether at home with. This sense of security must be recreated within the artificial situation that is the theatrical situation. We must therefore eliminate the objective blocking of the text which can occur if one has continuously to force oneself to remember it. The text must be learned by heart so perfectly that it flows without the least difficulty as if it were a spontaneous process, allowing the actor, through his action, to reach out in space, oblivious of the words he has learned. In reality, even if the words were written by someone else – or if, as in my case now where I am using words which are not my own, were not invented by me but were passed on to me by a culture and a tradition – these words assume life and presence through my whole being as personal reactions.

What we call stimulus is the starting point which allows the actor to continue freely alone. From this point of departure, the actor himself selects and develops his own images, his own stimuli to which he reacts. This is the second phase of the work process.

(Vocal improvisation)

That which we call stimulus is a concrete, precise yet suggestive image which appeals to the actor's fantasy. It is a starting point which allows the actor to take the original image and graft it onto his own fantasy, his own interior universe, thus developing his own images and associations which are vocal reactions.

In this way, although the point of departure, the initial image, is given from outside, decided by another, the whole process is personalized and becomes the individual expression of the actor and his universe.

If there are precise stimuli, there are also precise reactions, provided that there are no impediments. There may be objective impediments such as straining to remember the text, or psychological impediments stemming from a feeling of fear or lack of security. It is essential throughout this whole process to create a feeling of protection around those who are working. The results depend on this.

As I said before, if there are precise stimuli there are also precise reactions. Then a sonorous logic will become apparent, revealing itself through the rhythm, i.e., variations in tone, pauses, intensity, changes in volume, stress on particular parts of the sentences, micro-pauses before certain words and before breathing in, which instead of causing gaps in our speech, sharpen its sense and nerve.

This rhythm, this physical and vocal pulsation are signs that the whole body is alive. It is this pulsation which vibrates the fabric of sounds and meaning which is our body, present in and projected into space.

(Vocal improvisation)

Throughout the entire working process one must resist the temptation to try to obtain original results, to emit strange noises, inarticulate shouts, transforming our vocal reactions into a sonorous magma which may sound dramatic but is strained and artificial. You must forget your own voice and stretch out with all your body towards the stimulus and react to it.

Then the body lives, the voice lives, palpitates, vibrates like a flame, like a ray of sunshine which emanates from our body, illuminating and warming the space around it. From this modest point of departure and through regular work over the years, there springs our own vocal flora whose roots live in, *are* our body with its experience and its longings.

See pp. 39–40.

Chapter 14

Augusto Boal

THE STRUCTURE OF THE
ACTOR'S WORK

THE PRIMACY OF EMOTION

IN 1956 I STARTED working at the Arena Theatre of São Paulo, of which I was the artistic director until I had to leave Brazil in 1971. At this time, the Brazilian theatre was completely dominated by Italian directors, who used to impose pre-established forms on every play performed. To fight against this tendency, in concert with the actors we created an acting laboratory in which we set about a methodical study of the works of Stanislavski. Our first principle at that time was that emotion took precedence over all else and should be given a free rein to shape the final form of the actor's interpretation of a role.

But how can emotions 'freely' manifest themselves throughout an actor's body, if that very instrument (the body) is mechanised, automated in its muscle structures and insensible to 90 per cent of its possibilities? A newly discovered emotion runs the risk of being canalised by the mechanised patterns of the actor's behaviour; the emotion may be blocked by a body already hardened by habit into a certain set of actions and reactions.

How does this mechanisation of the actor's body come about? By repetition. The senses have an enormous capacity for registering, selecting and then hierarchising sensations. The eye, for example, can pick up an infinite variety of colours, whatever the object of its attention: a road, a room, a picture, an animal. There are thousands of greens, shades of green perfectly perceptible to the human eye. The same applies to hearing and sounds, and to the other senses and their sensations. A person driving a car sees an infinity of sensations stream past. Riding a bicycle involves an extremely complicated structure of muscular movements and tactile sensations, but the senses select the most important stimuli for this activity. Every human activity, from the very simplest onwards – walking, for instance – is an extremely complicated operation, which is possible only *because* the senses are capable of selection; even though they pick up all sensations, they present them to the consciousness according to a definite hierarchy, and this is repeated over and over again in our lives.

This becomes even more evident when a person leaves their habitual environment and visits an unknown town or country; the people dress differently, speak with another rhythm, the noises and the colours aren't the same, the faces are differently shaped. Everything seems wonderful, unexpected, fantastic. But after a few days, the senses once again learn to select and the routine starts all over. Let us imagine what happens when a (South American) forest-dwelling Indian comes to town or when a city-dweller gets lost in the forest. For the Indian the noises of the forest are perfectly natural, his senses are used to selecting from them; he can fix his bearings by the noise of the wind in the trees, by the brightness of the sun through the leaves. By contrast, what is natural and routine to us city-dwellers can drive the Indian mad, incapable as he is of selecting from the sensations produced by a big city. The same thing would happen to us if we got lost in virgin forest.

This process of selection and structuration results in a mechanisation because the senses always select in the same way.

When we began our exercises, we had not yet considered *social* masks; at that time we were considering mechanisation in its purely physical form, i.e. by always carrying out the same movements, each person mechanises their body to execute these movements as efficiently as possible, thus denying themselves the possibility of original action every time the opportunity arises.

Wrinkles appear because the repetition of particular muscle constructions eventually leaves its mark on the face.

What is a sectarian but a person – of the left or right – who has mechanised all their thoughts and responses?

Like all human beings, the actor acts and reacts according to mechanisms. For this reason, we must start with the 'de-mechanisation', the re-tuning (or de-tuning) of the actor, so that he may be able to take on the mechanisations of the character he is going to play. He must relearn to perceive emotions and sensations he has lost the habit of recognising.

11 The function of the actor

Forum Theatre demands a different style of acting. In certain African countries the people measure the talents of singers by the extent to which they can seduce their audiences into singing along with them. That is what should happen with good Forum Theatre actors. In their performances there must not be the slightest trace of the narcissism so commonly found in *closed* theatre shows. Because the presentation of the anti-model should, by contrast, principally express doubt; each action should contain its own negation; each phrase should leave open the possibility of saying the opposite of what is being said; each *yes* allows for an imagined *no*, or a *perhaps*.

During the forum proper, actors must be extremely dialectical. When they take up a counter-stance against a spect-actor/protagonist who wants to break the oppression, they must be honest and show that the oppression is not so easily defeated. They must show the difficulties which will appear, while retaining a manner which encourages the spect-actor to break the oppression. Which means that while still countering every phrase and action, they should awaken in the spect-actor other stances, other approaches. While impeding the attempt to break the oppression, they should rouse the spect-actor to achieve it.

If the actor is too firm, it can discourage or, worse still, frighten the spect-actor. If the actor is too soft and vulnerable, with no counter-arguments or counter-actions, it can mislead the spect-actor into believing that the problem posed by the play is easier to resolve than he or she thought.

In Berlin, at the Hochschüle der Kunst [*sic*], a forum showed a young man trying to convince his family to give him a certain sum of money a month. In order to achieve this, he had to undergo endless rituals, family conversations and reunions, discussions about the war, about the past, about members of the family who had disappeared, etc. The actors were so enthusiastic that every spect-actor who came forward was subjected to an avalanche of arguments, to such an extent that very soon the whole audience was up in arms and shouted in unison 'Stop – that's magic!', concluding that no family could be as fearsomely exasperating as that.

I repeat, the actors must be dialectical, must know how to give and take, how to hold back and lead on, how to be creative. They must feel no fear (which is common with professional actors) of losing their place, of standing aside. A great magician is someone who not only knows how to do magic, but also how to teach tricks to others. A great footballer loses no status by teaching someone else how to shoot with both feet.

One learns by teaching others. Pedagogy is transitive. Or it isn't pedagogy.

12 The repeated scene

Once the anti-model has been shown and the debate is under way, it is often the case that several spect-actors, one after another, want to break the same oppression. This means that the same scene will be shown several times. The only thing to be careful of is letting the show (however well constructed it may be) become monotonous. So, a word of advice: on each repetition the actors should accelerate the rhythm, so as to avoid showing exactly the same scene several times, or any more than necessary. Excessive repetition can diminish the audience's interest, enthusiasm and creativity.

13 Macrocosm and microcosm

In a good Forum Theatre show, the actors must be very much in tune with each other and ready for every eventuality. It can happen that the solution desired or suggested by a spect-actor may be unachievable within the 'microcosmic' world of the anti-model. To find the solution it is necessary to look elsewhere. How?

In Turin a young couple were searching for a flat. A letting agent asked them for their papers, their wage slips, asked them what their resources were, and so on. Then a man came in who wanted to rent the same flat as the venue for occasional liaisons with his mistress. He could have gone to a hotel, but he preferred the comfort of a flat. The agent, in view of the man's economic status, decided in his favour, instead of offering the flat to the young couple who really needed it. What was the solution? The young people broke into the 'flat' and occupied it. And what was the agent's next move? Calling the police.

However, in the anti-model there was no scene with the police. The agent dialled a telephone number and immediately an actor off stage answered; he turned himself into a police inspector. The other actors, assisted by a few spect-actors, immediately improvised the police station. The inspector decided to intervene, arresting the couple and sending them to the police station. There, the young man rang his lawyer. In the microcosm of the anti-model, of course there was no lawyer. No problem – an actor answered and once again, with the help of a few spect-actors, all in character, a lawyer's office sprang up. And now it was the lawyer's turn – he phoned the young people's parents. Actors and spect-actors improvised homes, families, parents and grandparents, uncles and aunts and neighbours. In a matter of minutes the whole room was involved in a huge scene in which almost everybody had a part.

This goes to show that the anti-model presents only a microcosm – but that that microcosm fits into the macrocosm of the whole of the society under examination. The whole of society can be involved and can enter into a Forum Theatre show, whatever the dimensions of the anti-model.

See p. 30.

Chapter 15

Moshe Feldenkrais

IMAGE, MOVEMENT, AND ACTOR:
RESTORATION OF POTENTIALITY

Translated and Edited by Kelly Morris

MIND-BODY UNITY

MY FUNDAMENTAL CONTENTION is that the unity of mind and body is an objective reality, that these entities are not *related* to each other in one fashion or another, but are an inseparable whole. To put this more clearly: I contend that a brain could not think without motor functions. It is probably language's serial formation in time which determines the serial genesis of our thought. Let me substantiate this: 1) It takes longer to think the numbers from twenty to thirty than from one to ten, although the numerical intervals are the same for each series. The difference lies in the fact that the time intervals are proportional to the time needed to utter the corresponding numbers aloud. This suggests that we actually mobilize the vocal apparatus. Thus, one of the purest abstractions is inextricably linked with muscular activity. Most people cannot think clearly without mobilizing the motor function of the brain enough to become aware of the word patterns representing the thought. 2) Macular vision—distinct, clear seeing—is limited to a very small area at a time. To perceive clearly the content of what we see while reading takes us the time required for the muscles of the eyes to scan the area under inspection. Here again, we see the functional unity of perception and motor function. 3) Consider feeling in detail. I may feel joyful, angry, afraid, disgusted. Everyone can, on seeing me, recognize the feeling I experience. Which comes first: the motor pattern or the feeling? I would like to stress the idea that they are basically the same thing. We cannot become conscious of a feeling before it is expressed by a motor mobilization, and therefore *there is no feeling so long as there is no body attitude.*

THE SELF-IMAGE AND REALITY

Each person has an impression of his own manner of speaking, walking, and carriage which seems personal and immutable—the only possible way—and he identifies himself with this image. His judgment of the spacial relationships and movements of his body seems innate, and he believes it is possible to change only the vitality, intensity, and capability of them. But everything important for social relations is acquired through a long apprenticeship: one *learns* to walk, to speak, to see the third dimension in a painting or photograph. It is by the chance circumstances of birth-place and environment that one acquires *specific* movements, attitudes, language, etc. The difficulty in changing a physical or mental habit is due partly to heredity and individuality, but mostly to the necessity of displacing an already-acquired habit.

It would be well at this point to perform a simple exercise, so that one may actu-ally *feel* the conditions and possibilities I am describing. Lie down on your back; mentally and methodically scan your entire body. You will discover that you can concentrate on certain parts more easily than others, and that you usually lose consciousness of these other parts during an action. In fact, certain parts almost never figure in the self-image during action.

For example, close your eyes and try to represent the width of your mouth with your index fingers. It is not unusual to discover an error of up to three hundred percent in exaggeration or underestimation. Keeping your eyes closed, try to represent with your hands the thickness of your chest, first with your hands in back and front, then by separating them laterally, and finally vertically. You will be amazed to see that your judgment changed with the positions of your hands and that for each attempt you produced a different result. The variation is often as much as one hundred per cent.

When this deviation between the conception of the self-image and the objective (or "real") facts is nearly one hundred per cent, the behavior of that part of the body is generally defective. For example: someone who holds his chest in a position of exaggerated exhalation will find that according to his self-image the chest seems two or three times thicker than it is in reality. Inversely, someone who holds a position of extreme inhalation will find the self-image underestimates the chest's thickness. A detailed examination of the whole body—particularly the pelvic and genital-anal region—will reveal even greater surprises.

If one simply thinks of his accustomed manner as an alternate term for "self-image," one comprehends the difficulty in perfecting a particular action. The self-image's habitual configuration is to a certain extent compulsive; the person could not act otherwise. He substitutes a habitual action for the proposed exercise without being conscious of not doing what he wished.

The difficulty, therefore, is not bound up with the substance of the habit, but with the temporal order—that is, the priority of the formed pattern which, in itself, is simply a product of chance. The question, then, is: is it possible to so change the body-attitude that new manners, different by choice, would be as fully personal as those previously acquired, without taking into account the person's past life?

It is important to understand that I do not intend the simple substitution of one action for another (which would be "static"), but a change in the *mode* of action, achieved through the "dynamic" of activity in general.

MOVEMENT AND POSTURE

Feldenkrais: Can *you* define good movement?

Schechner: No, except on stage I would say good movement is that which suits the part; but it's easier to recognize bad movement than to say what's good about good movement.

Feldenkrais: Yes, but when you say it should suit the part, you're not offering a definition, and you couldn't teach people good movement with a loose notion of what it is.

Schechner: What is good movement?

Feldenkrais: Well, good movement is more complex than it seems. First of all, it should be reversible. For instance, if I make a movement with my hand it will be accepted as good, as conscious, clear, and willed movement if I can at any point of the trajectory stop, reverse the movement, continue, or change it into something else.

Schechner: And you think that a basic definition of acting is the reversibility of the gesture?

Feldenkrais: Not only the gesture but the whole attitude. The actor should be able to stop, start again, or do something else. Only then can he play ten nights, one after the other, and do the same thing. Reversibility is one part of it. The next important thing is that the body should be maintained in a state of action where it can start a movement without preliminaries. For instance, suppose I normally stand with my feet wide apart. I have stability this way, but can't walk without first shifting around completely. Though this is the "best" posture by definition, I cannot move forward or backwards. This is the extreme case of *bad* posture. Now if I stand with a leg forward and back bent, I can of course walk forward or backwards. But if somebody asked me to jump, I couldn't do it without changing my position. But if I stand so that I can, without preliminaries, rise, stoop, move forward, backwards, right and left, and twist myself—then elementary demands of good posture are fulfilled. This is also true for the voice and the breath.

Schechner: So when you talk about movement, you're working with the voice, the breath, the movement, the eyes, the ears—the total body organism. You must be working with the total mental organism too.

Feldenkrais: Absolutely! They are one. I am working with the *human* organism.

MOSHE FELDENKRAIS (1904–1984)

Feldenkrais originally studied as an engineer. He enjoyed sports and trained in Ju Jitsu, which he also taught to others. The aggravation of an old football injury led him to carefully observe his body use in order to self-rehabilitate. This led to the formulation of the Feldenkrais method. From the 1960s onwards he ran workshops and courses around the world. His work in theatre and performance fields has included a period with Peter Brook and his international company in Paris.

See also: **Peter Brook.**

SUGGESTED FURTHER READING

Feldenkrais, M. (1980) *Awareness Through Movement*, Harmondsworth: Penguin.
Feldenkrais, M. (1985) *The Potent Self*, San Francisco: Harper & Row.

Saint Cyr, T. (1995) 'The Feldenkrais Method for Actors', available online at: http://www.
    feldenkrais.com/article_content.asp?edition=1&section=20&article=75. Accessed: 8
    April 2014.

Chapter 16

Dario Fo and Franca Rame

THEATRE WORKSHOPS AT THE RIVERSIDE STUDIOS

QUESTION: You've been talking about situations, rhythm etc. And then we've seen an example about situation. What I would like to know is if there are techniques to improve the rhythm and the acting, or is this something that is within yourself – you either have it, or you don't.

DARIO FO: Obviously, there are people who are naturally gifted in music, theatre, drawing etc. It's a natural thing in them. But then you also have training, exercises etc. Now, when I say "training", I do not mean that a person has to go to an Academy of Dramatic Art. There are very many great actors who have never been to acting school. The same goes for directors. The important thing is to train yourself in a given direction, and to create a discipline for yourself. But in order to create a discipline, you have to have an ideology. In my opinion, it is extremely dangerous to practise in the theatrical arts without knowing what *end* this practice is supposed to serve.

For example, there are very important drama schools which train you in gesture. I know them, and have given lessons at them. And what I have noticed is that the young people there have taken on only the *technique* of a given exercise. In the end they are just like empty egg-shells. I ask you! They know the techniques for laughing in 10 different ways: the abdominal laugh (*He demonstrates*); then the mid-abdominal laugh; then the head-laugh; then the falsetto laugh. They know how to do them all. But then, when they have to laugh for real, they are mechanical! The same goes for ways of using gesture – for example how to hold an object. This is important even when you are doing naturalistic representation. If I know how to hold this object properly, if I am able to construct it, even though it doesn't actually exist . . . (*He demonstrates*) You see! What did I do? I constructed the gesture of picking up the glass. I found a bodily equilibrium. My leg-position is passive, but is not dead. I make sure that all attention is concentrated on this gesture. I have prepared the form, the mould of this glass with my hand. I take the glass. Now at this point, the body-movement becomes more important. If I move my body wrongly in relation to the glass, it becomes not true. Then I put the glass down.

Now, note that if I take my hand away wrongly, I destroy the glass-object. I have to open my hand and leave the object there, so that it remains a real object.

Remember that all this also applies when you are handling real objects. If I have gestuality in my mind, then I have to apply it to reality as well. As you can see, I accelerate and augment the dimension of the object. This is the dimension of realism (He demonstrates), which is different from naturalism. If I act naturalistically, I would do it like this (He demonstrates again, with the glass) That's it. I don't move. You see, realism demands a heightening of reality. I could give you another example – how you sit yourself down. I don't necessarily need a seat, even . . . The dimension of my way of sitting determines my attitude, my way of being, according to how I sit. For instance, I could be extremely tired. This is how I might sit down. (He demonstrates) As you see, I look for the most comfortable position for my body. I've exaggerated a bit . . . really made a meal out of making myself comfortable . . . I may even speak while I'm doing it . . . but the important thing is that I invent, over and above what is the logical limit. I have made a transitional synthesis, and at the same time I have heightened certain situations.

DARIO FO (1926–) AND FRANCA RAME (1928–2013)

Fo trained as an architect, but after the Second World War he became an actor. From 1950, he worked with the Parenti company, performing revues and variety acts. During the early 1950s he wrote, directed and performed in several very successful revue shows, as well as collaborating with the French movement expert, Jacques Lecoq. In 1954 he married the actress Franca Rame. In 1968, Fo and Rame abandoned the official state theatre system and set up the Associazione Nuova Scena, which toured community venues. Over the following decades Fo has become internationally renowned for his political comedies, including *Accidental Death of an Anarchist, Can't Pay, Won't Pay*, and his own one man show, *Mistero Buffo*. In 1997, Fo received the Nobel Prize for Literature.

Born into a theatrical family, Rame made her theatrical debut in 1951. She met and married Dario Fo in 1954. In 1958 they co-founded the Fo-Rame company. In the 1970s Rame began writing her own pieces, often monologues which she would perform herself. In 1973, she was abducted and tortured by a fascist terrorist group. Her best known monologues are published in English as: *Waking Up, A Woman Alone, The Same Old Story* and *Medea*.

See also: **Jacques Lecoq, Bertolt Brecht, Augusto Boal.**

SUGGESTED FURTHER READING

Fo, D. (1991) *The Tricks of the Trade*, London: Methuen.
Fo, D. and Rame, F. (1983) *Theatre Workshops at the Riverside Studios, London*, London: Red Notes.

Ferrall, J. (2001) *Dario Fo & Franca Rame: Harlequins of the revolution*, London: Methuen.
Mitchell, T. (1999) *Dario Fo: People's court jester*, London: A & C Black.

Chapter 17

Jerzy Grotowski

ACTOR'S TRAINING AND TECHNIQUE

THE TRAINING CONSISTS of exercises worked out by the actors or adopted from other systems. Even those exercises which are not the result of the actor's personal research have been developed and elaborated in order to satisfy the precise aims of the method. The terminology pertaining to the chosen exercises is then altered. Once the actors adopt a given exercise, they themselves establish a name for it on the basis of personal associations and ideas. One tends consciously to use a kind of professional jargon since this has a stimulating effect on the imagination.

II – EXERCISES TO LOOSEN UP THE MUSCLES AND THE VERTEBRAL COLUMN

1   "The cat". This exercise is based on the observation of a cat as it awakes and stretches itself. The subject lies stretched out face downwards, completely relaxed. The legs are apart and the arms at right angles to the body, palms towards the floor. The "cat" wakes up and draws the hands in towards the chest, keeping the elbows upwards, so that the palms of the hands form a basis for support. The hips are raised, while the legs "walk" on tiptoe towards the hands. Raise and stretch the left leg sideways, at the same time lifting and stretching the head. Replace the left leg on the ground, supported by the tips of the toes. Repeat the same movements with the right leg, the head still stretching upwards. Stretch the spine, placing the centre of gravity first in the centre of the spine, and then higher up towards the nape of the neck. Then turn over and fall onto the back, relaxing.

2   Imagine you have a metal band around the chest. Stretch it by means of a vigorous expansion of the trunk.

3   Handstand with the feet together against the wall. The legs slowly open as wide as possible.

4   Resting position. Squatting with the head dropped forward and the arms dangling between the knees.

5   Upright position, with the legs together and straight. Flex the trunk towards the ground until the head touches the knees.

6   Vigorous rotation of the trunk from the waist upwards.

7   Keeping the legs together, jump up onto a chair. The impulse for the jump does not come from the legs but from the trunk.

8   Total or partial splits.

9   Starting from an upright position, bend the body backwards to form a "bridge" until the hands touch the ground behind.

10   Lying position stretched out on one's back. Roll the whole body vigorously to left and right.

11   From a kneeling position, bend the body backwards into a "bridge" until the head touches the ground.

12   Jumps imitating those of a kangaroo.

13   Sit on the floor with the legs together and stretched out in front, the body erect. The hands, placed at the back of the neck, press the head forward and downwards until it touches the knees.

14   Walk on the hands and feet, with the chest and abdomen facing upwards.

Note: It is equally incorrect to perform this series of exercises in an inanimate way. **The exercise serves the research**. It is not merely automatic repetition or a form of muscular massage. For example, during the exercises one investigates the body's centre of gravity, the mechanism for the contraction and relaxation of the muscles, the function of the spine in the various violent movements, analysing any complicated developments and relating them to the repertory of every single joint and muscle. All this is individual and is the result of continual and total research. Only the exercises which "investigate" involve the entire organism of the actor and mobilise his hidden resources. The exercises which "repeat" give inferior results.

All conscious systems in the field of acting ask the question: "How can this be done?". This is as it should be. A method is the consciousness of this "how". I believe that one must ask oneself this question once in one's life, but as soon one enters into the details it must no longer be asked for, at the very moment of formulating it, one begins to create stereotypes and clichés. One must then ask the question: "What must I **not** do?".

Technical examples are always the clearest. Let us take respiration. If we ask the question: "How should I breathe?", we will work out a precise, perfect type of breathing, perhaps the abdominal type. It is indeed a fact that children, animals, people who are closest to nature, breathe principally with the abdomen, the diaphragm. But then we come to the second question: "What sort of abdominal respiration is the best?". And we could try to discover among numerous examples a type of inspiration, a type of expiration, a particular position for the vertebral column. This would be a terrible mistake for there is no perfect type of respiration valid for everyone, nor for all psychical and physical situations. Breathing is a physiological reaction linked with specific characteristics in each of us and which is dependent on situations, types of effort, physical activities. It is the natural thing for most people, when breathing freely, to use abdominal respiration. The number of types of abdominal respiration, however, are unlimited. And of course there are exceptions. For example, I have met actresses who, because their thoraxes were too long, could not naturally use abdominal breathing in their work. For them it was therefore necessary to find another type of breathing controlled by the vertebral column. If the actor tries artificially to impose on himself the perfect, objective abdominal respiration, he blocks the natural process of respiration, even if his is naturally of the diaphragmatic type.

When I begin to work with an actor, the first question I ask myself is: "Does this actor have any breathing difficulties?". He breathes well; he has enough air to speak, to sing. Why then create a problem by imposing on him a different type of respiration? This would be absurd. On the other hand, perhaps he does have difficulties. Why? Are there physical problems? . . . Psychical problems? If he has psychical problems, what kind of problems are they?

For example, an actor is contracted. Why is he contracted? We are all contracted in one way or another. One cannot be completely relaxed as is taught in many theatre schools, for he who is totally relaxed is nothing more than a wet rag. Living is not being contracted, nor is it being relaxed: it is a process. But if the actor is always too contracted, the cause blocking the natural respiratory process – almost always of a psychical or psychological nature – must be discovered. We must determine which is his natural type of respiration. I observe the actor, while suggesting exercises that compel him into total psycho-physical mobilisation. I watch him while in a moment of conflict, play or flirtation with another actor, in those moments when something changes automatically. Once we know the actor's natural type of respiration, we can more exactly define the factors which act as obstacles to his natural reactions and the aim of the exercises is then to eliminate them. Here lies the essential difference between our technique and the other methods: ours is a negative technique, not a positive one.

We are not after the recipes, the stereotypes which are the prerogative of professionals. We do not attempt to answer questions such as: "How does one show irritation? How should one walk? How should Shakespeare be played?". For these are the sort of questions usually asked. Instead, one must ask the actor: "What are the obstacles blocking you on your way towards the total act which must engage all your psycho-physical resources, from the most instinctive to the most rational?". We must find out what it is that hinders him in the way of respiration, movement and – most important of all – human contact. What resistances are there? How can they be eliminated? I want to take away, steal from the actor all that disturbs him. That which is creative will remain within him. It is a liberation. If nothing remains, it means he is not creative.

One of the greatest dangers threatening the actor is, of course, lack of discipline, chaos. One cannot express oneself through anarchy. I believe there can be no true creative process within the actor if he lacks discipline or spontaneity. Meyerhold based his work on discipline, exterior formation; Stanislavski on the spontaneity of daily life. These are, in fact, the two complementary aspects of the creative process.

See pp. 39–40.

Chapter 18

Rudolf Laban

EFFORT TRAINING

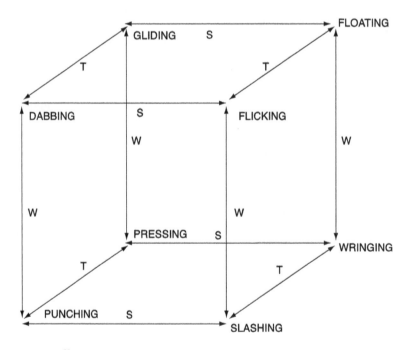

Figure 18.1 The Efforts

PSYCHOLOGICAL ASPECTS OF EFFORT CONTROL

THE CONTEMPORARY inclusion of industrial psychology as a part of work study arose from the recognition of the immense importance of the human factor and the unaccountable behaviour of individuals and groups within industrial concerns. Mechanical planning has been spoiled by the uncoordinated efforts of people who have had to perform the various tasks. Both the work study specialist and the industrial psychologist are able to profit from modern effort research.

Our arguments dealing with the economy and control of effort have made this clear so far as manual operations are concerned. An additional new light has, however, to be shed upon the psychological aspect of efforts appearing in work which is not manual or muscular. If we observe closely the distribution or economy of effort used by others, we get the following picture.

Time

People moving with easy effort seem to be freer than those moving with obviously stressed effort. The latter seem to struggle against something. We can learn more about what they are struggling against if we observe subjective movement – that is, those which do not deal with objects and have therefore no outer cause for struggle. But there is an obvious struggle visible in the sometimes painful deportment of a person.

It becomes gradually apparent that one of the main characteristics of effort is the presence or absence of rapidity. With this we have a clue concerning the nature of the struggle. Is it perhaps a fight against time? Time, or speed, is one of the factors of which the compound of effort is built up. This enables us to speak about an effort attitude towards time, in which either the struggling against or the indulging in time is prevailing.

Weight

We may also distinguish another main characteristic of effort, and this is the presence or lack of bodily force. Force is another of the factors of which efforts are built up. It is the degree of energy spent in overcoming one's own body weight, or that of an object, which expresses itself in the effort attitude towards the weight factor.

Someone's exaggerated effort may therefore be a struggle against time or weight, or both, while an easy effort may have its course in an almost complete neglect of any consideration of rapidity or of bodily force. Easy effort will show no struggle either against time or against weight, but rather indulgence in one or both of these factors. A person with an entire neglect of speed takes a lot of time. He or she is, so to speak, bathing, swimming or even submerging in a sea of time. The person whose bodily energy is lacking seems to enjoy his weightiness and to relax happily in being immersed in the general gravity of nature.

Now the strugglers against weight and the racers against time are surely different characters; and so also do those differ who are continuously immersed in a lot of time from those indulging in the experience of their own weight and in the weight of their surroundings.

Space

This is, however, not all that we can detect about the different attitude towards effort-elements. There are people who, without necessarily belonging to the groups of either time-racers or weight-forcers or their contrasts, appear, nevertheless, to move with stressed or easy effort. Since they do not appear either to swim in an ocean of time or to race against time, and as their attitude towards weight is also rather indifferent, what other kind of movement element are they stressing in their efforts? Easy movers might be observed to use a great deal of flexibility and twists in their efforts. That means, they apparently swim, circulate and twist most thoroughly through any possible region of space. Enjoying the space surrounding them makes them happy dwellers of a kingdom of which they know every corner.

But there are others who deal very sparingly with their moving space. Such people seem to take careful account of the extension and expansion of their movements, which appear to be as direct as possible.

It is as if they had an aversion against the manifold extensions of space. This aversion does not manifest itself so much in a tumultuous struggle, but rather in a kind of restriction in the use of many space directions. The need of an occasional excursion into space causes them a clearly visible and highly-stressed effort. These facts make it necessary to distinguish a special effort attitude towards space.

Flow

The three effort-attitudes towards the time factor, weight factor and space factor do not, however, cover all the basic phenomena observable. Persons do not move either suddenly or deliberately, weakly or forcefully, flexibly or directly only. There exists another factor, flow, which can be observed in people's movements, which together with the three factors mentioned above might give us a basis for a full account of effort phenomena. We can distinguish the flow of movement of a person, which can be free or bound, whatever velocity, space expansion or force the movements might have. With this observation we have discovered a fourth attitude towards the factors of movement, which, if prevailing in an effort, gives it the character of either a struggle against, or an indulgence in, the flow effort.

Some people seem to enjoy letting their movements flow whilst others show an obvious reluctance to do so. One can see how the latter endeavour to withhold and almost to stop the flow or progress of their movement at any moment of their action. This may cause them to make very large and perhaps roundabout movements. The reluctance is not directed against space, but they carefully abstain from letting movements flow freely. Their complicated movement-patterns are drawn in the air with a meticulous guidance which need not, however, be explicitly either slow or quick. Sometimes the shapes are traced with such withholding reticence that they are like a child's first attempts in writing and drawing. A real bound flow of this kind need not, however, be accompanied by any weight-accent – that is, a cramped use of force; it can be weak or entirely indifferent so far as weight is concerned.

People who indulge in flow find pleasure in the unrestricted freedom of fluency, without necessarily giving much attention to the various shades of the time, the weight and the space development of the movement. Movements with free flow cannot be easily interrupted or suddenly stopped; it takes time until the moving person gains the necessary control over the flow in order to stop. Those persons who tend to bind their flow will be able to stop their movements at any instant.

Having now distinguished the typical kinds of effort attitudes towards time, weight, space and flow, we can say that each of these may be either 'struggled against' or 'indulged in'. We have gained a vocabulary for the basic impressions we can receive from the observation of efforts.

RUDOLF LABAN (1879–1958)

Laban originally studied architecture in Paris, but became increasingly interested in the moving body and the dynamics of movement in space and time. He developed a notation system for the recording of dance and movement, and became the leading figure in the development of expressive dance (*ausdruckstanz*). In 1937 he relocated from Germany to England, where he taught first at Dartington in Devon and later in Manchester. In 1947 he published his work on 'efforts', in which he analysed movement in order to make it more efficient. He also applied these ideas to the generation of expressive movement for education and for performance.

See also: **Joan Littlewood.**

SUGGESTED FURTHER READING

Laban, R. (2011) *The Mastery of Movement,* Binsted: Dance Books.
McCaw, D. (2011) *The Laban Sourcebook,* London & New York: Routledge.

Bradley, K. (2008) *Rudolf Laban,* London & New York: Routledge.
Hodgson, J. (2001) *Mastering Movement: The Life and Work of Rudolf Laban,* London: Methuen.

Chapter 19

Jacques Lecoq

THE NEUTRAL MASK

THE NEUTRAL MASK

THIS IS THE BASIC mask that drives our understanding of all the other masks. It is through the neutral mask that we are able to wear other masks. It has no particular expression or characteristic, it doesn't laugh or cry, nor is it sad or happy. It is rooted in silence and calmness. The face should be simple, regular and without any hint of conflict. Anyone can make one out of papier mâché, using a plaster negative-mould, which is made from an original clay design. This is the best and most lasting way to make your own mask.

Making your own neutral mask is an excellent way of learning how to use it. The neutral mask is not at all like a mask made from the mould of a calm face; that would just be a sort of death mask. The first time that you put on a neutral mask it seems a heterogeneous sort of object that bothers and suffocates you. Gradually, however, you begin to feel hidden and you start to do things that you would never ordinarily do. Finally, once you have totally taken on the mask, you discover a new freedom that is greater than the naked face. Detached from your own face and words, both of which you can usually master in a social context, the body emerges as the only thing to guide you through the silence and you begin to feel its importance. There's no cheating with just your body. The neutral mask, which had originally allowed you to feel hidden, now exposes you. The mask that you wear in everyday life is gone, devoid of any purpose. You can feel each movement more intensely than before. You can no longer use your eyes to play psychological games and your whole head must now turn for you to look. Your gestures become bigger and slower. At the beginning, you felt stifled; now you breathe deeply.

The themes seem simple in description, difficult once you go deeper: wake up as though for the first time; discover the natural world through a journey; become what you see and recognise its rhythms (identification with animals, vegetation, the elements and materials). You can't have a neutral mask called Albert who wakes up in his bed. The neutral mask is a sort of common denominator for both men and women (there is a male mask, and also a different, female one). It unites us as living things and we can all see ourselves in it. It doesn't have a specific way of walking; it simply walks. It helps us discover the space around us, and the rhythm and gravity of things: the dynamics of fear, jealousy, pride and anger belong to us all. I have found that great actors, such as Michel Aumont, whom I persuaded to try on the mask, can bring the neutral mask to life without ever having tried it on before. The neutral mask is a tool that forces the actor to search deep within.

See p. 43.

Chapter 20

Kristin Linklater

HYPOTHETICAL FOUR-YEAR
ACTOR-TRAINING PROGRAM

IN THE FIRST YEAR, students have an hour a day of voice work and an hour a day of movement work consistently and continuously throughout the year. This work is an un-doing process. It begins to break down physical and vocal habits; it teaches an initial ability to relax tensions consciously. This ability slowly increases, expanding physical awareness, allowing more and more subtle connections between the mind and the body and a corresponding heightened state of being. Precise rapport between the approaches to the body and the voice is essential. While a student is attempting a deep re-programming of the route from motor impulse to muscle, it is important not to create chaos in the nervous system. If the student obeys the movement teacher's instructions to tuck in the behind, turn out the toes and support the torso with strong, contracted stomach muscles, and then goes into the voice teacher's class where the stomach must hang out, the knees go loose and the spine assume full responsibility for remaining upright, there will be confusion in the motor cortex if not general short-circuiting in the morale. It is important, too, that the gradual shift from *releasing* the body and the voice to developing their strengths be synchronized.

A similar synchronization is found with the acting work. Following the principle of release then development, basic acting consists of individual and group exercises to open up the imagination, break down reserves between people, liberate the emotions. This is delicate, very personal work, hovering on the boundary of psychotherapy. It is vital that there be a framework and a vocabulary that constantly refers the results back into the demands that acting will make without shirking the personal implications. There are several good improvisational approaches that can do the job effectively, each depending on the talent and understanding of the teacher, who must be able to provide the security and apply the pressure to get to the hidden core of a person. The aim of this basic work should be to remove habitual controls, to recognize and learn to follow impulses, to trust vulnerability, to explore and become familiar with different emotional conditions, and to begin to know how to enter and inhabit the interior world of self. The first two or three months of a first year's acting can be spent on such personal work without recourse to a written text.

The second step in acting makes use of two-character scenes from contemporary plays, preferably characters reasonably close to the age and experience of the students. (The improvisation classes continue with the emphasis on evolving group sensitivity and stretching imaginative horizons.) To begin with, in the scene work, the focus is on the personal processes between two people. The text is there to serve the student, so that the accurate interpretation of the scene as the author intended is subordinated to the ability of the student to personalize and make the words deeply true for him or herself. The two people involved (not yet "actors") learn to listen, to hear with their feelings, to make available the raw material of their lives in order to vitalize the exchange between them, discovering how to make words and actions that are not their own the outcome of an inner life that demands expression.

Balance is maintained between the emotional demands of such scenes and the stage of development the student has reached in voice work; hysterical screaming before the voice has been freed can set progress back considerably.

During the second half of the year several scenes are worked, each chosen to tackle a new area of personal exploration. By the end of the first year the students have a clearer idea of who they are and how they function, but may well feel that much has been taken away from them, leaving them in a sort of limbo. They are encouraged not to take a summer acting job, to take a vacation if possible, or, if they must earn money, to work at any job that has nothing to do with the theatre. The first summer is a gestation period. If they act according to what they have learned thus far they might never work again; if they act well enough to do a good job they will inevitably be going back to old tricks and patterns, thus effectively wiping out several months of de-conditioning.

There are other classes that can usefully take place in the first year: simple circus techniques such as juggling and tumbling. Ideally there should be two kinds of movement class. The Alexander technique marries perfectly with voice work and should be combined with more active movement exercises designed within the same philosophy (action results from the release of energy from an inner center.) Maximum effect with minimum effort is the criterion. Halfway through the year the voice teacher should add a class that aims to link the "technical" exercises with a text. Such texts must be very simple. They can be contemporary verse, a story written by the student, Japanese haiku, early Chinese poetry. As in the acting work the aim is to achieve a simple, personal connection between the words and self. To be able to talk.

In general the second year concentrates on development and consolidation. Voice and movement continue with at least an hour a day on pure release and strengthening, and additional longer sessions once or twice a week to explore the application of what is being achieved "technically" to creative and interpretative work. Content, something to be expressed through the voice and through the body, is introduced in vocal improvisation and movement improvisation on themes, or with stories. By the end of the year there will be combined sound and movement improvisation. In the acting area a step is taken from personalization toward fulfilling the needs of the scene. Two-person scenes are still the most useful for this, but now the student recognizes that the character in the play may react differently in a given situation from the natural reaction of the person playing it, and ways of rechanneling that person's raw psychological and emotional material in unfamiliar directions are examined. The practical application of whatever acting vocabulary that pins down the reality of a character's existence within the confines of a particular play is relentlessly rehearsed. How to give flesh and blood, psycho-emotional answers to questions such as "Who am I?," "Where am I going?," "Where am I coming from?,"

"What do I want?," "What's my objective?," "What's the scene objective?," "What's the plot objective?" How to depend on interaction with the other character. How to trust the life of one moment and then another. Each new scene chosen should stretch and mold personal reality to fill characters and situations further and further removed from the person playing it. Different emotions are explored, unfamiliar attitudes are examined. By doing.

Expansion into three- and four-person scenes is the next step, and in the second half of this year the more specialized aspects of character work are defined.

By the third year students are much more demanding. Whereas in the first two the teachers make the demands (in terms of vulnerability, discipline, stretch, work), in the third the students are beginning to feel their individuality and have a sense of themselves as *actors*. They begin to feel for themselves what their creative ambitions might be and how much work their bodies and their voices need to fulfill those ambitions. So they make demands of their teachers to help them with specific needs. It might seem that by the third year it would be possible to cut back on the "technical" work and concentrate more on plays, but in fact it is now that a thirty-hour day becomes necessary to accommodate the expansion of needs in all areas.

In general, the third year allows the student to practice the craft he or she has been learning in as many different kinds of plays as possible. Three or four different periods in theatre are explored in the course of the year, and two full-length plays performed for invited audiences. The emphasis in these productions is on the actors and the play, with only essentials in terms of costumes, sets, lights and props. A number of different periods can be explored in scene and act work, along with methods of doing background research on authors as well as the history, art, politics and social customs of the times.

In the third year students also extend their basic training in voice and body skills. Singing classes begin now, speech classes (dialects to be lost or acquired, problematic diction etc.), dance (period, folk, jazz), fighting (fencing, wrestling and whatever is "in" in Oriental fighting arts), acrobatics. Poetry speaking, (which has moved from contemporary through 19th century to 18th and 17th century, from narrative to lyric, from ballad to epic,) now gives way to a concentrated Shakespeare text class.

In the fourth year as many plays as possible are done before audiences and, if possible, taken on tour; outside directors are brought in to do productions; skills are sharpened and experimental work is encouraged alongside traditional theatre practice.

I do not see how an actor-training course that understands the importance of organic learning can cover the basic necessities of craft in under four years. By the end of that time a person has a groundwork of understanding from which to move out into the theatre and gradually become an actor through the next five or ten years of experience of plays. The training I have outlined may seem conventional but it is based on the belief that actors must be able to fulfill the classic traditions of the theatre before branching out into innovative experiment.

KRISTIN LINKLATER (1936–)

Kristin Linklater is a Scottish vocal coach, dialect coach, acting teacher, actor, theatre director, and author. She trained at the London Academy of Music and Dramatic Art (LAMDA), with Iris Warren. She has taught at LAMDA and at various other institutions. She is currently Head of Acting in the Theatre Arts Division of Columbia University.

See also: **Joseph Chaikin**, Michel **Saint-Denis**.

SUGGESTED FURTHER READING

Linklater, K. (2006) *Freeing the Natural Voice*, London: Nick Hern Books.
Linklater, K. (2010) *Freeing Shakespeare's Voice*, London: Nick Hern Books.

Martin, J. (1991) *Voice in the Modern Theatre*, London & New York: Routledge.

Chapter 21

Vsevolod Meyerhold

BIOMECHANICS

IN THE PAST THE actor has always conformed with the society for which his art was intended. In future the actor must go even further in relating his technique to the industrial situation. For he will be working in a society where labour is no longer regarded as a curse but as a joyful, vital necessity. In these conditions of ideal labour art clearly requires a new foundation.

We are accustomed to the rigid division of a man's time into *labour* and *rest*. Every worker used to try to expend as few hours as possible on labour and as many as possible on rest. Whereas such a desire is quite normal under the conditions of a capitalist society, it is totally incompatible with the proper development of a socialist society. The cardinal problem is that of fatigue, and it is on the correct solution of this problem that the art of the future depends.

In America at the present time much research is being devoted to the possible methods of incorporating rest in the work process instead of regarding it as a separate unit.

The whole question boils down to the regulation of rest periods. Under ideal conditions (taking account of hygiene, physiology and comfort) a rest of as little as ten minutes is capable of completely restoring a man's energy.

Work should be made easy, congenial and uninterrupted, whilst art should be utilized by the new class not only as a means of relaxation but as something *organically vital to the labour pattern of the worker. We need to change not only the forms of our art but our methods too.* An actor working for the new class needs to re-examine all the canons of the past. The very craft of the actor must be completely reorganized.

The work of the actor in an industrial society will be regarded as a means of production vital to the proper organization of the labour of every citizen of that society.

However, apart from the correct utilization of rest periods, *it is equally essential to discover those movements in work which facilitate the maximum use of work time.* If we observe a skilled worker in action, we notice the following in his movements: (1) an absence of superfluous, unproductive movements; (2) rhythm; (3) the correct positioning of the body's centre of gravity; (4) stability. Movements based on these principles are distinguished by their dance-like quality; a skilled worker at work invariably reminds one of a dancer; thus work borders on art. The spectacle of a man working efficiently affords positive pleasure. This applies equally to the work of the actor of the future.

In art our constant concern is the organization of raw material. Constructivism has forced the artist to become both artist and engineer. Art should be based on scientific principles; the entire creative act should be a conscious process. The art of the actor consists in organizing his material; that is, in his capacity to utilize correctly his body's means of expression.

The actor embodies in himself both the organizer and that which is organized (i.e. the artist and his material). The formula for acting may be expressed as follows:

$N = A_1 + A_2$ (where N = the actor; A_1 = the artist who conceives the idea and issues the instructions necessary for its execution; A_2 = the executant who executes the conception of A_1).

The actor must train his material (the body), so that it is capable of executing instant-aneously those tasks which are dictated externally (by the actor, the director).

In so far as the task of the actor is the realization of a specific objective, his means of expression must be economical in order to ensure that *precision* of movement which will facilite *the quickest possible realization of the objective.*

The methods of Taylorism[1] may be applied to the work of the actor in the same way as they are to any form of work with the aim of maximum productivity.

The conditions (1) that rest is embodied in the work process in the form of pauses, and (2) that art has a specific, vital function and does not serve merely as a means of relaxation, make it obligatory for the actor to utilize his time *as economically as possible.* Art is allocated a specific number of time units in the worker's timetable which must be utilized to the maximum effect. This means that one must not fritter away 1½–2 hours in making up and putting on one's costume.

The actor of the future will work without make-up and wear an overall, that is, a costume designed to serve as everyday clothing yet equally suited to the movements and concepts which the actor realizes on the stage.

The Taylorization of the theatre will make it possible to perform in one hour that which requires four at present.

For this the actor must possess: (1) *the innate capacity for reflex excitability,* which will enable him to cope with any emploi within the limits of his physical characteristics; (2) 'physical competence', consisting of a true eye, a sense of balance, and the ability to sense at any given moment the location of his centre of gravity.

Since the art of the actor is the art of plastic forms in space, he must study the mechanics of his body. This is essential because any manifestation of a force (including the living organism) is subject to constant laws of mechanics (and obviously the creation by the actor of plastic forms in the space of the stage is a manifestation of the force of the human organism).

The fundamental deficiency of the modern actor is his absolute ignorance of the laws of *biomechanics.*

It is quite natural that with the acting methods which have prevailed up to now, the 'inspirational' method and the method of 'authentic emotions' (essentially they are one and the same, differing only in their means of realization: the first employs narcotic stimulation, the second – hypnosis), the actor has always been so overwhelmed by his emotions that he has been unable to answer either for his move-ments or for his voice. He has had no control over himself and hence been in no state to ensure success or failure. Only a few exceptionally great actors have succeeded instinctively in finding the correct method, that is, the method of building the role not from inside outwards, but vice versa. By approaching their role from the outside, they succeeded in developing stupendous technical mastery. I am speaking of artists like Duse, Sarah Bernhardt, Grasso, Chaliapin, Coquelin.

There is a whole range of questions to which psychology is incapable of supplying the answers. A theatre built on psychological foundations is as certain to collapse as a house built on sand. On the other hand, a theatre which relies on *physical elements* is at very least assured of clarity. All psychological states are determined by specific physiological processes. By correctly resolving the nature of his state physically, the actor reaches the point where he experiences the *excitation* which communicates itself to the spectator and induces him to share in the actor's performance: what we used to call 'gripping' the spectator. It is this excitation which is the very essence of the actor's art. From a sequence of physical positions and situations there arise those 'points of excitation' which are informed with some particular emotion.

Throughout this process of 'rousing the emotions' the actor observes a rigid framework of physical prerequisites.

Physical culture, acrobatics, dance, rhythmics, boxing and fencing are all useful activities, but they are of use only so long as they constitute auxiliary exercises in a course of 'biomechanics', the essential basis of every actor's training.

['The Actor of the Future and Biomechanics',
a report of Meyerhold's lecture in the Little Hall of the
Moscow Conservatoire, 12 June 1922;
in Ermitazh, Moscow, 1922, no 6, pp. 10–11.]

Notes

1   Term derived from the name of Frederick Winslow Taylor.

VSEVOLOD MEYERHOLD (1874–1940)

Meyerhold originally studied law, but became an acting student under Nemirovich-Danchenko. He worked at the Moscow Art Theatre, including performing as Treplov in Chekhov's *The Seagull*. He experimented with new theatre styles up until 1917 and the Russian Revolution. In 1920 he founded his own theatre and experimented with scenic construction and highly physical styles of performance, based on his system of biomechanics. His major productions included: *The Bedbug, The Government Inspector*, and *Mystery-Bouffe*. He was arrested and executed in 1940, after his avant-garde approach fell foul of Stalin's insistence on socialist realism.

See also: **Konstantin Stanislavski.**

SUGGESTED FURTHER READING

Braun, E. (ed.) (1969) *Meyerhold on Theatre,* London: Eyre Methuen.

Leach, R. (1989) *Vsevolod Meyerhold,* Cambridge: Cambridge University Press.
Pitches, J. (2003) *Vsevolod Meyerhold,* London & New York: Routledge.

Chapter 22

Michel Saint-Denis

VOCAL IMAGINATION AND IMPROVISATION

VOCAL IMAGINATION

AS **WE USE IMPROVISATION** in the training of an actor to develop the *physical* imagination needed to arrive at physical acting, just so we should develop in the actor the *vocal* imagination needed to arrive at vocal "acting." From the fusion of these two elements, the total actor of today will emerge.

In the early part of the training, the discipline of physical acting—in improvisation—and the discipline of vocal acting—in the voice and speech classes— run separately, but parallel. Gradually, they join and become one.

I cannot stress enough the importance of developing vocal imagination. This should be accomplished through exercises that aim at spontaneous vocal, but *non-verbal*, reactions to feelings, moods, and provocations. These are devised as an anti-dote to the exercises in pure technique. Students often become somewhat inhibited by being made too conscious of technique. These exercises help to break down those inhibitions without neglecting pure technique. There should be a continuous flow and exchange between vocal technique and vocal imagination.

I don't think it is an exaggeration to say that speech has become more and more mechanical. Many people, and particularly the visually-educated young people of today, speak without really relating thought and feeling to words and their real meaning. Speech has also become separated from the senses, from the body, but the senses and the body cannot be so separated and an awareness of this affinity should be developed before any demands are made on the student's use of words. The awareness, the perception of the functioning of the senses has become blunted and therefore does not produce the chemistry that leads to vitality of speech and communication.

The fundamental, the most important branch of our training is Improvisation.

What do we mean by "Improvisation" and why do we attach such a basic importance to it? We believe that through it the student discovers for himself the true essence, the real substance, of acting. It is here that he will find the relationship between the reality of his own inner life, both intellectual and emotional, and its physical expression, the means through which he can convey this reality to others. He must, as it were, first discover *himself*, then bring to the surface what was covered— by education and other factors—and *dare* to show it. This means to give of himself *totally*.

It is during Improvisation that the student should, step by step, become aware of what I like to call his own "inner chemistry," that oscillation between the subjective and objective.

It is here too that he can experience the very fact of acting: this will enable him to connect his work on improvisation with his later work on the interpretation of a text and to use the one for the animation of the other. If as a student he has fully experienced this, the imaginative actor will never forget the satisfaction he experienced in finding in himself the essence and the resources of acting. His interpretation will benefit deeply from this creative experience.

He will gradually learn how to arouse his subconscious in such a way that he can safely lose himself in the character he is creating without ever losing the control that concentration and observation have taught him. But this control is only achieved during the latter part of his training, as it demands years of experience.

We do not practice improvisation for its own sake; it is not there to corrupt the text but to invent a way to "uncork" it.

The student will have to learn how to prepare and repeat an improvised scenario just as one repeats a text of a play when performing it, rendering it with complete spontaneity each time.

The student should also come to feel the necessity of bringing to a text the same creative attitude which he has learned from his work in Improvisation.

The contribution which improvisation makes to interpretation is a very vital one: it must be understood that improvisation is a channel through which the imagination flows to reach life in interpretation. The passage from improvisation to interpretation is often a difficult one which takes time to learn to apply.

THE STUDENT IN ACTION AS HIMSELF

It might be useful here to describe the basic elements in the progression of the work on improvisation.

At first the student is asked only to present those elementary activities of everyday life that he is familiar with from his own personal experience. The student is not to invent characters; he is to be himself. He presents the ordinariness of life, but there is sufficient margin here for invention. Because of the absence of real objects, the student is obliged to find the physical means of presenting true reality. But this must be faithfully presented. If the actor is having breakfast, the non-existent table must be at a constant height from the floor in the eyes of the imagination. One must recognize whether the actor is eating eggs or toast and jam, whether what he is drinking is hot or cold. These become exercises in observation, invention and control.

The teacher gives the student his subject matter, but invention of the precise action, the way he is going to show the action in space, the manner in which he gives reality to it—all these problems have got to be solved by the student. The bareness of the rehearsal room makes this work very hard for the student at first; he will need some help and encouragement from his teacher.

The dramatic imagination of the student, so far, is in a comparatively rudimentary state, but it will come more into play and modify the physical representation of the action when specific exterior circumstances, and later, various moods, are suggested to the student. This new phase will make the student feel the interdependence of an idea and its physical expression, without any reference yet being made to the psychology of character.

For many students this stage creates difficulties of enormous proportions; it places them face to face with seemingly contradictory demands upon their feelings and the expression of them. Precision of physical action is continuously called for, even when the rhythm of the action is complicated by new moods or changes in emotions coming to the surface.

To help maintain this precision, certain complementary exercises should be introduced. These involve a return to the observation of the real world, the use of memories and work on rhythm and stage-space. All this is done in order to nourish the physical action and to avoid recourse to cliché, artificiality, or to the use of excessive concentration, which can paralyse expression.

ANIMALS

> D. W. Griffith advised me to watch animals as much as people, to try to find out how they communicate with each other—*without words.*
>
> LILLIAN GISH

This series of exercises allows for the most complete and striking transformations, which go much further in the physical modification of the self, and oblige the student to explore unknown regions of his imagination. These exercises transform the student into something very far from himself and this sometimes can have a profound influence on his later work.

For the exercise to be successful and useful, the choice of the animal is crucial. According to his nature and temperament, the student, with the help of his teacher, selects an animal with which he feels a certain affinity; certainly not one which might disturb him too much emotionally.

To start this work of transforming his body, the student begins by precise observation of the chosen animal or by activating his memory of animals he has seen. He must not reduce these observations to the obvious, but rather *select* those elements that can register on the stage and which capture the temperament, the essence of the animal. He must not try *to be* the animal in the abstract; he must get the feeling of the animal in his body and *lend himself* to it.

He should choose a certain action and mood natural to the animal. The action should be simple; just to cross from one end of the room to the other should be sufficient.

He must work in detail to establish his transformation *physically*: how does this animal stand? or run? what kind of mood can be given to it? where does it live? The student must decide on an action and sketch the moves lightly. If he does a four-legged animal, for instance a horse, he must synchronise the movements of the four legs as he walks or trots; he should explore the way a horse holds and moves its head; how, really, does a horse snort?

It is not necessary to do such animals on all fours; sometimes they are best represented by working on two legs, as I once saw a student do a cow. Standing on her two legs, with her torso slightly bent forward and with her arms hanging down, the student established the cow by making a kind of comment on the cow's body:

the way she chased insects away by a movement of her head; the way she munched her food, with an inward look in her eyes. The cow was completely believable.

Animal exercises allow the most complete, striking transformations because the subjects are tangible and very distinct from human nature. All will go well if the choice of the animal is right and if the student's concentration, though intense and focused, remains light.

We are, as a matter of fact, stretching Stanislavski's concept of concentration to its limit. Realism is a logical result of such concentration. But, in this exercise, we have moved far beyond realism.

To us, a mask is a temporary instrument which we offer to the curiosity of the student in the hope that, through literally *shielding* his timidity, it may help his concentration, diminish his self-consciousness, strengthen his inner feelings and lead him to develop his physical powers of outward dramatic expression.

Mask work is central to the training precisely because it enables the student to warm his feelings and cool his head; at the same time it permits him to experience, in its most startling form, the chemistry of acting. At the very moment when the actor's feelings beneath the mask are at their height, the urgent necessity to control his physical actions compels him to detachment and lucidity.

We do not wish in any way to imitate the Greeks, the Japanese or the Chinese, nor use masks that seem copies from a past tradition. The basic masks should be specifically designed for this work and be of normal human size with distinct features, representing the four ages of man:

- Adolescence
- Adulthood
- Mature Age
- Old Age

They must not be abstract, but they must be clear and easy to read from a distance.

It is the concrete experience of the mask which counts more than anything else. The student must go through this experience in good faith, leaving himself open to all its possibilities. What we are trying to do is to make the student discover inside himself the forces which will allow him to bring to light *reality* in all its fullness; that is to say, the luminous reality of the stage. In order to do this, words are not sufficient.

A mask is a tangible object. It is a presence which encounters one's own—face to face. By the imposition of such an external object on one's face, one will actually feel possessed by a foreign presence, without, however, being dispossessed of one's own self. When one puts a mask on one's face, one receives a strong impulse from it which one must learn how to obey naturally. Because one's own face is not seen, all expression depends on the body, but this expression cannot be released in a valid and dramatic way except by complete concentration on, and openness to, the sensations created by the mask. In other words, in these exercises the mask is the energising force.

Once the actor has acquired the elementary technique that is needed in using a mask, he will begin to realize that masks dislike agitation, that they can only be animated by controlled, strong, and utterly simple actions which depend upon the richness of the inner life within the calm and balanced body of the performer.

The student must not try to force himself to do anything interesting or fantastic; what he does must be simple and clear. The mask obliges him to eliminate everything unnecessary.

As his inner feelings accumulate behind the mask, the actor's face relaxes. This, together with his awareness that his eyes and facial characteristics are concealed as well, will help to simplify his physical, outward expression at the same time that it is being utilized to the utmost.

Without question this work is an excellent introduction to playing classical drama: it is a preparatory school for the tragedy and drama of the great styles.

A mask is an inanimate object that can have no life without the actor's existence; the mask absorbs the actor's personality, on which it feeds. Behind the mask the actor's inner feelings group themselves as in a closed container. Submission to the lesson of the mask helps an actor of talent to master a broad, inspired and objective way of acting. This has, in fact, been the aim of all our previous exercises in improvisation, but probably it has never been realised before with this much clarity and power.

MICHEL SAINT-DENIS (1897–1971)

Saint-Denis began in theatre as a pupil and assistant to his uncle, Jacques Copeau. He was a core member of Les Copiaus, Copeau's troupe in Burgundy, and later formed the Compagnie des Quinze. In the 1930s he moved to London where he became established as a director and teacher. He was one of the original three founding directors of the Royal Shakespeare Company, and founded five drama schools including leading institutions in London, New York, Strasbourg and Montreal.

See also: **Jacques Copeau.**

SUGGESTED FURTHER READING

Saint-Denis, M. (1982) *Training in the Theatre,* New York: Theatre Arts.
Saint-Denis, M. (2008) *The Rediscovery of Style and Other Writings,* London & New York: Routledge.

Baldwin, J. (2003) *Michel Saint-Denis and the Shaping of the Modern Actor,* Westport, CT: Praeger Publishers.
Baldwin, J. (2010) 'Michel Saint-Denis: Training the complete actor', in Hodge, A. (ed.) (2010) *Actor Training,* London & New York: Routledge.

Chapter 23

Tadashi Suzuki

THE GRAMMAR OF THE FEET

THE WAY IN WHICH the feet are used is the basis of a stage performance. Even the movements of the arms and hands can only augment the feeling inherent in the body positions established by the feet. There are many cases in which the position of the feet determines even the strength and nuance of the actor's voice. An actor can still perform without arms and hands, but to perform without feet would be inconceivable.

Nō has often been defined as the art of walking. The movements of the actor's feet create the expressive environment. The basic use made of the feet in the nō consists of a shuffling motion. The actor walks by dragging the feet, turns around in a shuffle-like motion, and strikes a rhythm with his feet in the same way. The upper parts of his body are practically immobile; even the movements of his hands are extremely limited. Whether the actor is standing still or in motion, his feet are the center of interest. These feet, encased in *tabi* (white bifurcated socks) provide one of the most profound pleasures of the nō, as they move from a position of repose forwards and backwards, left and right, up and down with their own independent rhythm. Such patterns of foot motion can be created out of the intimate relationship of the feet of the actor with the surface of the nō stage. The very life of the art depends on the fixing and deepening of the relationships of the feet to the stage in order to render the expressiveness of foot movements all the more compelling. In fact, this kind of ambulatory art is involved in all theatrical performance.

Classical ballet, for example, is equally dependent on the feet, as is the traditional Japanese *kabuki*. In *kabuki* (except in the domestic plays, where the characters often sit), much of the audience's pleasure comes from watching the actors' foot movements, which are often more pronounced than in the nō. The *hanamichi* (the runway that connects the auditorium with the *kabuki* stage) is particularly well suited to emphasize the art of the feet.

Since the coming of the modern theatre to Japan, however, the artistic use of foot movements has not continued to develop. This is too bad, because realism in the theatre should inspire a veritable treasure house of walking styles. Since it is commonly accepted that realism should attempt to reproduce faithfully on the stage the surface manner of life, the art of walking has more or less been reduced to the simplest forms of naturalistic movement. Yet any movement on the stage is, by definition, a fabrication. Since there is more room within realism for a variety of movements than in the nō or in kabuki, these various ambulatory possibilities should be exhibited in an artistic fashion. One reason the modern theatre is so tedious to watch, it seems to me, is because it has no feet.

Since Japan's modern theatre attempts to take European drama and wed it theatrically to lifestyles of contemporary Japan, there is no room for the movements of bare or naked feet. Actors, because they must wear shoes to perform, have, in a manner of speaking, lost their feet.

When an actor puts on shoes, the movements of his feet are limited. Stamping, sliding, walking pigeon-toed, walking bowlegged—all of these are virtually denied him. When an actor does struggle to make such movements, the sinews in his ankle or his Achilles tendon will pain him, and his feet will develop blisters. Even in the West, specially designed footwear has been developed for the classical ballet which somewhat resembles the footwear used in the traditional Japanese theatre arts. Japanese tabi, which have served so long in that capacity, can still be put to good use on the stage today. We occasionally wear tabi in our everyday life, but they always suggest a certain formality. The modern theatre does nothing to promote the expressiveness of the feet; the feet are merely used as they are in ordinary life. In the nō, where ghosts serve as the protagonists, the art of the foot exists; but in the modern theatre, which purports to show living beings, there are none. How ironic, since in Japanese folklore the ghost is represented invariably as footless.

A performance begins when the actor's feet touch the ground, a wooden floor, a surface, when he first has the sensation of putting down roots; it begins in another sense when he lifts himself lightly from that spot. The actor composes himself on the basis of his sense of contact with the ground, by the way in which his body makes contact with the floor. The performer indeed proves with his feet that he is an actor. Of course, there are many ways in which the human body can make contact with the floor, but most of us, excepting small children, make contact with the lower part of the body, centering on the feet. The various pleasures that an actor feels as he comes in contact with the ground—and the growth in the richness of change in his bodily responses when he is in contact with the ground—constitute the first stage in his training as an actor.

In training the actors in my company, I have one exercise in which I have them stamp their feet in time to rhythmic music for a fixed period. Stamping may not be the most accurate term, for they loosen their pelvic area slightly, then move themselves by striking the floor in a vehement motion. As the music finishes, they use up the last of their energy and fall to the floor. They lie flat, in a hush, as though they were dead. After a pause, the music begins again, this time gently. The actors rise in tune with this new atmosphere, each in his or her own fashion, and finally return to a fully vertical standing position. This exercise is based on motion and stillness, and the contrasting expulsion and containment of bodily force. By means of strengthening breath support, this exercise develops a concentration of strength in the body.

The essential element in the first musical portion of this training exercise is the continuous pounding of the floor, using an even, unremitting strength without loosening the upper part of the body. If the actor loses his concentration on his legs and loins and so misses the sense of being toughened or tempered, he will not be able to continue on to the end with a unified, settled energy, no matter how full of energy he may feel. What is more, if the actor does not have the determination to control any irregularities of breathing, then toward the end of the exercise his upper body will of necessity begin to tremble, and he will lose the rhythm. In either case, the energy produced as the feet strike the floor spreads into the upper body. I ask that the actors strike the floor with all the energy possible; the energy that is not properly absorbed will rise upwards and cause the upper part of their bodies to tremble. In order to minimize such a transfer, the actor must learn to control and contain that energy in the pelvic region. Focusing on this part of the body, he must learn to gauge continuously the relationship between the upper and lower parts of his body, all the while continuing on with the stamping motion.

Of course, the idea that an actor can learn to control the apportionment of his energy, unifying it through his pelvic region, is hardly unique to my training exercises. All physical techniques employed for the stage surely involve such a principle. What I believe I have added, however, is the idea of stamping the foot—forcing the development of a special consciousness based on this striking of the ground. This concept arises from my conviction that an actor's basic sense of his physicality comes from his feet.

In ordinary life, we have little consciousness of our feet. The body can stand of its own accord without any sense at all of the relationship of feet to earth; in stamping, we come to understand that the body establishes its relation to the ground through the feet, that the ground and the body are not two separate entities. We are a part of the ground. Our very beings will return to the earth when we die.

TADASHI SUZUKI (1939–)

Suzuki is the director of the Suzuki Company of Toga, which he founded in 1984. He invented the Suzuki Method of Actor Training, which emphasizes the placement of the feet, the connection with the ground, and the actor's ability to transcend limitations. With Anne Bogart he co-founded SITI (Saratoga International Theatre Institute) in 1992.

See also: **Anne Bogart, Tina Landau.**

SUGGESTED FURTHER READING

Suzuki, T. (1993) *The Way of Acting*, New York: Theatre Communications Group.

Allain, P. (2003) *The Art of Stillness: The Theater Practice of Tadashi Suzuki*, Basingstoke: Palgrave Macmillan.
Climenhaga, R. (2010) 'Anne Bogart and SITI Company: Creating the moment', in Hodge, A. (ed.) (2010) *Actor Training*, London & New York: Routledge.

Chapter 24

Yevgeny Vakhtangov

CONSCIOUSNESS, THE SUBCONSCIOUS AND THE ORGANIC OUTER TECHNIQUE

SUBCONSCIOUS PERCEPTION AND EXPRESSION

CONSCIOUSNESS DOES NOT CREATE anything—ever ... Only the subconscious does. It has an independent ability to choose material for the creative process, bypassing the conscious mind. Apart from that, one can consciously send material for the creative process into the realm of his subconscious. From this standpoint, any rehearsal is only productive when in it one seeks or provides material for the next rehearsal; it is in the intervals between rehearsals that the subconscious processes the acquired material. One cannot create anything out of nothing, which is why one cannot play a role without work—"out of inspiration."

Inspiration is the moment when our subconscious has combined material from the preceding work. At the mere call of our conscious mind, but without its involvement, the subconscious will give everything one single form.

Fire that accompanies this moment is a natural condition, just as several chemical elements being combined into one form naturally produce heat.

Mental elements combined into a particular form amenable for a given individual cause an inflow of energy at the moment of their expression. This energy warms up, lights up, and breathes life into the form. Everything that is invented consciously does not carry the signs of fire. Everything that is created within the subconscious realm and formed subconsciously is accompanied by the extraction of this energy; it is chiefly this very energy that carries an infectious power.

This infectiousness can be described as a subconscious captivation of the perceiving party's subconscious. It is the sign of talent. He who consciously feeds his subconscious and expresses the results of its work in a subconscious way is a talent.

He who subconsciously feeds his subconscious and engages in a **subconscious expression** is a genius.

He who expresses consciously is a master.

He who is deprived of the ability to perceive subconsciously or consciously, and yet dares to express is a mediocrity. For he does not have an individuality. For he, who deposited zero into his subconscious (the creative realm), will express zero.

From November 3, 1917, notebook entry.

ON ACTOR CULTIVATION

Actor cultivation must consist of enriching the actor's subconscious with varied abilities: freedom, concentration, seriousness, **stage intelligence**, artistry, activity, expressiveness, gift of observation, quickness to adapt, etc. There are an infinite number of these abilities.

The subconscious, equipped with such a supply of means, will forge a near perfect creation from the material it receives.

Ideally, an actor should, together with his partners, analyze and digest the text and proceed onto the stage to create the character.

This is [how it should be] in the ideal, once an actor cultivated all necessary means, or abilities. An actor must be an improviser. This is what we call talent.

God only knows what goes on in theatre schools. The main mistake the schools make is that they take it upon themselves *to teach how to act*, while they should be *cultivating actors*.

From October 22, 1918, notebook entry.

ON CONSCIOUS AND SUBCONSCIOUS ELEMENTS IN TRAINING

The important thing is not to play an *étude* well but to resort to all aspects of our system of training as frequently and as consciously (as strange as it may sound) as possible. This is necessary so that you develop a subconscious habit of using all the abilities we "cultivate."

This can be compared to learning a foreign language.

From November 10, 1918, entry in the
Gunst Studio's Diary of Independent Works.

ON PLASTICITY OF MOVEMENT

Actors should train in *plastique* not so that they can dance or acquire a beautiful gesture or posture but in order to imbue their body with the feeling of plasticity (cultivate it). Moreover, plasticity is present not just in movement but in a piece of fabric tossed by a nonchalant hand, in the surface of a frozen lake, in a cozily sleeping cat, in suspended garlands, and in a still marble statue.

Nature does not know things not plastic: a breaking wave, a swaying branch, a galloping horse (a wretched nag even), the succession of day and night, a sudden whirlwind, flying birds, a tranquil mountainous expanse, a waterfall, madly leaping, the heavy step of an elephant, a hippopotamus's ugly form—all of it is plastic: there is no clumsiness here, no embarrassment, no awkward tension, deliberateness or staleness. There is nothing stiff or dead about a cat fast asleep, but, oh my God!, how stiff is an eager young man darting to get a glass of water for his sweetheart.

Actors should engage in long and diligent work to consciously *cultivate* the habit of plasticity so that later they can unconsciously *express* themselves in a plastic way. This applies to their ability to wear a costume, adjust the volume of their voice, achieve physical transfiguration (through a visible external form) into the form of the character they portray, allocate their muscular energy efficiently, and model themselves into anything in gesture, voice, or musical speech. Actors should also be able to achieve plasticity in the logic of their feelings.

From October 30, 1918, notebook entry.

PLASTIQUE CLASS

I am in bed; I cannot come to you; I won't see you for a long time, and yet I need to tell you how vital it is to train in *plastique*, and how vital it is to *know how* to train in it, so as to understand the essence of "plasticity" as one of the most essential actor's qualities. You must learn how to sense *modeling*, and the *sculpture* of the role, scene, play; without the quality of plasticity one is unable to do this. It is almost impossible to acquire the quality of plasticity unless you train in *plastique* skillfully.

This is in short.

You will find a detailed and fascinating account of it in a wonderful book by S. Volkonsky, *The Man on the Stage*, published by the Apollon publishing house. Read it, and you will be attending the *plastique* class as eagerly as you now attend your speech class and acting exercises.

Next time I will tell you about *solfeggio*.

Ye. Vakhtangov

From November 8, 1918, letter to the Gunst Studio.

ON THE SPOKEN WORD

A phrase must first be cleared grammatically. All words must be finished, but some words must be said *lovingly*.

Feelings must be threaded through your *favorite* word.

Do not color the nearest words, but rather go along the line of action.

Speech and tone must be placed in the vowels.

In a poem, if you try to achieve a singsong quality, or color words and phrases, the inner meaning will be lost.

In text analysis, one should be first guided by the thought, searching for the *most important words*.

One must give the right meaning to the word—then the feeling will come.

To start with, one says the words of the scene in a grammatically sound manner—the feeling will follow.

Dull speech results from a mere recitation of facts, without the emotional experience.

When the quality [of speech] turns out to be dull, one must consult the compass—the through action.

YEVGENY VAKHTANGOV (1883–1922)

Vakhtangov began his education at Moscow State University, but struggled with his studies due to his interest in theatre. After training as an actor he joined the Moscow Art Theatre in 1911. He was influenced by Stanislavski and Meyerhold, and his own work sought to find a meeting point between Stanislavski's psychophysical approach and Meyerhold's theatrical techniques. Stanislavski recognized his talent and encouraged him to teach his new techniques based on fantastic realism at the Art Theatre. Important productions include: *The Dybbuk* and *Princess Turandot*. He died of stomach cancer at the age of 39.

See also: **Konstantin Stanislavski**.

SUGGESTED FURTHER READING

Malaev-Babel, A. (ed.) (2011) *The Vakhtangov Sourcebook*, London & New York: Routledge.

Malaev-Babel, A. (2012) *Yevgeny Vakhtangov: A Critical Portrait*, London & New York: Routledge.
Worrall, N. (2008) *Modernism to Realism on the Soviet Stage: Tairov-Vakhtangov, Okhlopkov*, Cambridge: Cambridge University Press.

Chapter 25

Phillip Zarrilli

BEGINNING WITH THE BREATH

(RE)DISCOVERING THE BODY AND MIND THROUGH PRACTICE

TRAINING THE ACTOR TO "stand still while not standing still" necessarily means a transformation of the practitioner's relationship to his body and mind in practice, and also of how one conceptualizes the relationship between body and mind. I begin with my own experience of this process of transformation to illustrate the commonplace confusions as well as the idiosyncrasies characteristic of this twofold process. My story takes place between the fields of play on which many American males of my age were enculturated to particular practices and paradigms of the body-mind relationship, and Kerala, South India's *kalaris* or gymnasia-cum-temples and stages where practitioners of *kalarippayattu* and *kathakali* dance-drama are enculturated to a very different understanding and practice of the body-mind relationship.

Before I first traveled to India in 1976 I had very little movement or dance training. My experience of my body was based on a variety of sports: baseball, track, wrestling, basketball, soccer, and (American) football. I assumed that they promoted good health while making me assertive and self-confident. But I also intuitively knew that my high school football training promoted aggressive and potentially violent attitudes and behavior. While being psychophysically shaped by my training in sports, I was philosophically, ethically, and ideologically becoming a pacifist.

But my body remained separate, that is, it would not be "pacified." It had been shaped by a masculine culture of the body which assumed an overarching and directive "will" which, through sheer determination and/or aggression, could shape the body per se, and/or make use of the body to impose that will on someone/ something else. Consequently, I unthinkingly forced my body to shape itself to a discipline such as football or soccer, and/or I tried to use that body as a means to an end, that is, for winning. My sports body was the objective or neutral biomedical, physiological body observable from the outside. As my body was a "thing" to be mastered, male culture gave me permission to keep this body sequestered and separate from my beliefs and values. Separate from my biomedical/sports body, I inhabited an *other* body—the personal and private body which was a repository of my feelings. It too existed in a state of tension with my beliefs and ethical values, and also remained separate from my biomedical/sports body.

My (separate) mind was manifest in my will to mastery, in my reflexive consciousness which could watch my sports body from the outside and in my beliefs and values which attempted, through my active will, to impose themselves on either or both bodies. None of these fragmented experiences of my body and mind nor their implicitly dualistic paradigms helped me to inhabit and/or understand either in a way that led me to achieve an integration between them which, at least intellectually, I eventually sought both in performance and in life.

Consequently, when I first went to India in 1976, I was totally unprepared for the psychophysiological experiences I was to undergo. For my first six months I was immersed in studying *kathakali* dance-drama for approximately eight hours of intensive daily training at the Kerala Kalamandalam under M. P. Sankaran Namboodiri. For an additional three months I began four to six hours of daily training in the closely related martial art, *kalarippayattu*, under Gurukkal Govindankutty Nayar of the CVN Kalari, Thiruvananthapuram.

Over the months and years of observing masters of both *kathakali* and *kalarippayattu*, I began to notice the ease with which they embodied their dynamic arts, manifesting an extraordinary focus and power. In *kathakali* that power is manifest in the full-bodied aesthetically expressive forms through which the actor channels his energy as he realizes each state of being/doing (*bhava*) appropriate to the dramatic context. In *kalarippayattu* that focus and power is manifest not only in performance of the fully embodied forms of exercise but also in the fierce and potentially lethal force of a step, kick, or blow.

When masters of either the dance-drama or martial art performed their complex acrobatic combinations of steps, kicks, jumps, turns, and leaps, as Govindankutty Nayar liked to describe it, they "flowed like a river." At that time, my body did anything but flow. The serpentine, graceful, yet powerfully grounded fluidity of movement seemed an unapproachable state of embodiment. My overt physical ineptitude was matched by my equal naivety about how to learn through my body, and how that body was related to my mind. I physically attacked both *kathakali* and *kalarippayattu* exercises. I tried to force the exercises into my body; my body into the forms. I was determined to make myself learn each exercise, no matter how difficult. There in the Indian *kalari* was my Akron, Ohio, Buchtel Griffin high school football coach yelling at me: "Zarrilli, hit him harder. Get up off your ass and let's see you move! And I mean really move this time! Get up and do it again—right, this time!"

Although characteristic of American male sports, this willful, aggressive, assertive approach to one's body-in-training is not restricted to Americans. Many males undergoing training suffer the same problem with the same result—unnecessary tension. Whenever an individual willfully asserts an intention on an action, the body will be full of tension and the mind full of the aggressive attempt to control and assert the will.

Gradually, after years of practice, the relationship of my body and mind in practice and my understanding of that relationship began to alter. When demonstrating the martial art or when acting, I found myself able more consistently to enter a state of readiness and awareness—I no longer attacked the activity or the moment. Rather than being directed to an end or goal, my body and mind were being positively integrated and cultivated for engagement in what I was doing in the present moment. My tensions and inattentions gradually gave way to sensing myself simultaneously as flowing yet power-full, centered yet free, released yet controlled. I was beginning to actualize what Benedetti described as "stillness at my center." I was learning how to "stand still."

Simultaneously, through the long process of repetition of basic forms of practice, I gradually began to sense a shift in the quality of my relationship to my bodymind in exercise or on stage—I was discovering an internal energy which I was gradually able to control and modulate physically and vocally whether in performance or when extending my breath or energy through a weapon when delivering a blow. I was moving from a concern with the physical, external form to awareness of the subtler internal (psycho-) dimension of how to fully embody an action. My body and mind were beginning to become one *in practice*. I was able to enter a state of heightened awareness of and sensitivity to my bodymind and breath in action within, and simultaneously keep my awareness and energy open to the immediate environment. I was beginning to discover how *not* to stand still, while standing still.

I emphasize *beginning* because every day of practice during my initial periods of training in India I watched a master such as Govindankutty Nayar actualize this optimal state of "standing still while not standing still." For example, when he performed the *kalarippayattu* lion pose, behind the momentary stasis was a palpable inner fullness reflected in his concentrated gaze and in his readiness to respond—animal-like—to anything that might happen in the immediate environment. Govindankutty Nayar was inhabiting a state in which, like Lord Brahman the thousand-eyed, "the body becomes all eyes" (*meyyu kannakuka*). From my perspective, when the "body is all eyes" one is "standing still yet not standing still." This is the optimal state of readiness that the actor ideally inhabits.

PHILLIP ZARRILLI (1947–)

Zarrilli began his training in the Indian art of kalarippayattu in 1976. He was the first Westerner to undertake an extensive program of this training. He has also studied kathakali and t'ai chi ch'uan. He has taught at the University of Wisconsin-Madison and more recently at the University of Exeter (2000–2010). He now runs the Llanarth Group in Wales.

See also: **Tadashi Suzuki, Yoshi Oida.**

SUGGESTED FURTHER READING

Zarrilli, P. (2008) *Psychophysical Acting: An intercultural approach after Stanislavski*, London & New York: Routledge.
Zarrilli, P., Daboo, J. and Loukes, R. (2013) *Acting: Psychophysical phenomenon and process*, Basingstoke: Palgrave Macmillan.

PART IV

Character and Composition

Introduction to Part IV: The Self and the Fictive Other in Creation, Rehearsal and Performance

Bella Merlin, University of California, Riverside, USA

FROM THE ANCIENT GREEKS to twenty-first-century Hollywood, the significance of character in the composition of a dramatic story has been paramount. Essentially, 'character' can be said to refer to the construction of a persona – fictive or fact-based – represented through the actor's body, voice, and imagination. That said, the concept of character has altered significantly over the last century, as narrative form and structure have shifted – in other words, as the audience's relationship with the dramatic material has changed. In the realm of psychological realism (the dominant aesthetic in film, television and much story-based theatre), the actor seeks to merge self with scripted role to draw the audience into the narrative flow. Over the last one hundred years, however, particular playwrights and practitioners have actively challenged that notion of character. Amongst others, Yevgeny Vakhtangov's experiments with fantastical realism, Brecht's 'estrangement' (or alienation), and Robert Wilson's experimental theater might be seen as key pioneering movements in foregrounding composition over character. In the post-modern and post-dramatic canons, contemporary scholars even pronounce the death of character.[1] Nonetheless, training schools across the globe still tend to focus on the transition from the actor's autobiographical self to a created role.[2] In fact, most actors thrive on this challenge: how do we transform our own bodies, voices and emotional repertoires into a vast array of dramatic characters in a diversity of styles and media? Which compositional strategies may be used – whether the character is already scripted or we are devising it from scratch? Whether the aesthetic is traditional or experimental?

The extracts in this section address that challenge from a number of perspectives. Although the writers reflect a host of different acting schools – some more physical, some more psychological – the overall mission is to develop an actor with enhanced psycho-physical awareness, regardless of genre.[3] While some extracts are clearly in the realm of actor training, most blur the edges of training and performance, as they include the impact of director, writer and audience on the actor's choices.

Drawing together 'character' and 'composition' into Part IV highlights the fact that, as actors, we can only really fine-tune our psychophysical choices for characters within the compositional context of time, space and place. Ultimately our portrayal of a character is relational: to the given circumstances of the script, to the intentions of the writer, to our onstage partners, to the performance space, and to the audience. In other words, building a character works diametrically from the inside out (using our inner and physical resources) and from the outside in (incorporating the dimensions and dynamics of the stage, as well as the playwright's dramaturgy and the director's production score).

Although the extracts are collated alphabetically, I use this introductory essay to tease out the (semi-chronological) way in which an actor might use their content when creating a role. The journey takes us from the first moments of training the acting instrument, through composing a performance in rehearsal, to performing that role in a final production. When we boil it down to its most basic, there are two fundamental approaches to building a character depending on how we want to affect our audience. Either we want the audience to forget that they're seeing actors create roles so that they can empathize with the characters' journeys, or we want overtly to remind them that they're watching performers so that they can take critical stock of the presented situation. In the first instance, psychophysical transformation is at the core (as is arguably the case with Stella Adler and Michael Chekhov). (As previously mentioned, this is the main aesthetic with most television and film acting today.) In the second instance, the way in which the scenic composition juxtaposes different actions is more significant (as is arguably the case with Dario Fo and Bertolt Brecht): rather than being swept on a narrative journey, the audience is invited to compare, contrast, question and reassess the behaviours of the characters/performers. (This is the main aesthetic with most political theatre and performance art.) Of course, there are myriad gradations in between these two fundamental approaches, as we will see elucidated in the extracts in Part IV.

TRAINING THE CREATIVE IMPULSE TOWARDS CHARACTER AND COMPOSITION

The process of building a character (be it physically or psychophysically) involves transitioning from our daily selves to our creative – or 'extra-daily' – selves, and evolving our personal dramaturgical toolkits. We begin, therefore, with director, Eugenio Barba's article, 'An Amulet Made of Memory: The Significance of Exercises in the Actor's Dramaturgy' (1997). Born in Italy in 1936, Barba's adopted hometown became Holstebro, Denmark, where he founded the Odin Teatret (1964) and the International School of Theatre Anthropology (1979): the former is devoted to staging dramatically arresting works, and the later is devoted to theatre research.[4] Barba's eclectic mixture of eastern and western practices informs his lifelong investigation into acting and performing. In the 'Amulet' extract, Barba pinpoints (through a list of ten 'characteristics') the fundamental purposes of *exercises*, which are essentially the tools through which we train the self and subsequently build a character. He combines hands-on practicum with useful philosophies, basically asking: What is the point of exercises? For Barba, exercises provide the opportunity for us to use our 'body-minds' (i.e. our psychophysical instruments comprising body, brain, imagination and emotions) to release a specific creative energy that will shift us from our daily self to our extra-daily self. It is our extra-daily self that will ultimately deliver our performance to the audience. The simple tasks of an exercise don't have any great meaning in themselves: instead, their simplicity trains our ability to fill every moment with what Stanislavsky called 'adaptation' or 'a constant state of inner improvisation'.[5] In terms of *composition*, the rhythms and chains of association inherent in exercises become a score (or subscore) of physical actions: in other words, exercises themselves can be the starting point for composing a piece. In terms of *character*, the reason for placing this extract first is that, through exercises (says Barba), we *learn not to learn to act*: as actors, we have to get out of our own way before we can start transforming into characters or performed roles.

If Barba's 'Amulet' extract invites us to start by learning *not* to learn to act, the extract from *Sanford Meisner on Acting* (1987) addresses the next basic step: how to train our impulses. Sanford Meisner (1905-1997) emerged from the American Method of the 1930s, as one of twenty-eight actors selected to form the Group Theatre by New York pioneers, Harold Clurman, Lee Strasberg and Cheryl Campbell in 1931. Heavily influenced by the Moscow Art Theatre's tours to the USA in the 1920s, the Group Theatre sought 'truth' in an actor's portrayal of character and onstage composition.[6] However, Meisner strayed away from the Group's emphasis on affective memory and in 1935 he began teaching at the Neighborhood Playhouse School of Theatre. There, he experimented with 'living truthfully under given imaginary circumstances' (Meisner & Longwell 1987: 15) and evolved his Meisner Technique. This extract explains the most famous aspect of his Technique: the Repetition Exercise. The Repetition Exercise is used to train actors to respond instinctively and impulsively to their partners rather than serving up an intellectual manipulation of what they think the response should be. In many ways, this exercise integrates fundamental actor training with the first steps of building a character, as Meisner uses two key principles to train a sense of creative freedom: (1) we shouldn't do anything unless something happens to make us do it; and (2) whatever we do must depend on our onstage partner. (These are exactly the same two principles that we might adopt in rehearsal when building a character from a playwright's text.) We can apply the quality of play that arises from the Repetition Exercise to almost any compositional style or genre, as Meisner's improvisation-based training encourages heart-felt impulses, rather than head-led considerations.

Equally multivalent are the practices proposed in Robert Pasolli's extract from *A Book on the Open Theatre* (1970). Two words are used here that appear frequently in the other extracts, often with slightly different biases but always of importance to character and composition: 'transformation' and 'improvisation'. Actor-director, Joseph Chaikin (1935–2003) left the provocative avant-garde Living Theatre in 1963 to join a group of students who had formed the Open Theatre in New York.[7] With a desire to create collaborative, ensemble theatre, Chaikin and his actors sought an acting style that wasn't as autobiographically introspective as the American Method or as compositionally anti-realistic as the Theatre of the Absurd. This extract is called 'transformation', and it focuses on training an actor's sense of playfulness and willingness to jump from one set of given circumstances to another, thereby continuously changing character and compositional style. As with Meisner, the emphasis is on following our instincts and responding to our onstage partner, though Chaikin and Meisner's intentions might be subtly different. Meisner's background in the American Method encourages connected listening between two or more people, with a logical sequence of interdepending actions and reactions. Chaikin's aesthetic arguably works away from behavioural logic and sequence. At any moment in a Chaikin-based improvisation, we can completely transform the identity of our character, as well as where they are, when they're there, or what their objectives might be. Our scene partner has to adapt to these transformations – not worrying about a rational or psychological justification, but by allowing a more pliable, instinctual acceptance of the given circumstances to inform the improvisational choices. Because identities can shape-shift at a moment's notice – even to that of an animal, a machine or an abstraction – a playful attitude towards embodying a wide range of characters and emotions is developed. Because style can change at any moment – from grand opera to Chekhovian realism – compositional skills are dynamically trained. This definition of 'transformation' (which builds an actor's confidence towards improvisation) is unquestionably relevant to any actor training today, regardless of genre or medium.

We can clearly see with Barba, Meisner and Chaikin the strands of actor training that strengthen impulse and instinct, playfulness and improvisation, and how we have to integrate our own bodies, minds and imaginations before we can focus on building a fictional character. The next three extracts from Fo and Lecoq take us deeper into the realm of physicality, combining character and composition in body and space.

TRAINING BODY, MIND AND PSYCHOLOGY TOWARDS CHARACTER AND COMPOSITION

In this discussion so far, we've placed the training of impulse and improvisation at the beginning of an actor's work on a role. However, Italian performer, Dario Fo (1926-) cites learning how to 'move the limbs with unaffected elegance and awareness' (Fo 1991: 35) as the first discipline in actor training. 'Elegance and awareness' covers the gamut of movement for Fo, from basic breathing to complex acrobatics to mime and gesture; after all, simple movement through space and time forms the starting point in many respects for composing a theatre piece. As an actor, director, writer, political activist, and Nobel Prize winner in Literature (1997), Fo understands the power of theatre from all facets of performance making. He draws heavily on 'illegitimate' theatre including the *guillari* (medieval Italian strolling players) and *commedia dell'arte*, and he worked for many successful years with his actress-writer-activist wife, Franca Rame, until her death in 2013. Fo's performances – not least his one-man show, *Mistero-Buffo* (1973) – are precise in their encapsulation of character, extremely physical and mercurial in their composition, and full of improvisation. His synthesis of popular theatre and political activism is potent, and his ability to conjure up characters through mime and caricature, while preserving a recognizable reality in his acting, is masterful. The extract from Fo's book *Tricks of the Trade* (1991) focuses on the dialogue between gesture and mask: although Fo rarely uses actual masks, he has evolved an extensive physical and facial versatility. In terms of gesture, Fo breaks the grip of American Method realism, whereby a vernacular of realistic ticks and 'paranoiac twitches' are often used as shortcuts into character. Instead, he urges actors to allow the mask of the character to synthesize body and gesture into a vocabulary of movements that is simultaneously *expanded* to a dramatic size and *condensed* to a psychological essence. With regard to developing a character's physicality, there are some excellent ideas in this extract. So many actors remain gridlocked in their bodies, relying on their face and voice to do much of the work: Fo's idea that the pelvis can be the fulcrum of a character is simple and liberating.[8]

That said, many young actors in the twenty-first century earn their living through film and television, where a repertoire of realistic details can be the very tools that furnish their screen careers. The sucking on a cigarette, the scratching of the nose, the chewing on a toothpick are the visual details that the film camera loves. Indeed, many movie actors *do* inhabit their own masks and earn a living from doing so. Robert de Niro, Bruce Willis, Jennifer Aniston: each has a mask that encourages a certain range of gestures (more or less limited) and body centres (more or less predictable), and that fixity in itself sustains their careers. The modern film industry has in many respects created a new *dramatis personae* of Arlechinos, Pantelones and Columbinas.

A similar juxtaposition between physical character work and cinematic choices is raised in the next extract, Jacques Lecoq's *The Moving Body* (2000). As we read these extracts, it's worth remembering that the compositional choices made in building a character for screen are markedly different from those made for stage. Lecoq raises this point when distinguishing between character and personality, and the osmosis between the two: 'It may be possible for this kind of osmosis to work in the cinema, in psychological close-ups, but theatre performance must be able to make an image carry from stage to spectator' (2000: 61). Jacques Lecoq (1921–1999) spent eight years in Italy, where he worked with Dario Fo and studied the *commedia dell'arte* traditions. An actor, mime, and gymnast, he founded L'École Internationale de Théâtre Jacques Lecoq in 1956, where the training is based on the principles of playfulness, complicity, and openness. Offering practical tactics rather than philo-sophical theories, Lecoq points out that the first year of his training is aimed towards 'character acting', an actor training drawn from work with the neutral mask, an exploration of rhythm, and improvisations based on natural elements, animals and abstractions (such as colours). With an emphasis on 'physical characterisation', improvisation is used extensively to develop characters (as with Chaikin and the Open Theatre), and there are very specific steps outlined in Lecoq's extract for undertaking this. For example, students are required to find three characteristics or 'lines of force', which define a character; these three words then form the compositional 'home' from which the nuances of the character emerge. It's also worth noting the importance of the onstage partner when creating a character: as with Meisner, Lecoq highlights the fact that character cannot be separated from situation. Essentially, we are who we are *in relation* to others and our environment. The impact of composition is vividly explored in the 'stylistic constraints' exercise, where up to five actors play up to ten characters in a 'cabaret' space of two metres square. It's also fun! Indeed (whether it's always possible or not) Lecoq declares that 'It is essential to have fun and our school is a happy school' (2000: 65) where theatre always retains its playful dimensions. Although Lecoq's work is highly theatrical, it is possible to apply his principles – particularly the lines of force – to smaller-scale, screen work as well as bold, physical compositions.

TRAINING COMPOSITION

The creation of character for any medium (screen or stage) and genre (from musical theatre to black-box realism) depends fundamentally on the composition of bodies in space – and that includes the bodies of the viewers as well as the bodies of the performers. It also depends on the movement of bodies *through* space. This becomes crystal clear in 'Viewpoints and Composition: What are they?' – the extract from

Bogart and Landau's *The Viewpoints Book*. As with most actor training, the writers express that their concepts are not original, but rather (what they call) 'timeless and belong[ing] to the natural principles of movement, time and space' (2005: 7). This notion in itself raises questions about the basics of actor training. Many trainers seek to evolve principles and practices, which are drawn from fundamental human behaviours, the body's anatomy and social dynamics, and are therefore (seemingly) widely applicable. However, practice inevitably changes over time and according to context. (Indeed, I envision certain actor training principles shifting dramatically over the next few years in response to technological advances and dependencies.) That said, there is arguably a broad relevance and application regarding this extract's contents. Anne Bogart (1951–) – an internationally acclaimed director – encountered choreographer, Mary Overlie,[9] at NYU in 1979. There, she evolved Overlie's Six View Points of dance into Viewpoints – 'a philosophy translated into a technique for (1) training performers; (2) building ensemble; and (3) creating movement for the stage' (2005: 7). Over the last twenty years, Bogart has worked tirelessly as a professional theatre maker and an educator – in the graduate Directing programme at Columbia University, New York, and in the creation of the Saratoga International Theatre Institute (SITI) with Japanese practitioner, Tadashi Suzuki. The principles of Viewpoints are succinct: the two main Viewpoints of Time and Space are divided into nine subsets, all of which are designed to sharpen a performer's aware-ness. These are set out so clearly that they are immediately implementable, both in training and in creating characters. Equally clear are the descriptions of Composition, its purposes being as diverse as: to generate a vocabulary within an ensemble; to create an original piece of theatre; to reveal to ourselves our impulses and intuitions; and to dialogue with other art forms. Used as a part of actor training, the very nature of Composition is multivalent: it's the fine balance between process and result, between inner feelings and outer expression. Indeed, of all the writings included in this chapter, Bogart and Landau's extract is most explicit in its definition of Composition. For any student of acting or directing, Viewpoints are essential anchor-points.

The six extracts examined so far have all featured the fundamentals of *actor training* in conjunction with creating a character and composition. The next three extracts can be situated more overtly in the realm of *rehearsal*.

CHARACTER, COMPOSITION AND REHEARSAL

Among the actors-cum-trainers cited in this chapter, the one who has sashayed most expansively between diverse characters and various media is Michael Chekhov (1891–1955).[10] Described by Stanislavsky as his most brilliant student, Chekhov acted, directed and experimented at the Moscow Art Theatre from 1911 to 1928 when he was forced to leave Soviet Russia due to his political and personal ideologies. Thereafter he travelled the world, inspiring audiences and student-actors in Germany, France, Latvia, Lithuania and the UK, where he set up the Theatre Studio at Dartington Hall in 1936. He ended his days in Hollywood, having made his name in movies including his Oscar-nominated performance in Hitchcock's *Spellbound* (1945) and having written his inspirational *To the Actor* (2002), from whence this extract on 'Character and Characterization' comes. Like Fo, Chekhov's choices for characterizations were always physically very expressive, while simultaneously bearing great psychological truth. Famed for resisting Stanislavsky's experiments with affective memory, Chekhov refocused the actor's attention on imagination as the means of igniting body, feelings and impulses in a subtle, non-disruptive way. Two of his most impactful and immediate tools – the imaginary body and imaginary centres – are outlined here. With both of these tools, Chekhov combines physicality and psychology, encouraging us as actors to see the differences between our own personalities and the characters that we're playing (as indeed did Lecoq), and allowing the *psychological* differences to find *physical* expression through our bodies. The joy of working with Chekhov's methods is his sense of play and amusement (again like Lecoq, he incorporated various aspects of clowning into his training). Also his writings are very accessible: as an actor and a teacher of acting (often working in a second language), Chekhov understood the importance of igniting a student's imagination when learning new tools. The heading to this extract – *Transformation* – brings to the fore one of the terms that recurs through these extracts. While Pasolli uses the term to train the actor's ability to adapt rapidly from one set of given circumstances to another, Chekhov uses it as the goal towards which many professional actors strive, particularly in film, television and narrative-driven theatre.

Like Chekhov, Stella Adler (1901–1992) is one degree of separation from Stanislavsky, having studied with him briefly but significantly in Paris in 1934. Also like Chekhov, her style of writing is very accessible, combining her understanding of how to act (on stage and screen) with her desire to communicate her love of acting to her students. Born into a celebrated theatre family, Adler was among the first members of the Group Theatre, along with Sanford Meisner and co-founders Lee Strasberg and Harold Clurman (who later became her second husband). With a successful career on the Broadway stage and in Hollywood films, Adler opened her Stella Adler Studio of Acting in 1949 (schools currently exist in New York and Los Angeles). The two key principles explored in this extract are the 'role of props' in bringing a character to life, and our 'attitude' to our partner in a scene. Both of these tools have great application for a twenty-first-century actor, both in theatre and film. It could be argued that unless we give a prop 'dignity' by understanding how it works and personalizing its significance, it remains a lifeless object rather than a valuable partner. In other words, props are important in the composition of a scene, as we can use them to texture a score of physical actions that can counterpoint the scripted dialogue. With regard to the importance of our onstage partner, there are obvious links to Adler's fellow actor-teacher, Sanford Meisner. Adler encourages you to develop an 'attitude towards your partner' – 'and you know the partner's attitude towards everything. Dialogue exists not on cue but when you understand and react to your partner' (Adler 2000: 180). Take nothing for granted, Adler insists, because having an attitude creates drama.[11] Adler's personality oozes off the page: since her books are largely drawn from classes and discussions, there's an immediacy to the writing, even if the structure is a little loose at times. Throughout these extracts, we see potent connections between those practitioners whose ethos lies predominantly in the psychological realm of acting and those who are more in the physical realm. For example, Adler's use of animal imagery, and her ability to leap from one set of given circumstances to another, echo some of the exercises we see in both Lecoq and Pasolli.

When it comes to composing a score in rehearsal, Barba's extract from *On Directing and Dramaturgy: Burning the House* (2010) is especially useful, if a little dense. There are three terms in particular, which warrant some unpacking – 'real actions', 'improvisation' and 'score'. In terms of 'real actions', Barba harks back to the material of his earlier extract ('An Amulet Made of Memory') with some echoes of Meisner's training of impulses. When, as actors, we are so relaxed in our rehearsal process that we can react spontaneously to the given circumstances of the scene, we unlock – moment by moment – the precise actions needed to carry the narrative forward. These real actions are 'the smallest perceptible impulses' (Barba 2010: 26) which produce a definite change in us as actors as well as having a direct effect on our audiences. This kind of kinetic connection between actor and audience is very hard to commit to paper – which is why Barba's words can seem a little philosophical at times. However, he is addressing something profoundly important. In terms of composition and character, Barba is essentially saying that when we allow ourselves to be in a constant state of 'improvisation' (inner and outer), we unlock an appropriate 'score' of physical actions that manifests the character's personality and nature. In other words, the score of physical actions *is* the character. Historically, this connects Stanislavsky's Method of Physical Actions of the early twentieth century with a later twentieth-century aesthetic that foregrounds what might loosely be called 'physical theatre'. For Stanislavsky, it could be argued that the emphasis was predominantly behavioural: we *are* our behaviour, and it is only by what we say and do that other people have a sense of who we are. For Barba, it could be argued that the emphasis is predominantly compositional: the score of actions is all you need to read and know the character. Although the score of actions initially emerges through improvisations, it can then be fixed and rendered repeatable. Here again, Barba shows how actor training and rehearsal of a role are just different facets of the same process: our task as actors is to be able to repeat precisely and frequently – night after night, take after take – exactly the same score. Yet if we're fully psychophysically aware, that score will never be an empty shell, a form without content: it will always be filled with dynamic rhythm and powerful affect. The director can then help us 'elaborate' this score, as he or she can use every 'fragment of living tissue' to shape the emerging production, making it increasingly specific and appropriate to the final composition. There are some immensely valuable tools in this extract, the contents of which are (as suggested) very closely connected to Stanislavsky's Method of Physical Actions.[12] Although Barba's writing is much more dense than, say, Adler's or Chekhov's, it's well worth taking the time to understand the ways in which he elucidates the process of how (in Stanislavsky's terminology) we create a *line of thought* (the subscore) and a *line of action* (a score of physical actions) which weave together to create an actor's *through-line of action*. This in itself *is* the composition of the character.[13]

CHARACTER IN PERFORMANCE COMPOSITION

The final three extracts directly address the journey on which we take our audience in performance. The first – 'Performance Text' from Erik Exe Christoffersen's *The Actor's Way* (1993) – posits that character and composition only exist during the transient and elusive experience of a live performance. Christoffersen's book takes us back to Odin Teatret and Eugenio Barba's work. As a dramaturg and scholar, he defines an actor's dramaturgy as 'the flow of energy' that exists between actor and spectator in the very moment of incarnating a role. With regard to composition, this extract offers a subtle reminder of the differences between live and recorded media: in theatre, the performance composition – lights, actions, text, changes in space – is a polyphony, drawing the spectators' attention in diverse directions. In other words, for all the work that we put into preparing our selves, preparing a role, and preparing a production composition, we can never entirely guide the spectators' unified gaze towards the same moment in the way that a film frame can. What Christoffersen excitingly highlights here is that character and composition are almost intangible and highly mercurial: they're really only the network of tensions between the actor and the spectator caused by movements in space and time, which once executed are gone forever. Dramaturgy is in effect dynamic energy: it's the ephemeral dialogue that only live theatre can create between its actors and observers.

The nuances of that dialogue depend on the playwright's intention – or 'super-task' – which in turn influences the stylistic composition of a production. Two of the most misinterpreted tools from Russian acting pioneer, Konstantin Stanislavsky (1863–1938) – the 'supertask' of the writer and the corresponding 'throughaction' of the actor – form the contents of this extract from *An Actor's Work* (2008). In Jean Benedetti's new translation of Stanislavsky's classic text, these tools are actually made extremely clear. In terms of character and composition, the play-wright's supertask is the unbreakable link between actor, director, playwright, and audience. It comprises what Stanislavsky calls the 'great, life-giving goals' (2008: 307) of a writer that are then converted into stimulating, compelling onstage tasks for the actors; these tasks collectively bring together all the strands of the play. So, once we've pinpointed the motivating drive underpinning why a playwright wrote a particular piece, we can start to ignite all the mental, emotional, and physical qualities in ourselves that connect to the playwright's scripted characters. In this way, the supertask becomes the marriage of the author's play with the actor's person-ality. As the co-founder of the Moscow Art Theatre, Stanislavsky's supertask throughout his life was to produce a systematic way of enabling actors to penetrate a text. Because he was always trying to demystify acting processes, Stanislavsky devoted hours and pages to finding the right way of addressing actors. This extract demonstrates his semi-autobiographical narrative style, in which he adopts both the roles of the all-knowing director, Tortsov, and the naïve student, Kostya. 'Throughaction' is essentially the precursor to the 'score' of physical actions discussed by Barba and the 'performance text' discussed by Christoffersen. It is the precise, repeatable (but spontaneously driven) series of minute actions that harmonizes all the compositional elements into the play's overarching meaning. All too often Stanislavsky is allied with psychological realism and narrative-driven plays; yet, his own acting, directing and teaching career was filled with non-realistic pieces including operetta, Shakespeare, Molière, and fairy stories, not to mention social dramas and larger-than-life comedies. Frequently (and somewhat misrepresentatively), his acting theories are placed on one side of a seesaw with Bertolt Brecht's on the other, where never the twain can meet. So, Stanislavsky's approach is labelled 'identification with a character' and Brecht's approach is labelled 'alienation from a character', which makes for neat packaging rather than comprehensive understanding of their prac-tices. Indeed, their similarities regarding building a character *in rehearsal* are pronounced; it is the composition and presentation of character *in performance* that differentiates their practices.

German-born Bertolt Brecht (1898–1956) was a playwright and a director, and – unlike Stanislavsky, who largely distracted himself from Soviet politics – he was very politically active. He was not an actor, nor was he really an actor trainer. However, he was a man of words, and was therefore very articulate in writing about what he wanted theatre and acting to be. As a result, he is seminal in contemporary actor training for encouraging an approach to character that was non-psychological in performance, not to mention a compositional aesthetic that stirred people into action rather than whirling them into fictional realms. In this extract from *Brecht on Theatre* (1969), we see that the 'Alienation Effect' – the process of enabling something familiar to be seen in a new, strange way – still requires actors *in the process of rehearsal* to unlock the psychology of their characters. While creating the role, we should have an 'attitude' towards our character (not dissimilar to the practice put forward by Adler), and that attitude should be one of incredulity and contradiction. As we start remembering the lines, we also remember what astounds us about the character and what we want to contradict in the character's behaviour. In other words, throughout the process of creating the role, we remain in a curious, questioning dialogue with it. This questioning becomes so inextricably built into our interpretation of the character, that the audience sees that anything the character does is just one of a range of options. In terms of composition, therefore, the audience is presented with juxtapositions, rather than through-lines, in order that they too can question their own choices and behaviours in everyday life – and change them. In fact, the 'not . . . but . . .' idea described here is very useful when working on any role from any play for sharpening choices and highlighting composition. Perhaps one of the key phrases in the extract is that we never try to persuade ourselves (and thereby others) that our performance 'amounts to a complete transformation'. In many respects, this is nothing new. Even with Chekhov's definition of transformation, no actor or actor trainer would truly advocate forgetting either the existence of the audience or the technicalities of the production.[14] This extract is possibly one of the most useful contributions to figuring out the difference between the ideas advocated by Brecht and those proposed by more psychologically orientated practitioners. He is clear that the A-effect doesn't mean a performance should be compositionally stylized: it should actually be as natural and earthy as possible. The main aesthetic difference in composing the character is that we don't imply that our character's way of behaving is fixed or universal or decreed by destiny (in the way that the ancient Greek tragedies implied). Rather, we are all free to take different choices, we are all free to change society, we are aware that specific socio-historical conditions cause us to behave in certain ways, and that should be remarkable.

We see from many of these writings that composing a character is steeped in a paradox: how do we perform a fixed, repeatable score with an inner quality of improvisation? While the extracts are collated in alphabetical order, we sense an inherent through-line in their content that addresses that paradox: from the training of impulse and improvisation to the director's adjustments to action-scores to the final performance-demands of a writer's supertask. Although there are distinct differences in the aesthetics of the various contributors, character and composition inevitably go hand-in-hand, integrating body, imagination, impulse, and emotions, and of course, the energetic exchange between actors and audience.

PROVOCATIONS

1   For actors like myself – who are essentially more interested in the embodi-
    ment of pre-written characters within a narrative than the presentation
    of post-dramatic compositions – how does the definition of composition
    shift? When is a character 'composed' of actions and behaviours that
    are consciously negotiated and embodied by the actors, and when
    is 'character' less relevant than the composition of bodies in space and
    time?

2   What relevance does traditional storytelling retain in twenty-first-century
    theatre?

3   What significance does composition have in the framing of film and
    television pictures? Does the screen actor need to concern him or herself
    with the compositional arc of a character, or simply commit to the playing
    of actions in a scene?

4   Will Stanislavsky's 'system' remain the bedrock of much western actor
    training (and an increasing number of non-western training systems)[15]
    into the next few decades, or will our understanding of human and
    cognitive processes evolve new paradigms of actor training and thoughts
    about character and composition?

Notes

1   See Fuchs (1996), regarding changes in composition and dramatic form in the last decades of the twentieth century.

2   Institutions, from the Royal Academy of Dramatic Arts in London to Yale School of Drama in New York to the Actor Prepares School of Acting in Mumbai to the National Institute of Dramatic Art in Sydney, place emphasis on transformation into character and on what is often loosely termed 'living truthfully' in a performance.

3   The term 'psychophysical' essentially refers to the holistic integration of body, mind, imagination, emotions, intellect, and what might be called 'spirit' or 'energy' – within and between actors. For a fuller understanding of the term, see Merlin (2001) and Zarrilli (2008).

4   Barba & Savarese (2005) is a vivid and visual investigation into performance vocabulary and composition from around the world.

5   See Stanislavski (2013: 193–209).

6   Mel Gordon's *Stanislavsky in America: An Actor's Workbook* (2010) is a handy guide to the transition of Stanislavsky's processes into America, with an excellent chapter on the Group Theatre.

7   Chaikin's own book, *The Presence of the Actor* (1993) contains many accessible insights into his acting and directing processes.

8   Here again, Barba and Savarese's *Dictionary of Theatre Anthropology* can be particularly useful, especially in their chapter on Equivalence and the shift of weight and balance within the body to construct character from a variety of eastern and western styles, both realistic and non-realistic.

9   As Overlie's website biography describes, Viewpoints were developed as a 'conceptual articulation for postmodern performance and a teaching system that is applicable to directing, choreographing, dancing, acting, improvisation, and analysis' (http://www.sixviewpoints.com/Biography.html).

10 Chekhov's autobiography, *The Path of the Actor* (2005), is a charming, witty and poignant insight into his professional work, as well as his metaphorical and literal itinerancy.

11   This idea of 'attitude' is subtle and connects with the idea of 'world view'. As actors, we are trying to plant images in our listener's heads in order that they may see the world through our lens, i.e. share our world view. By having an 'attitude' towards them, we develop a proactive connection to them: we have specific reasons for why we need to change their world view, and therefore have a clearer understanding of what strategies we need to adopt in order to achieve that change in perception.

12   See *The Complete Stanislavsky Toolkit* (Merlin 2010) for a comprehensive overview of the Method of Physical Actions and Stanislavsky's final legacy of Active Analysis.

13   In our chapter on *The Seagull* in *Russians in Britain: British Theatre and the Russian Tradition of Actor Training* (Pitches 2012), entitled 'Re-visioned directions: Stanislavsky in the 21st Century', Katya Kamotskaia and I present a detailed analysis of creating the line of thought and the line of action.

14   In her excellent book, *Stanislavsky in Focus* (2008), Sharon M. Carnicke is very articulate about Stanislavsky's term *perezhivanie* – living through a role. To 'live through a role' involves as much awareness of the actual given circumstances of the audience and the technical requirements of the performance, as the immersion in the fictional given circumstances of the character and the dramatic narrative.

15   See Hodge (2010) and Margolis & Renaud (2011).

Bibliography

Adler, S. (2000) *The Art of Acting*, New York: Applause.

Barba, E. (1997) 'An Amulet Made of Memory: The Significance of Exercises in an Actor's Dramaturgy', *TDR* 41:4, Winter.

Barba, E. (2010) *On Directing and Dramaturgy: Burning the House*, London & New York: Routledge.

Barba, E. & Savarese, N. (eds) (2005) *A Dictionary of Theatre Anthropology: The Secret Art of the Performer*, 2nd edition, London & New York: Routledge.

Bogart, A. & Landau, T. (2005) *The Viewpoints Book*, New York: Theatre Communications Group.

Carnicke, S. M. (2008) *Stanislavsky in Focus*, London & New York: Routledge.

Chaikin, J. (1993) *The Presence of the Actor*, New York: Theater Communications Group.

Chekhov, M. (2005) *The Path of the Actor*, edited by Kirilov, A. & Merlin, B., London & New York: Routledge.

Christoffersen, E. E. (1993) *The Actor's Way*, London & New York: Routledge.

Fo, D. (1991) *Tricks of the Trade*, London: Methuen.

Fuchs, E. (1996) *The Death of Character: Perspectives on Theater after Modernism*, Bloomington: Indiana University Press.

Gordon, M. (2010) *Stanislavsky in America: An Actor's Workbook*, London & New York: Routledge.

Hodge, A. (ed.) (2010) *Actor Training*, 2nd Edition, London & New York: Routledge.

Lecoq, J. (2000) *The Moving Body*, London: Methuen.

Margolis, E. and Renaud, L.T. (eds) (2011) *The Politics of American Actor Training*, London & New York: Routledge.

Meisner, S. & Longwell, D. (1987) *Sanford Meisner on Acting*, New York: Vintage.

Merlin, B. (2001) *Beyond Stanislavsky: The Psycho-Physical Approach to Actor Training*, London: Nick Hern Books.

Merlin, B. (2010) *The Complete Stanislavsky Toolkit*, London: Nick Hern Books.

Pasolli, R. (1970) *A Book on the Open Theatre*, New York: Avon.

Pitches, J. (ed.) (2012) *Russians in Britain: British Theatre and the Russian Tradition of Actor Training*, London & New York: Routledge.

Stanislavsky, K. (2008) *An Actor's Work* trans. Benedetti, J., London & New York: Routledge.

Stanislavski, C (2013) *An Actor Prepares*, trans. Reynolds Hapgood, E., London: Bloomsbury Revelations Edition.

Willett, J. (ed.), (1969) *Brecht on Theatre: The Development of an Aesthetic*, London: Methuen.

Zarrilli, P. (2008) *Psychophysical Acting: An Intercultural Approach after Stanislavski*, London & New York: Routledge.

Chapter 26

Stella Adler

THE ART OF ACTING

EVERY OBJECT YOU BRING on stage has to tell you about the circumstances of the character you're playing and the world in which he lives. You have to understand and personalize every object you work with. You have to handle every object imaginatively. You bring a book onto the stage. We have to have some sense of what kind of book it is. Is it a volume of an encyclopedia? Is it the Bible? The way you carry it has to tell us something.

As actors we have to have the ability of children to make believe. A child believes that a stick he has between his legs as he hops up and down is a horse. That indeed is what all acting is made up of — the conviction of the child that the stick is a horse. As an actor you are responsible for this belief. If it's good enough for Dickens, for Balzac, it's good enough for us.

Before using a prop you have to know what the life of the prop is. If you have a gun, you should know how to take it apart, how to clean it, where to put it, how to use it. The gun has its own life, which you have nothing to do with. That life you have to understand as well as a policeman knows the life of his nightstick.

You cannot possibly use a sword unless you study with a specialist for six months. A whole tradition surrounds the wearing of a sword. How do you take it out? How do you put it back in its scabbard? What do you clean steel with? If you don't know how to clean an object and how to put it away, you don't know how to use it.

My brother Luther Adler once played a benefit performance at Madison Square Garden. The action called for him to pick up a gun from a table and shoot a man, but there was no gun on the table. He picked up an imaginary gun and fired it, and the man fell. Because he had this sense of perfection in what he was doing, because he could convince himself, the audience was convinced that a gun had been fired and the shot had killed a man.

In Moscow I watched one of Russia's great actors performing on a stage that was bare except for a stepladder. Seated on the ladder, which was meant to represent the bank of a river, he was supposed to be fishing. There was no pole, no line, no fish hook. But in the way he held his hand and lifted his arm, you could see the pole, the line hanging in the water, the twitch of the line as the fish took hold of the hook. It was genius.

Each prop has its own truth and its own nature. As actors you have to understand every prop. Unfortunately in most young students a sense of giving every prop its dignity does not exist. You cannot use a prop unless you give it dignity and unless you have a liking for it. You must work with it until you know you can use it.

Personalize the props you use by endowing them with some quality that comes from you. Personalize the rose you are about to pin on your dress by shaking drops of water off it or by taking a thorn off its stem. When you put a sweater in a drawer, personalize the sweater by noticing a loose thread and fixing it.

You also have to ask the object what it demands of you. The person who wears a high hat has to know how it lives. The high hat lives in a box, and that box gives you its nature and its value. Do you know how to brush this hat or put it down? Do you know you have to use both hands to put it on? It's made to be worn straight. The person who wears it has a controlled speech, a controlled walk, a controlled mind. You must not bring your own out-of-control culture into the wearing of the hat. In the society of that hat, the human being as well as the clothes were under strict control.

Your job as an actor is to make the world of the play as real as your own, maybe more-so. You're born into your circumstances. If you're ambitious, you can change them, but most of us accept them without thinking.

When you go on stage you can't take anything for granted. You have to examine the circumstances with great care and great understanding. That's the only way you'll feel comfortable there. One of the advantages of concentrating on the circumstances you build on stage is that you won't worry about the audience. When you find yourself worrying about them, it's because you're not absorbed in the world of the play.

Actors are undercover agents. You must constantly spy on people, studying their character elements. You must see which are related to the character's profession or appropriate to his nationality or age. Acting is hard because it requires not just the study of books, though that can be important too, but constant study of human behavior.

One dependable comfort is that you are never alone on stage. You have the circumstances of the play to work with. You have the set. You have your props and your costume.

You also have your fellow actors.

You always have partners on stage, and you have an attitude toward your partner. In all cases your partner is needed to give you your action; and you have to know the partner's attitude toward everything. Dialogue exists not on cue but when you understand and react to your partner.

I'm going to select two actors from the class and ask them to go up on stage and play two monkeys living in the same cage. Certain behavioral traits will very soon appear. Each monkey will shortly develop an attitude toward the other, whether it's hostility, jealousy, affection or some other response.

Resist the tendency to start acting right away. Let the action come from some place that prompts it. Beware of behavioral cliches ("monkey business"), don't start fighting before fighting is actually justified — that is, before either has taken any action against the other. If one snatches a banana away from the other, then the anger is provoked, and the fighting will be more interesting.

Acting is reacting, and shouldn't arise out of a false response. And the reacting always presumes the presence of a partner.

Actually, the two monkeys, before they do anything together, should live for a time separately, so that each develops an individual character. Allow an opinion of the other to form slowly and naturally. The attitude will develop, and the audience will develop its attitude toward the characters.

Now let's put a few more actors on the stage and divide them up between dogs and chickens. Find some way to relate to each other. First, each group of animals must learn to live in its circumstances. Is it a farmyard? If so, the attitude will be different than an open field.

In any case, the attitude between you should not be combative. Since fighting is the cheapest thing you can do on stage, it's better to use your imagination and find some other obvious way dogs and chickens can live together. If the dogs refrain from bothering the chickens, it will be more interesting, and real attitudes will emerge.

What you think of a person stimulates you to behave in a certain way toward him. Herein lies the wisdom of acting. It's not what a person says but your reaction to what he says that creates your attitude toward the person. Without this attitude you don't exist on the stage.

What does it mean to have an attitude toward your partner and where does it come from? From your reactions to what you see, what confronts you, what you're exposed to.

We can illustrate this on the most primitive level. If you see a snake on the ground, would you go over and pick it up? Having already developed an attitude toward the snake, from what you know or have heard or read about snakes, going back to the earliest Biblical reference, you wouldn't.

One develops an attitude toward everything — even toward the snake. As an intern at the hospital, you quickly become aware the operation has failed. Your actions are to check the X-rays, the patient's chart and the EKG. You see everything's gone wrong. Now you have an attitude toward the doctor in charge.

Suppose you have a very wealthy friend. Her husband, whom she didn't much care for, has died. In his memory she gives money to various institutions and dedicates a number of memorials to him. Now she wants to remarry, but not for love. She wants a companion.

How do you feel about her? One attitude might be you'd like to exploit her money yourself. We can add a little information. She likes to give parties and even invites people she doesn't know well. She is regularly accustomed to spending $400 or $500 a night inviting people to dinner. What do you really think of her? Are you developing an attitude toward her? Do you think her values are distorted, or that she's lonely, or do you resent her money? Do you feel she's mixed up, wasteful and stupid?

Now suppose, to bring it closer to home, this woman comes to me and says she wants to direct a play using the students in this class for the cast. My reaction to her proposal is: Why not? She has money. Why shouldn't she direct a play? I invite her to come and direct members of this class in a play. What would your reaction be?

She wants to be treated professionally. She asks the actors to take minimum pay since none is a member of Actors Equity. After the performance, she also wants to give a lecture on the playwright. I agree to all her conditions.

Now which of you wants to be in this woman's play. Not so fast. And not so emotional. What's that? To allow a woman to buy her way in is opposed to everything the theatre stands for — it's selling out. I see. Brad, what do you think? That you feel perfectly capable of taking from the woman's direction what's right and helpful and leaving out what's useless. So you think it's all right for her to come.

Isn't it interesting that each of you has developed an attitude toward this woman before she has even appeared and thus a drama has been created.

By the variety of our responses to the way people express themselves, we develop an attitude toward a person. If I say, "Oh, no, I wish I could come, but I can't," that expresses one attitude. The attitude changes when you say, "Oh, I do wish I could come, darling. I can't." The first is sincere and felt. The second is less genuine, even a little false.

In a play you can't really work unless you develop an attitude toward your partner.

To speak on stage you must be provoked by something that will *make* you speak. Unless somebody says something or you hear a noise or you're stimulated in some other way, you must not speak. In saying a line, your natural tendency is to wait for an answer. This is called "sitting on your partner." It's something you mustn't do. Don't wait for the dialogue, and don't suddenly push your partner into an answer. As you exchange dialogue, thoughts of your own can come, unexpectedly. For example, in the country, I said to my husband one day, "It's too cold. I don't want the dog to go out. Did they ever catch the man who killed Lincoln?"

This last has nothing to do with what we were talking about, but it's natural to have irrelevant thoughts, even though they may come as a complete surprise to your partner. If you actually talk to him, he must answer. But if you simply say something not conditioned on a response, he may or may not answer you.

Each time you must react as if for the first time. Each time, you must create the images that lead you to speak while adhering to the theme and reacting to your partner. If you remain with the theme and never fail to respond to the partner, you have a play.

Resist the impulse to make the play fit you. You must fit the play.

STELLA ADLER (1901–1992)

Adler was born into a theatrical family. In 1922 she saw Stanislavski's company perform in New York, and was later introduced to his ideas by two members of his company, Richard Boleslavsky and Maria Ouspenskaya. In 1931, she joined the Group Theatre, with Strasberg, Crawford and Clurman (whom she later married). In 1934 she studied with Stanislavski in Paris, where she learnt that he had moved away from his previous emphasis on emotion memory. From this period, she broke away from the Method approach and developed her own techniques which she taught for many years at her own studio.

See also: **Konstantin Stanislavsky, Sanford Meisner.**

SUGGESTED FURTHER READING

Adler, S. (1988) *The Technique of Acting*, Toronto: Bantam.
Adler, S. (2000) *The Art of Acting*, New York: Applause.

Krasner, D. (2010) 'Strasberg, Adler and Meisner: Method Acting', in Hodge, A. (ed.) (2010) *Actor Training*, London & New York: Routledge.
Oppenheim, T. (2006) 'Stella Adler Technique', in Bartow, A. (2006) *Training the American Actor*, New York: Theatre Communications Group.

Chapter 27

Eugenio Barba

AN AMULET MADE OF MEMORY;
ON DIRECTING AND DRAMATURGY

AN AMULET MADE OF MEMORY

EXERCISES ARE SMALL LABYRINTHS that the actors' body-minds can trace and retrace in order to incorporate a paradoxical way of thinking, thereby distancing themselves from their own daily behavior and entering the domain of the stage's extra-daily behavior.

Exercises are like amulets, which the actor carries around, not to show them off, but to draw from them certain qualities of energy out of which a second nervous system slowly develops. An exercise is made up of memory, body-memory. An exercise becomes memory, which acts through the entire body.

Inner life and interpretation

There are at least ten characteristics that distinguish an exercise and explain its effectiveness as dramaturgy reserved for the nonpublic work of actors, i.e., the work on oneself:

1 Exercises are primarily a pedagogical fiction. The actor learns not to learn to be an actor or, in other words, learns not to learn to act. Exercises teach how to think with the entire body-mind.
2 Exercises teach how to carry out a real action (not "realistic," but real).
3 Exercises teach that precision in form is essential in a real action. An exercise has a beginning and an end, and the path between these two points is not linear but fraught with peripeteias, changes, leaps, turning points, and contrasts.
4 The dynamic form of an exercise is a continuity constituted by a series of phases. In order to learn the exercise precisely it is divided up into segments. This process teaches how to think of continuity as a succession of minute but well-defined phases (or perceptible actions). An exercise is an ideogram made

up of strokes and, like all ideograms, must always follow the same succession. But each single stroke can vary in thickness, intensity, and impetus.

5 Each phase of an exercise engages the entire body. The transition from one phase to another is a "sats."

6 Every phase of an exercise dilates, refines, or miniaturizes certain dynamisms of daily behavior. In this way these dynamisms are isolated and "edited"; they become a montage and underline the play of tensions, contrasts, oppositions— in other words, all the elements of basic dramaticity that transform daily behavior into the extra-daily behavior of the stage.

7 The different phases of the exercise make the actor experience his or her own body not as a unity but as a center for simultaneous actions. In the beginning, this experience coincides with a painful sense of expropriation of the actor's own spontaneity. Later it turns into the fundamental quality of the actor: a presence ready to be projected in diverging directions and capable of attracting the attention of the spectator.

8 Exercises teach how to repeat. Learning to repeat is not difficult as long as it is a question of knowing how to execute a score with ever greater precision. It becomes difficult in the next phase. Here the difficulty lies in repeating continuously without becoming dull, which presupposes discovering and motivating new details, new points of departure within the familiar score.

9 The exercise is the way of refusal: it teaches renunciation through fatigue and commitment to a humble task.

10 An exercise is not work on the text but on oneself. It puts the actor to the test through a series of obstacles. It allows the actor to get to know him- or herself through an encounter with his or her own limits, not through self-analysis.

Exercises teach how to work on what is visible through using repeatable forms. These forms are empty. At the beginning, they are filled with the concentration necessary for the successful execution of each single phase. Once they have been mastered, either they die or they are filled by the capacity for improvisation. This capacity consists in the ability to vary the execution of the diverse phases, the images behind them (for example, to move like an astronaut on the moon), their rhythms (to different music), the chains of mental associations.

In this way a subscore develops from the score of the exercise.

The value of the visible (the score) and the invisible (the subscore) generates the possibility of making them carry on a dialogue, creating a space within the design of movements and their precision.

The dialogue between the visible and the invisible is precisely that which the actor experiences as inner life and in some cases even as meditation. And it is what the spectator experiences as interpretation.

* * *

ON DIRECTING AND DRAMATURGY

Real actions, improvisation and score

When in the training or during rehearsals I divided any situation (like writing a letter and putting it into an envelope, peeling an apple or picking up a coin from the ground) into smaller and smaller segments, I reached an indivisible point, a barely perceptible atom: a minute dynamic form which nevertheless had consequences for the tone of the whole body. This minute dynamic form was called *a real action* by me and my actors. It could be microscopic, just an impulse, however it radiated within the whole organism and was immediately sensed by the nervous system of the spectator.

At Odin Teatret, the dramaturgy of the actor was not a way of interpreting, but a technique to perform *real actions* in the fiction of the scenic space.

It has been fertile for our work that the actor's actions followed a dynamic logic which was independent from the narrative meaning. This logic often referred to the capacity to display the *equivalent of the energy* (quality of tensions, dynamic design, effort, acceleration, manipulation, etc.) necessary for an action from his score, even when this action was modified. For example, the actor had slapped someone, but the director had changed it into a caress. Although the actor moulded the dynamic design as if to caress, she kept the original tensions of striking a blow. The real dynamic *information* was thus retained, but appeared in a different *form*. The spectator's kinaesthetic sense (or empathy) recognised the dynamisms of striking a blow, but this sensorial information did not correspond to what he was seeing: a caress.

It is undeniable that, in the daily reality as in the extra-daily one of theatre, a *real action*, even if reduced to its impulse, possesses a strength of sensorial persuasion which produces an *organic effect* – that is, one of life and immediateness – on the spectator's nervous system. It suffices to think of the feints in boxing and dribbling in football which are precise impulses of real actions provoking an instant response in the adversary.

Although sport is the practice which allows us to understand best what a real action is, I defined it to myself in a less competitive way: a gentle breath of wind on an ear of corn. The corn is the attention of the spectator. It is not shaken as by a gust in a storm, but that gentle breath is just enough to upset its perpendicularity.

When I indicated the action to an actor, I suggested recognising it by elimination, distinguishing it from a simple 'movement' or 'gesture'. I told him: an action is your smallest perceptible impulse and I identify it by the fact that even if you make a microscopic movement (the tiniest displacement of the hand, for example) the entire tonicity of your body changes. A real action produces a change in the tensions in your whole body, and subsequently a change in the perception of the spectator: then your action is sensed, kinaesthetically, in an analogous way. The action originates in the spinal cord. It is not the wrist which moves the hand, not the shoulder or elbow which moves the arm, but the dynamic impulse is rooted in the torso.

It is obvious that the organic action was not enough. If, in the end, it was not enlivened by an inner dimension, then the action remained mute – *did not communicate* – and the actor appeared to be predetermined by the form of his score.

The character's personality, nature, profession and psychology could be important information and a concrete point of departure for performing real actions. But at Odin Teatret, the actors reached this objective using, above all, various improvisation techniques to create *a score of real actions*.

In general, the term 'improvisation' refers to at least three quite different procedures. Improvisation may be understood as the creation of actor's material. It is a process which gives life to a succession of physical or vocal actions starting out from a text, a theme, images, mental or sensorial associations, a painting, a melody, memories or fantasies.

In the second procedure, improvisation is synonymous with variation. The actor develops a theme or a situation by alternating and combining material which is already incorporated. The elements, previously assimilated, appear 'spontaneously' and assume different meanings according to the options, relationships, succession, rhythm and context. This was the type of improvisation used by European actors from the *commedia dell'arte* until Stanislavski and the reformers of the twentieth century.

The third procedure is far more subtle. Here improvisation means individualisation. Evening after evening the actor infuses life into the character's actions, repeating a score which is often fixed down to the smallest detail. It would appear that everything is established and that possibilities for variations or new choices are excluded. Nevertheless this type of improvisation is the most common in an actor's daily practice. It is the capacity 'to interpret' their scores every evening with different nuances – as a pianist might interpret a composition by Beethoven.

At Odin Teatret, the term *score* referred to:

- the general design of the form in a sequence of actions, and the evolution of each single action (beginning, climax, conclusion);
- the precision of the fixed details of each action as well as of the transitions connecting them (*sats*, changes of direction, different qualities of energy, variations of speed);
- the dynamism and the rhythm: the speed and intensity which regulated the *tempo* (in the musical sense) of a series of actions. This was the metre of the actions with their micro-pauses and decisions, the alternation of long or short ones, accented or unaccented segments, characterised by vigorous or soft energy;
- the orchestration of the relationships between the different parts of the body (hands, arms, legs, feet, eyes, voice, facial expression).

The creation of a score with the subsequent phases of working out, developing and eliminating or adding details took place according to an exacting process in which I recognised the actor's patience and refusal of easy solutions. This attitude and awareness had been incorporated in the training: the incisiveness of scenic presence depended on the inner justification, on precision and the ability to preserve the smallest details.

A score began to live only after it was fixed and repeated over a long period of time.

The score was the objective demonstration of the subjective world of the actor. It allowed the meeting with the director who *elaborated* it according to shared artisanal criteria. The score was the search for order so as to give space to Disorder.

The term *elaborate* was fundamental in our working jargon and in our practice. This word had multiple meanings implying different and even opposing working procedures, for example, developing and expounding the actor's material resulting from an improvisation or a sequence of actions which he had deliberately structured. But *elaboration* also signified the distillation of this material through radical modifications and cuts. It involved the working out of variations, the polishing and care for details in order to make them stand out, the alteration of the actions' form while preserving their original tensions (their dynamic information). Elaboration encompassed changes in the rhythm and in direction in space, the establishing of micropauses between one action and another and an arrangement of the different parts of the body (feet, arms, facial expressions) which differed from the original material.

So when I write that as a director I *elaborated* the actor's material, I mean that I was using one of these technical procedures.

When an actor improvised, he went fishing for material from which later to distil (to elaborate) a score. It would have been foolish to fish with nets with holes through which fish brought to the surface could escape. For me, an improvisation had value only if I was able to utilise its entirety as a fragment of living tissue to be inserted and developed into the overall organism of the performance.

One of my first requests to the actors was that they had to learn to repeat an improvisation. They had to be able to replicate their improvisation in the exact same variety of postures and dynamisms, introverted and extroverted attitudes, temporary halts, hesitations, accelerations and plurality of rhythms. It was easy to improvise, much harder to memorise the improvisation. The actor reconstructed step by step what he had done with the help of fellow actors who had noted down his patterns of gestures and actions, their directions, the increase and decrease of speed, sudden stops and prolonged pauses. It often happened that we recorded the improvisation with a video. Everything was on the screen, in every detail, with the actor's frequent surprise and often dismay because he was unable to believe that he had performed that particular gesture or grimace. It was as if these belonged to somebody else. It took time to take on this behaviour which was felt as extraneous, and make it one's own again through assiduous repetition.

Perseverance, concentration and knowledge of procedures for remembering were necessary to fix an improvisation. I demanded that the actor render perceptible concrete or imagined situations, real or psychic events, the landscapes and epochs that he had crossed in the inner reality of the improvisation. But the flora and fauna of his inner microcosm, which had surfaced during this process, were a friable and fugitive reality like snow ready to melt.

To my eyes, it was a sign of experience and skill to know how to preserve the snow of the improvisation, without letting it melt or become slush. It was this ability to fix an improvisation that characterised the Odin actors. An aspect of their craft consisted in making an inner process perceptible through precise vocal and physical actions.

In the organic dramaturgy, precision was for me the essential sensory information which induced a reaction in the spectator. The precision revealed the need for a determined action and at the same time its inner coherence.

We used or we invented techniques for remembering that allowed us to reconstruct and recreate the whole variety of impulses, gradations, dynamisms and forms of an improvisation.

A thread guided the actor in finding again the direction of the paths which divided and merged together in his body-mind while improvising. It was a thread made of stimuli, of mental energy and somatic memory, absolute subjectivity and imaginative freedom, permeated by timelessness and biographic episodes.

This thread was the subscore. It was what the actor heard, saw and reacted to. In other words, the way he recounted the improvisation to himself through actions. This tale involved rhythms, sounds and tunes, silences and suspensions, fragrances and colours, people and clusters of contrasting images: a stream of stimuli or inner actions which turned into precise dynamic forms.

See pp. 25–6.

Chapter 28

Anne Bogart and Tina Landau

VIEWPOINTS AND COMPOSITION: WHAT ARE THEY?

VIEWPOINTS, COMPOSITION: WHAT DO these terms mean? The following definitions reflect our understanding and use of them. Even in the context of the work of such pioneers as Mary Overlie and Aileen Passloff, it is impossible to say where these ideas actually originated, because they are timeless and belong to the natural principles of movement, time and space. Over the years, we have simply articulated a set of names for things that already exist, things that we do naturally and have always done, with greater or lesser degrees of consciousness and emphasis.

VIEWPOINTS

- Viewpoints is a philosophy translated into a technique for (1) training performers; (2) building ensemble; and (3) creating movement for the stage.
- Viewpoints is a set of names given to certain principles of movement through time and space; these names constitute a language for talking about what happens onstage.
- Viewpoints is points of awareness that a performer or creator makes use of while working.

We work with nine Physical Viewpoints, within Viewpoints of Time and Viewpoints of Space. The bulk of this book focuses on the Physical Viewpoints, though Vocal Viewpoints, which we developed later, are addressed in Chapter 9. The Vocal Viewpoints are specifically related to sound as opposed to movement. Physical and Vocal Viewpoints overlap each other and constantly change in relative value, depending on the artist or teacher and/or the style of the production. The Physical Viewpoints are:

Viewpoints of time

Tempo

The rate of speed at which a movement occurs; how fast or slow something happens onstage.

Duration

How long a movement or sequence of movements continues. Duration, in terms of Viewpoints work, specifically relates to how long a group of people working together stay inside a certain section of movement before it changes.

Kinesthetic response

A spontaneous reaction to motion which occurs outside you; the timing in which you respond to the external events of movement or sound; the impulsive movement that occurs from a stimulation of the senses. An example: someone claps in front of your eyes and you blink in response; or someone slams a door and you impulsively stand up from your chair.

Repetition

The repeating of something onstage. Repetition includes (1) *Internal Repetition* (repeating a movement within your own body); (2) *External Repetition* (repeating the shape, tempo, gesture, etc., of something outside your own body).

Viewpoints of space

Shape

The contour or outline the body (or bodies) makes in space. All Shape can be broken down into either (1) *lines*; (2) *curves*; (3) a *combination* of lines and curves.
    Therefore, in Viewpoints training we create shapes that are round, shapes that are angular, shapes that are a mixture of these two.
    In addition, Shape can either be (1) *stationary*; (2) *moving* through space.
    Lastly, Shape can be made in one of three forms: (1) the body in space; (2) the body in relationship to architecture making a shape; (3) the body in relationship to other bodies making a shape.

Gesture

A movement involving a part or parts of the body; Gesture is Shape with a beginning, middle and end. Gestures can be made with the hands, the arms, the legs, the head, the mouth, the eyes, the feet, the stomach, or any other part or combination of parts that can be isolated. Gesture is broken down into:

1   BEHAVIORAL GESTURE. Belongs to the concrete, physical world of human behavior as we observe it in our everyday reality. It is the kind of gesture you see in the supermarket or on the subway: scratching, pointing, waving, sniffing, bowing, saluting. A Behavioral Gesture can give information about character, time period, physical health, circumstance, weather, clothes, etc. It is usually defined by a person's character or the time and place in which they live. It can also have a thought or intention behind it. A Behavioral Gesture can be further broken down and worked on in terms of *Private Gesture* and *Public Gesture*, distinguishing between actions performed in solitude and those performed with awareness of or proximity to others.

2   EXPRESSIVE GESTURE. Expresses an inner state, an emotion, a desire, an idea or a value. It is abstract and symbolic rather than representational. It is universal and timeless and is not something you would normally see someone do in the supermarket or subway. For instance, an Expressive Gesture might be expressive of, or stand for, such emotions as "joy," "grief" or "anger." Or it might express the inner essence of Hamlet as a given actor feels him. Or, in a production of Chekhov, you might create and work with Expressive Gestures of or for "time," "memory" or "Moscow."

Architecture

The physical environment in which you are working and how awareness of it affects movement. How many times have we seen productions where there is a lavish, intricate set covering the stage and yet the actors remain down center, hardly exploring or using the surrounding architecture? In working on Architecture as a Viewpoint, we learn to dance with the space, to be in dialogue with a room, to let movement (especially Shape and Gesture) evolve out of our surroundings. Architecture is broken down into:

1   SOLID MASS. Walls, floors, ceilings, furniture, windows, doors, etc.
2   TEXTURE. Whether the solid mass is wood or metal or fabric will change the kind of movement we create in relationship to it.
3   LIGHT. The sources of light in the room, the shadows we make in relationship to these sources, etc.
4   COLOR. Creating movement off of colors in the space, e.g., how one red chair among many black ones would affect our choreography in relation to that chair.
5   SOUND. Sound created by and from the architecture, e.g., the sound of feet on the floor, the creak of a door, etc.

Additionally, in working with Architecture, we create *spatial metaphors*, giving form to such feelings as I'm "up against the wall," "caught between the cracks," "trapped," "lost in space," "on the threshold," "high as a kite," etc.

Spatial relationship

The distance between things onstage, especially (1) one body to another; (2) one body (or bodies) to a group of bodies; (3) the body to the architecture.

What is the full range of possible distances between things onstage? What kinds of groupings allow us to see a stage picture more clearly? Which groupings suggest an event or emotion, express a dynamic? In both real life and onstage, we tend to position ourselves at a polite two- or three-foot distance from someone we are talking to. When we become aware of the expressive possibilities of Spatial Relationship onstage, we begin working with less polite but more dynamic distances of extreme proximity or extreme separation.

Topography

The landscape, the floor pattern, the design we create in movement through space. In defining a landscape, for instance, we might decide that the downstage area has great density, is difficult to move through, while the upstage area has less density and therefore involves more fluidity and faster tempos. To understand floor pattern, imagine that the bottoms of your feet are painted red; as you move through the space, the picture that evolves on the floor is the floor pattern that emerges over time. In addition, staging or designing for performance always involves choices about the size and shape of the space we work in. For example, we might choose to work in a narrow three-foot strip all the way downstage or in a giant triangular shape that covers the whole floor, etc.

COMPOSITION

- Composition is a method for creating new work.
- Composition is the practice of selecting and arranging the separate components of theatrical language into a cohesive work of art for the stage. It is the same technique that any choreographer, painter, writer, composer or filmmaker uses in their corresponding disciplines. In theater, it is writing on your feet, with others, in space and time, using the language of theater.
- Composition is a method for generating, defining and developing the theater vocabulary that will be used for any given piece. In Composition, we make pieces so that we can point to them and say: "That worked," and ask: "Why?" so that we can then articulate which ideas, moments, images, etc., we will include in our production.
- Composition is a method for revealing to ourselves our hidden thoughts and feelings about the material. Because we usually make Compositions in rehearsal in a compressed period of time, we have no time to think. Composition provides a structure for working from our impulses and intuition. As Pablo Picasso once said, making art is "another way of keeping a diary."
- Composition is an assignment given to an ensemble so that it can create short, specific theater pieces addressing a particular aspect of the work. We use Composition during rehearsal to engage the collaborators in the process of generating their own work around a source. The assignment will usually include an overall intention or structure as well as a substantial list of

ingredients which must be included in the piece. This list is the raw material of the theater language we'll speak in the piece, either principles that are useful for staging (symmetry versus asymmetry, use of scale and perspective, juxta-position, etc.) or the ingredients that belong specifically to the Play-World we are working on (objects, textures, colors, sounds, actions, etc.) These ingredients are to a Composition what single words are to a paragraph or essay. The creator makes meaning through their arrangement.

- Composition is a method for being in dialogue with other art forms, as it borrows from and reflects the other arts. In Composition work, we study and use principles from other disciplines translated for the stage. For example, borrowing from music, we might ask what the rhythm of a moment is, or how to interact based on a fugue structure, or how a coda functions and whether or not we should add one. Or we'll think about film: "How do we stage a close-up? An establishing shot? A montage?" And we'll ask: "What is the equivalent in the theater?" In applying Compositional principles from other disciplines to the theater, we push the envelope of theatrical possibility and challenge ourselves to create new forms.

- Composition is to the creator (whether director, writer, performer, designer, etc.) what Viewpoints is to the actor: a method for practicing the art.

ANNE BOGART (1951–) AND TINA LANDAU (1962–)

After graduating from her Masters degree at NYU Tisch School of Arts, Bogart worked with Mary Overlie and adapted her Six View Points into a system she called Viewpoints that uses improvisation, ensemble working and compositional strategies to create theatre performance material. In 1992, together with Tadashi Suzuki, she founded the SITI (Saratoga International Theatre Institute) Company. The company aims to create new work, train young actors and encourage international collaboration.

Landau is an American playwright and theatre director. She studied at Yale and Harvard universities before working professionally. In 1997 she became a member of Steppenwolf Theatre Company in Chicago where she has directed many productions. She continues to teach and work with Viewpoints, having co-authored *The Viewpoints Book* with Anne Bogart.

See also: **Tadashi Suzuki.**

SUGGESTED FURTHER READING

Bogart, A. (2007) *And Then, You Act*, London & New York: Routledge.
Bogart, A. and Landau, T. (2005) *The Viewpoints Book*, New York: Theatre Communications Group.

Climenhaga, R. (2010) 'Anne Bogart and SITI Company: Creating the moment', in Hodge, A. (ed.) (2010) *Actor Training*, London & New York: Routledge.
Overlie, M. (2006) 'The Six Viewpoints', in Bartow, A. (2006) *Training of the American Actor*, New York: Theatre Communications Group.

Chapter 29

Bertolt Brecht

SHORT DESCRIPTION OF A NEW TECHNIQUE OF ACTING WHICH PRODUCES AN ALIENATION EFFECT

THE FIRST CONDITION FOR the achievement of the A-effect is that the actor must invest what he has to show with a definite gest of showing. It is of course necessary to drop the assumption that there is a fourth wall cutting the audience off from the stage and the consequent illusion that the stage action is taking place in reality and without an audience. That being so, it is possible for the actor in principle to address the audience direct.

It is well known that contact between audience and stage is normally made on the basis of empathy. Conventional actors devote their efforts so exclusively to bringing about this psychological operation that they may be said to see it as the principal aim of their art. Our introductory remarks will already have made it clear that the technique which produces an A-effect is the exact opposite of that which aims at empathy. The actor applying it is bound not to try to bring about the empathy operation.

Yet in his efforts to reproduce particular characters and show their behaviour he need not renounce the means of empathy entirely. He uses these means just as any normal person with no particular acting talent would use them if he wanted to portray someone else, i.e. show how he behaves. This showing of other people's behaviour happens time and again in ordinary life (witnesses of an accident demonstrating to newcomers how the victim behaved, a facetious person imitating a friend's walk, etc.), without those involved making the least effort to subject their spectators to an illusion. At the same time they do feel their way into their characters' skins with a view to acquiring their characteristics.

As has already been said, the actor too will make use of this psychological operation. But whereas the usual practice in acting is to execute it during the actual performance, in the hope of stimulating the spectator into a similar operation, he will achieve it only at an earlier stage, at some time during rehearsals.

To safeguard against an unduly 'impulsive', frictionless and uncritical creation of characters and incidents, more reading rehearsals can be held than usual. The actor should refrain from living himself into the part prematurely in any way, and should go on functioning as long as possible as a reader (which does not mean a reader-aloud). An important step is memorizing one's first impressions.

When reading his part the actor's attitude should be one of a man who is astounded and contradicts. Not only the occurrence of the incidents, as he reads about them, but the conduct of the man he is playing, as he experiences it, must be weighed up by him and their peculiarities understood; none can be taken as given, as something that 'was bound to turn out that way', that was 'only to be expected from a character like that'. Before memorizing the words he must memorize what he felt astounded at and where he felt impelled to contradict. For these are dynamic forces that he must preserve in creating his performance.

When he appears on the stage, besides what he actually is doing he will at all essential points discover, specify, imply what he is not doing; that is to say he will act in such a way that the alternative emerges as clearly as possible, that his acting allows the other possibilities to be inferred and only represents one out of the possible variants. He will say for instance 'You'll pay for that', and not say 'I forgive you'. He detests his children; it is not the case that he loves them. He moves down stage left and not up stage right. Whatever he doesn't do must be contained and conserved in what he does. In this way every sentence and every gesture signifies a decision; the character remains under observation and is tested. The technical term for this procedure is 'fixing the "not . . . but" '.

The actor does not allow himself to become completely transformed on the stage into the character he is portraying. He is not Lear, Harpagon, Schweik; he shows them. He reproduces their remarks as authentically as he can; he puts forward their way of behaving to the best of his abilities and knowledge of men; but he never tries to persuade himself (and thereby others) that this amounts to a complete transformation. Actors will know what it means if I say that a typical kind of acting without this complete transformation takes place when a producer or colleague shows one how to play a particular passage. It is not his own part, so he is not completely transformed; he underlines the technical aspect and retains the attitude of someone just making suggestions.

Once the idea of total transformation is abandoned the actor speaks his part not as if he were improvising it himself but like a quotation. At the same time he obviously has to render all the quotation's overtones, the remark's full human and concrete shape; similarly the gesture he makes must have the full substance of a human gesture even though it now represents a copy.

Given this absence of total transformation in the acting there are three aids which may help to alienate the actions and remarks of the characters being portrayed:

1   Transposition into the third person.
2   Transposition into the past.
3   Speaking the stage directions out loud.

Using the third person and the past tense allows the actor to adopt the right attitude of detachment. In addition he will look for stage directions and remarks that comment on his lines, and speak them aloud at rehearsal ('He stood up and exclaimed angrily, not having eaten: . . .', or 'He had never been told so before, and didn't know if it was true or not', or 'He smiled, and said with forced nonchalance: . . .'). Speaking the stage directions out loud in the third person results in a clash between two tones of voice, alienating the second of them, the text proper. This style of acting is further alienated by taking place on the stage after having already been outlined and announced in words. Transposing it into the past gives the speaker a standpoint from which he can look back at his sentence. The sentence too is thereby alienated without the speaker adopting an unreal point of view; unlike the spectator, he has read the play right through and is better placed to judge the sentence in accordance with the ending, with its consequences, than the former, who knows less and is more of a stranger to the sentence.

This composite process leads to an alienation of the text in the rehearsals which generally persists in the performance too. The directness of the relationship with the audience allows and indeed forces the actual speech delivery to be varied in accordance with the greater or smaller significance attaching to the sentences. Take the case of witnesses addressing a court. The underlinings, the characters' insistence on their remarks, must be developed as a piece of effective virtuosity. If the actor turns to the audience it must be a whole-hearted turn rather than the asides and soliloquizing technique of the old-fashioned theatre. To get the full A-effect from the poetic medium the actor should start at rehearsal by paraphrasing the verse's content in vulgar prose, possibly accompanying this by the gestures designed for the verse. A daring and beautiful handling of verbal media will alienate the text. (Prose can be alienated by translation into the actor's native dialect.)

Gesture will be dealt with below, but it can at once be said that everything to do with the emotions has to be externalized; that is to say, it must be developed into a gesture. The actor has to find a sensibly perceptible outward expression for his character's emotions, preferably some action that gives away what is going on inside him. The emotion in question must be brought out, must lose all its restrictions so that it can be treated on a big scale. Special elegance, power and grace of gesture bring about the A-effect.

A masterly use of gesture can be seen in Chinese acting. The Chinese actor achieves the A-effect by being seen to observe his own movements.

Whatever the actor offers in the way of gesture, verse structure, etc., must be finished and bear the hallmarks of something rehearsed and rounded-off. The impression to be given is one of ease, which is at the same time one of difficulties overcome. The actor must make it possible for the audience to take his own art, his mastery of technique, lightly too. He puts an incident before the spectator with perfection and as he thinks it really happened or might have happened. He does not conceal the fact that he has rehearsed it, any more than an acrobat conceals his training, and he emphasizes that it is his own (actor's) account, view, version of the incident.

Because he doesn't identify himself with him he can pick a definite attitude to adopt towards the character whom he portrays, can show what he thinks of him and invite the spectator, who is likewise not asked to identify himself, to criticize the character portrayed.

The attitude which he adopts is a socially critical one. In his exposition of the incidents and in his characterization of the person he tries to bring out those features which come within society's sphere. In this way his performance becomes a discussion (about social conditions) with the audience he is addressing. He prompts the spectator to justify or abolish these conditions according to what class he belongs to.

The object of the A-effect is to alienate the social gest underlying every incident. By social gest is meant the mimetic and gestural expression of the social relationships prevailing between people of a given period.

It helps to formulate the incident for society, and to put it across in such a way that society is given the key, if titles are thought up for the scenes. These titles must have a historical quality.

This brings us to a crucial technical device: historicization.

The actor must play the incidents as historical ones. Historical incidents are unique, transitory incidents associated with particular periods. The conduct of the persons involved in them is not fixed and 'universally human'; it includes elements that have been or may be overtaken by the course of history, and is subject to criticism from the immediately following period's point of view. The conduct of those born before us is alienated from us by an incessant evolution.

It is up to the actor to treat present-day events and modes of behaviour with the same detachment as the historian adopts with regard to those of the past. He must alienate these characters and incidents from us.

Characters and incidents from ordinary life, from our immediate surroundings, being familiar, strike us as more or less natural. Alienating them helps to make them seem remarkable to us. Science has carefully developed a technique of getting irritated with the everyday, 'self-evident', universally accepted occurrence, and there is no reason why this infinitely useful attitude should not be taken over by art. It is an attitude which arose in science as a result of the growth in human productive powers. In art the same motive applies.

As for the emotions, the experimental use of the A-effect in the epic theatre's German productions indicated that this way of acting too can stimulate them, though possibly a different class of emotion is involved from those of the orthodox theatre. A critical attitude on the audience's part is a thoroughly artistic one. Nor does the actual practice of the A-effect seem anything like so unnatural as its description. Of course it is a way of acting that has nothing to do with stylization as commonly practised. The main advantage of the epic theatre with its A-effect, intended purely to show the world in such a way that it becomes manageable, is precisely its quality of being natural and earthly, its humour and its renunciation of all the mystical elements that have stuck to the orthodox theatre from the old days.

BERTOLT BRECHT (1898–1956)

Brecht emerged as a poet and playwright in the 1920s in Germany. His ideas on 'epic' theatre developed from his work on an adaptation of *Edward II* in 1924, and were further stimulated by his studies of Marx and his collaboration with the dramaturg Erwin Piscator. His most successful plays include: *The Threepenny Opera, Mother Courage and Her Children, The Life of Galileo, The Resistable Rise of Arturu Ui* and *The Caucasian Chalk Circle*. He wrote extensively on his ideas on epic theatre, which have been very influential in the development of political theatre.

See also: **Augusto Boal, Dario Fo.**

SUGGESTED FURTHER READING

Willett, J. (ed.) (1981) *Brecht on Theatre*, London: Methuen.

Thomson, P. (2010) 'Brecht and actor training: on whose behalf do we act?', in Hodge, A. (ed.) (2010) *Actor Training*, London & New York: Routledge.
Thomson, P. and Sacks, G. (eds) (1994) *The Cambridge Companion to Brecht*, Cambridge: Cambridge University Press.
Unwin, S. (2014) *The Complete Brecht Toolkit*, London: Nick Hern Books.
Willett, J. (1977) *The Theatre of Bertolt Brecht*, London: Methuen.

Chapter 30

Michael Chekhov

CHARACTER AND CHARACTERIZATION

Transformation – that is what the actor's nature, consciously or sub-consciously, longs for.

AS YOU WILL NEVER MEET TWO PERSONS precisely alike in life, so you will never find two identical parts in plays. That which constitutes their *difference* makes them *characters*. And it will be a good starting point for an actor, in order to grasp the initial idea about the character he is going to perform on the stage, to ask himself: "What is the *difference* – however subtle or slight this difference may be – between myself and the character as it is described by the playwright?"

By doing so you will not only lose the desire to paint your "self-portrait" repeatedly but discover the main psychological characteristics or features in your character.

Then you face the need to incorporate these characteristic features that make the difference between yourself and the character. How will you approach this task?

The shortest, most artistic (and amusing) approach is *to find an imaginary body for your character*. Imagine, as a case in point, that you must play the role of a person whose character you define as lazy, sluggish and awkward (psychologically as well as physically). These qualities should not necessarily be pronounced or emphatically expressed, as perhaps in comedy. They might show themselves as mere, almost imperceptible indications. And yet they are typical features of the character which should not be overlooked.

As soon as you have outlined those features and qualities of your role – that is, compared with your own – try to imagine *what kind of body* such a lazy, awkward and slow person would have. Perhaps you will find that he might possess a full, plump, short body with drooping shoulders, thick neck, long arms hanging listlessly, and a big, heavy head. This body is, of course, a far cry from your own. Yet you must look like that and do as it does. How do you go about effecting a true resemblance? Thus:

You are going to imagine that in the same space you occupy with your own, real body there exists another body – the imaginary body of your character, which you have just created in your mind.

You clothe yourself, as it were, with this body; you put it on like a garment. What will be the result of this "masquerade"? After a while (or perhaps in a flash!) you will begin to feel and think of yourself as *another person*. This experience is very similar to that of a real masquerade. And did you ever notice in everyday life how different you feel in different clothes? Are you not "another person" when wearing a dressing gown or an evening dress; when in an old, worn-out suit or one that's brand-new? But "wearing another body" is more than any raiment or costume. This assumption of the character's imaginary physical form influences your psychology ten times more strongly than any garment!

The imaginary body stands, as it were, *between* your real body and your psychology, influencing both of them with equal force. Step by step, you begin to move, speak and feel in accord with it; that is to say, your character now dwells within you (or; if you prefer, you dwell within it).

How strongly you express the qualities of your imaginary body while acting will depend on the type of play and on your own taste and desire. But in any case, your *whole being, psychologically and physically*, will be changed – I would not hesitate to say even *possessed* – by the character. When really taken on and exercised, the imaginary body stirs the actor's will and feelings; it harmonizes them with the characteristic speech and movements, it transforms the actor into another person! Merely discussing the character, analyzing it mentally, cannot produce this desired effect, because your reasoning mind, however skillful it may be, is apt to leave you cold and passive, whereas the imaginary body has the power to appeal directly to your will and feelings.

Consider creating and assuming a character as a kind of quick and simple game. "Play" with the imaginary body, changing and perfecting it until you are completely satisfied with your achievement. You will never fail to win with this game unless your impatience hurries the result; your artistic nature is bound to be carried away by it if you do not force it by "performing" your imaginary body prematurely. Learn to rely upon it in full confidence and it will not betray you.

Do not exaggerate outwardly by stressing, pushing and overdoing those subtle inspirations which come to you from your "new body." And only when you begin to feel absolutely free, true and natural in using it should you start rehearsing your character with its lines and business, whether at home or on the stage.

In some cases you will find it sufficient to use only a part of your imaginary body: long, depending arms, for example, might suddenly change your whole psychology and give your own body the necessary stature. But always see to it that your *entire* being has transformed itself into the character you must portray.

The effect of the imaginary body will be strengthened and acquire many unexpected nuances if you add to it the *imaginary center* [. . .].

So long as the center remains in the middle of your chest (pretend it is a few inches deep), you will feel that you are still yourself and in full command, only more energetically and harmoniously so, with your body approaching an "ideal" type. But as soon as you try to shift the center to some other place within or outside your body, you will feel that your whole psychological and physical attitude will change, just as it changes when you step into an imaginary body. You will notice that the center is able to draw and concentrate your whole being into one spot from which your activity emanates and radiates. If, to illustrate the point, you were to move the center from your chest to your head, you would become aware that the thought element has begun to play a characteristic part in your performance. From its place in your head the imaginary center will suddenly or gradually co-ordinate all your movements, influence the entire bodily attitude, motivate your behavior, action and speech, and tune your psychology in such a way that you will quite naturally experience the sensation that the thought element is germane and important to your performance.

But no matter where you choose to put the center, it will produce an entirely different effect as soon as you change its *quality*. It is not enough to place it in the head, for example, and leave it there to do its own work. You must further stimulate it by investing it with various desired qualities. For a wise man, let us say, you would imagine the center in your head as big, shining and radiating, whereas for a stupid, fanatic or narrow-minded type of person you would imagine a small, tense and hard center. You must be free from any restraint in imagining the center in many and different ways, so long as the variations are compatible with the part you are playing.

Try a few experiments for a while. Put a soft, warm, not too small center in the region of your abdomen and you may experience a psychology that is self-satisfied, earthy, a bit heavy and even humorous. Place a tiny, hard center on the tip of your nose and you will become curious, inquisitive, prying and even meddlesome. Move the center into one of your eyes and notice how quickly it seems that you have become sly, cunning and perhaps hypocritical. Imagine a big, heavy, dull and sloppy center placed outside the seat of your pants and you have a cowardly, not too honest, droll character. A center located a few feet outside your eyes or forehead may invoke the sensation of a sharp, penetrating and even sagacious mind. A warm, hot and even fiery center situated within your heart may awaken in you heroic, loving and courageous feelings.

You can also imagine a movable center. Let it sway slowly before your forehead and circle your head from time to time, and you will sense the psychology of a bewildered person; or let it circle irregularly around your whole body, in varying tempos, now going up and now sinking down, and the effect will no doubt be one of intoxication.

See p. 33.

Chapter 31

Dario Fo

THE TRICKS OF THE TRADE

GESTURE AND GESTICULATION

LEARNING HOW TO MOVE the limbs and the trunk with unaffected elegance and awareness ought to be the first element in the training of the actor. An apprenticeship in the movement-related techniques of breathing, right up to performance in acrobatics, ought to be the central plank of our profession, even more than voice training. I have seen several highly rated directors break down in tears when confronted with the awkwardness of some actors who were simply incapable of controlling their gestures. There are actors who try to hide their sheer lack of naturalness by sticking their hands in their pockets, by fidgeting with their cuffs and lapels or by continually smoothing their hair.

There are actors, like the Americans of one particular school, who, in order to avoid the problems of on-stage awkwardness, have created a kind of mimic-gestural repertoire of a level which is, in my view, positively subnormal. Obviously I have in mind the products of some of the great schools like the Actors Studio, where gestures are fired out in a sequence of paranoiac twitches, all too often bereft of any connection with real life and intended to display purely abstract virtuoso flourishes. You know the kind of thing I mean: rubbing eyes and noses, scratching heads with greater or lesser vehemence, sticking hands into pockets to incredible depths, and so on.

The real problem concerns the matching of the gesture to the mask. What is the purpose of the mask? To magnify and simultaneously give the essence of the character. It obliges you to widen and develop your gestures, which must not be arbitrary if you want the audience, your immediate mirror, to follow you and to grasp the flow of the piece, especially when dealing with a gag, a routine or a comic situation.

FIRST LECTURE ON SYNTHESIS

The mask, in bringing the movement of the whole body into play, imposes the need to identify the essence of a gesture, because if, in order to heighten a particular effect, a multiplicity of senseless gestures are performed, the result is to destroy the value of the original gesture itself. It is crucial to select gestures in full awareness of the choice. The movement, the general attitude, the positioning of the body must be duly pondered and reduced to the bare essential.

Finally we arrive at the topic which underlies both Commedia dell'Arte, and, strange as it may appear, a substantial part of oriental theatre. The moment anyone puts on a mask to play a stock character in Commedia, he realises that the entire performance hinges on the pelvis, the source of all movements. For instance, the figure of the old man is characterised by the springy forward stretch of the pelvis. The eighteenth-century (supposedly classical) Harlequin moves with his belly protruding to the front and his buttocks to the rear, and so is forced into a position which imposes a continual, bent double dance with occasional hops.

PELVIS – CENTRE OF THE UNIVERSE

The early or seventeenth-century Harlequin, on the other hand, positions himself on his trunk, moving 'off-balance' with a hip movement which is, however, walked, not danced.

This hip movement has, however unlikely it may seem, an equivalent in eastern theatre. In Japan, *kaza*, for example, means 'hip' or 'stomach' and *kabuki* is a composite expression which stands for 'theatre of the hip'. The same definition could be applied to the theatre of Commedia dell'Arte – theatre of the hip, theatre of a unified approach, linked to this essential fulcrum. Only continual exercise with the mask can convince us of the truth of this definition.

This implement not only imposes a quest for the essential but also forces the wearer to eschew all form of mystification. Bernard Shaw once said: 'Give a hypocrite a mask to wear, and he will be rendered incapable of further lying.' Perfect; the mask obliges people to tell the truth. Why? Because the mask cancels the prime element – the face, with all the expressions we formulate and employ with such ease – used to give expression to any form of mystification. When the face is removed from the equation, people are compelled to speak in a language free of formulas and of fixed stereotypes – in the language of the hands, of the arms and of the fingers. No one is accustomed to lying with their body. We never bother to check the gestures we make while speaking. If you pay sufficient heed, and if you know the language, you are bound to notice that many people say one thing with their mouth which they contradict with their hands and arms, thereby revealing themselves as liars. In other words, Bernard Shaw hit the nail on the head. The use of a mask is an extraordinarily effective means of checking your own gestures. A word of warning, however; never place yourself in front of a mirror, because the results are likely to be unfortunate. To gain a reflection of your own gestures, it is better to use your imagination, and to bear in mind that the best mirror of all is an audience.

See p. 84.

Chapter 32

Jacques Lecoq

CHARACTERS

STATES, PASSIONS, FEELINGS

ALL THE WORK ACCOMPLISHED in the first year is moving towards one
main objective: character acting. Just as they have taken on different elements,
colours, insects, students must be able to take on characters, even if this involves a
more difficult approach. When we begin the work on characters, I am always afraid
the students will fall back on personality, in other words talk about themselves, with
no element of genuine play. If character becomes identical with personality, there is
no play. It may be possible for this kind of osmosis to work in the cinema, in psychological close-ups, but theatre performance must be able to make an image carry from
stage to spectator. There is a huge difference between actors who express their own
lives, and those who can truly be described as players. In achieving this, the mask will
have had an important function: the students will have learned to perform something
other than themselves, while nevertheless investing themselves deeply in the performance. They have learned not to play *themselves* but to play *using* themselves. In this lies
all the ambiguity of the actor's work.

In order to avoid the phenomenon of osmosis, and to give us purchase on that
elsewhere which we so desire, we make considerable use of animals. Each character can
be compared, in part, to one or more animals. If we take a character based on the
pretentiousness of the turkey, we must be sure that the turkey is indeed evident in the
actor's playing. Rather than a simple encounter between actor and character, we have
a relationship which is always triangular: in this case the turkey, the actor and the
character.

I begin by asking students to come up with a first character freely inspired by
someone observed in the street or in their own circle. They simply have to have fun
being a different character. We start by defining *characteristics*. These are not to be
confused with the character's passions, nor with motivating states, nor even with the
situations in which it finds itself, but consist of the *lines of force* which define it. Their
definition must be reducible to three words. A given character might be: 'proud,
generous and quick-tempered'. In this way we simplify the definition as far as

possible in order to establish the basic structure which will permit the actor to play the character. With three sticks we can create a first space: a hut is already a home! Two elements would not be enough, because they would not be able to balance. For a character, just as for a house, the rules of architecture require a tripod. Once the three elements have been defined, we can begin searching for nuances: 'he is proud but brave'; he is 'quick-tempered but kind'. Little by little, the actors develop their own nuances, their own complexities, and thus their characters are built on firm foundations with a clearly defined structure.

The students come to class in character, appropriately dressed. Some of them make the journey from home in character and occasionally we do not even recognise them, so great is their physical transformation. We treat them as if they were new students and they are put into the introductory classes on movement or acrobatics. This is amusing but tiring, and so we agree on a signal which will allow them to stop playing and to relax briefly before going on. For, try as one may, characters always tend to revert towards personalities. We must remember that the students are improvising in their own words and cannot rely on the distancing effect of a text written by an author. This is why I insist on them presenting a genuine dramatic character, in other words, a character stemming from real life, not a real-life character. The difference is subtle but essential.

When they show themselves, one by one, in front of the others, we question them about their identity: their name, age, family situation, origins, work, etc., and they have to reply. After this we place them in situation so that their character can reveal itself. For, of course, character cannot be separated from situation. It is only through situation that character can reveal itself. 'Bring us to life!' is the cry of Pirandello's Six Characters in Search of an Author.

STYLISTIC CONSTRAINTS

These improvisations are explored through group work, after which the students continue the work along the same lines on their own, in their auto-cours. I group them into 'companies' of five, asking each company to play ten characters. Anything becomes possible: separation of voices and images, multiplication of screens, etc. 'Hotel Paradiso'[1] is a richly suggestive theme, with doors which slam, cupboards for hiding in, mistaken identities of all kinds. Here we are approaching both the virtuosity and the pleasure of play, and for me these are the most important dimensions of acting. In this exercise, as in its predecessors, my pedagogic purpose is always to oblige the students to play characters which are as distant as possible from themselves.

I conclude this introduction to characters by asking a group of actors, organised into a company, to perform a scene with sets, costumes, objects and a number of characters. Since this tends to make them spread out and take up a lot of space, I counter this tendency by a constraint: they can use only a very restricted space, measuring one metre by two. On this small, limited stage they must bring huge areas to life.

> Two people, lost in an immense forest, search in vain for one another, then at last meet up. Physically they can be fifty centimetres apart while dramatically the distance is hundreds of metres; they can call to one another across a valley, or from the tops of hills, while all the time standing back to back.

This exercise is performed with two actors, then with three, four or five. The upper limit is seven actors on two square metres. The exercise comes out of the cabaret tradition in which the imposition of extreme spatial constraints encourages the invention of dramatic forms. I recall the performance of a Western, complete with horses, chase sequences, saloon-bar fights, all done with tremendous verve on the tiny stage of the *Rose Rouge*, a famous post-war Parisian cabaret. But above all we conclude our work on characters with a reminder that the theatre must always retain its playful dimension. It is essential to have fun and our school is a happy school. Not for us, tortured self-questioning about the best way to walk on stage: it is enough that it be done with pleasure.

Note

1   English title of *L'Hôtel du libre échange* – a farce by Feydeau.

See p. 43.

Chapter 33

Sanford Meisner

THE PINCH AND THE OUCH

"**TODAY WE'RE GOING TO** talk about beginnings. I have an exercise that I'm going to demonstrate to you. It is basic and vital, and it may clarify something. John, stand up. I want to show you where you begin. There are two basic principles involved here, which you can write down if you wish."

He leaves the desk to stand beside John, who is a head taller than he.

" *'Don't do anything unless something happens to make you do it.'* That's one of them. The second is: *'What you do doesn't depend on you; it depends on the other fellow.'* John," he asks, "how are you on learning a script? Are you pretty good? You're fast? Here's your text: 'Mr. Meisner.' Can you learn that? Can I hear that?"

" 'Mr. Meisner,' " John says simply.

"Not bad." The class laughs. "Now, I said don't do anything until something happens to make you do it, and I said that what you do doesn't depend on you but on the other fellow, didn't I? Now, you've got a script. Do you remember it?"

"Yes."

"What is it, please?"

" 'Mr. Meisner.' "

"Perfect. Would you mind turning around?"

Sensing what is to come, the class begins to titter.

"What are you laughing at? I haven't done it yet!"

Then he reaches up and gives John's back a big pinch.

" 'Mr. *Meisner!*' " John shouts, jumping away from him. There is laughter and scattered applause.

"That," Meisner says, "is the illustration of what I just told you. 'Don't do anything until something happens to make you do it. And what you do doesn't depend upon you; it depends on the other fellow!' Did I force that screech out of you?"

"Yes, in a manner of speaking."

"That's justification. Okay, John, sit down."

* * *

"You know, in the early days of the Group Theatre, the actors used to do what they called 'improvisations.' "

Meisner leans back in a comfortable armchair angled before the unlit fireplace in his paneled office. The class was a long one, and outside a red sun is about to set. Scott Roberts, a large leather briefcase across his knees, sits on the daybed against the wall.

"These were general verbalizations of what we thought was an approximation of our situation in the play. We were retelling what we remembered of the story of the play using our own words. I came to the realization that this was all intellectual nonsense. A composer doesn't write down what he thinks would be effective; he works from his heart.

"I decided I wanted an exercise for actors where there is no intellectuality. I wanted to eliminate all that 'head' work, to take away all the mental manipulation and get to where the impulses come from. And I began with the premise that if I repeat what I hear you saying, my head is not working. I'm listening, and there is an absolute elimination of the brain. If you say, 'Your glasses are dirty,' and I say, 'My glasses are dirty,' and you say, 'Yes, your glasses are dirty,' there is no intellectuality in that."

Meisner glances for a moment at the framed black-and-white photograph of Eleonora Duse which stands on his small mahogany desk.

"Then I came to the next stage. Let's say I say to you, 'Lend me ten dollars.' And you say, 'Lend you ten dollars?' 'Yes, lend me ten dollars.' And that goes on for five or six times until—and this is vital—your refusal sets up an impulse in me which comes directly out of the repetition and it makes me say to you, 'You're a stinker!' That's repetition which leads to impulses. It is not intellectual. It is emotional and impulsive, and *gradually* when the actors I train improvise, what they say—like what the composer writes—comes not from the head but truthfully from the impulses."

"I know," Scott says. "But the problem is that on a superficial level all this repetitive back-and-forth can seem boring. Vincent, for example, the guy who's Anna's partner, told me before class that the repetition exercise drives him nuts."

"Ah, please," Meisner says with a dismissive wave of his hand, "Vincent comes from California, for God's sake, where he claims to have studied with one of the legion of teachers who claim to have studied with me! Look, I'll tell you why the repetition exercise, in essence, is *not* boring: it plays on the source of all organic creativity, which is the inner impulses. I wish I could make that clear!"

He pauses for a moment. "Of course, if I were a pianist and sat for an hour just making each finger move in a certain way, the onlooker could very well say, 'That's boring!' And it would be—to the onlooker. But the practitioner is somebody who is learning to funnel his instincts, not give performances. The mistake we made in the Group was that our early improvisations were performances of how we remembered the original play.

"You know, a friend of mine who owns the house in which Joan Sutherland has an apartment says, 'Sometimes she drives me crazy with the repetition of the scales, but then I hear the purity of the tones and all is forgiven.' I'm a very nonintellectual teacher of acting. My approach is based on bringing the actor back to his emotional impulses and to acting that is firmly rooted in the instinctive. It is based on the fact that all good acting comes from the heart, as it were, and that there's no mentality in it."

SANFORD MEISNER (1905–1997)

In 1931, Meisner, along with Lee Strasberg, Harold Clurman and Cheryl Crawford, co-founded the Group Theatre in New York. He eventually rejected the Method's emphasis on affective memory. He worked at the Neighbourhood Playhouse from 1935, and when the Group Theatre disbanded in 1940 he continued his teaching and developed his own approach to actor training. He taught at the Neighbourhood Playhouse until 1990; his former students include many leading actors and writers.

See also: **Konstantin Stanislavsky, Stella Adler.**

SUGGESTED FURTHER READING

Meisner, S. and Longwell, D. (1990) *Sanford Meisner on Acting*, New York: Vintage.

Hart, V. (2006) 'Meisner Technique: Teaching the work of Sanford Meisner', in Bartow, A. (2006) *Training of the American Actor*, New York: Theatre Communications Group.
Krasner, D. (2010) 'Strasberg, Adler and Meisner: Method Acting', in Hodge, A. (ed.) (2010) *Actor Training*, London & New York: Routledge.
Shirley, D. (2010) '"The Reality of Doing": Meisner Technique and British Actor training', in *Theatre, Dance and Performer Training*, 1: 2, 199–213.

Chapter 34

Odin Teatret: Erik Exe Christoffersen

DRAMATURGY: PERFORMANCE TEXT

PERFORMANCE TEXT

A THEATRE PERFORMANCE IS a flow of energy between the actors and the spectators given form in a particular way in accordance with a particular goal.

The performance text is the wave of meaning elements which make up the theatre performance. What is particular about this 'text' is that it exists only when it is seen by the spectators. Unlike a book, a film, or a painting, it cannot be separated from its own production. The 'performance text' is a series of expressive elements, which are present at the same time, just as all the expressive elements of a painting are present at the same time – in contrast to written drama, which can only be acquired by being gone through from beginning to end. The spectators can see and experience many elements at the same time and are free to choose where to direct their attention. The performance is a polyphony of the actors' actions, use of text, changes in the lights, changes in the space, which are not necessarily subject to a common point of view.

The spectators are 'led' through the performance's inner life or logic. This occurs not only with respect to the performance's action (the plot, the story), which could be called the performance's linear dimension (horizontal progression), but also with respect to the performance's simultaneous or spatial dimension (vertical progression). The performance's dynamic is a balance between these poles and the spectator's attention is stretched between a time dimension and a space dimension.

One could say that on one level the actor performs 'acting people' and this is perhaps what the spectator 'sees', but on another level the actor does something which has nothing to do with either drama itself or its characters: the actor creates a network of tensions between himself or herself and the space and in relationship to the spectators.

Let us take as an example a scene with five actors. The focus shifts between them. The technique which one actor uses to bring himself or herself in or out of focus or to create focus for another actor may perhaps be a distortion of balance or a kind of movement which attracts or deflects attention. The actor plays 'the role' but creates also something which is part of the theatre situation itself: movement-forms in space which create the context for what the spectator experiences as the 'performance text'.

The term 'dramaturgy' derives from the Greek, *drama-ergon*, and refers to the inner or invisible energy of an action. An action is a work, an activity. The dramaturgy of a performance is the way an action is told or shown and becomes functional as dramatic energy.

The actor's dramaturgy is that particular and individual way in which the action, the 'character', the prop is brought alive. It is the way the actor uses the text and the subtext, the tone colours of the words, the way sounds and movements are created, the space filled with presence, directions, and different kinds of energy. And it is the way in which the spectator's attention is caught and held as the actor enters into a dialogue relationship with the spectator's daily logic.

ERIK EXE CHRISTOFFERSEN (1958–)

Christoffersen graduated from the Department of Drama at the University of Aarhus, Denmark, where he is now Associate Professor in the Department of Aesthetics and Communication. He has worked closely with Eugenio Barba and Odin Teatret in the past.

See also: **Eugenio Barba.**

SUGGESTED FURTHER READING

Christoffersen, E. E. (1993) *The Actor's Way*, London & New York: Routledge.

Chapter 35

The Open Theatre: Robert Pasolli

TRANSFORMATION

A **TRANSFORMATION IS A** radical change in the circumstances of an impro-visation made by the actors improvising. For example: two actors are teenage brothers arguing over who gets to sleep in the lower bunk of their new double-decker bed. Claims, counterclaims; threats, entreaties. Abruptly the older brother starts acting like a wild animal, say, a lion. He has transformed his identity. His partner must transform too. He might become a small animal trapped by the lion or, conversely, a hunter stalking the lion. His change in identity establishes a new set of circumstances, which he and his partner then elaborate improvisationally.

Several things are important. The actors must let things happen; that is, they must follow their instincts, breaking out of the established circumstances as frequently and freely as they can. They must accept whatever changes their partners initiate, finding a way to join in; they must cooperate with even bewildering changes.

Transformation taps the unconscious resources of the actor, who, in jumping from one set of circumstances to another, relies on links between given and potential situations which he would not necessarily understand rationally. Thus the device mines levels of meaning in a given situation which might not be otherwise evident. Transformation is a way rapidly and with minimal discussion to invent situations for improvisation (where improvisation itself is the goal). In terms of acting training, transformation develops the actor's ability to handle a wide range of situations, acting styles, and emotions. It also heightens the actor's sensitivity to partners. Since trans-formation takes the actor out of himself, it is a very good way to break the grip of the Method and the dependence on psychological motivation and logical transition between situations which it imposes on the actor. Transformation frees the actor to be the child (now I'm the grass, now I'm the queen, now I'm the king of the moun-tain, now I'm a cloud).

In transformation, the actor is not limited to changing his identity (the who). He can change the place of action (the where), the clock time or epoch (the when), or the relationship between himself and his partners as defined by what goes on between them (the what). In fact, transforming the who often automatically entails other changes. In exercising transformation, it is useful to limit the change to one element, for this makes greater demands on the actors. In such cases, however, it is important for the actor initiating a transformation to leave it somewhat undefined, so that his partner has some latitude in getting himself into the new circumstances. As an improvisation, however, transformation is richest when the choices for change are wide open. Here the actor's unconscious cues can function most fully. As such, the improvisation can include machines, animals, and personified abstractions as well as recognizable characters. The Open Theatre has frequently presented "open transformations" in public as ensemble improvisations.

During a "style transformation" the theatrical or sociological style of a scene is transformed (restoration comedy to soap opera to Brechtian *lehrstücke* to Hollywood melodrama) in the course of an improvisation. The "singing transformation" is a variation of the style transformation in which the actors improvise on a line of text or brief dialogue, perhaps from a scene in progress (madrigal to Verdi aria to hillbilly croon). "Rescue-squads" is a device where an actor or actors enter an improvisation as it is flagging, transforming the situation as they go in. The original actors stay or leave depending on their instincts for fitting into the situation initiated by the rescue-squad. These ensemble improvisations are entertaining virtuoso pieces. But the fullest development of the transformation device occurs in connection with playwriting and character conception, for which see Megan Terry's plays *Calm Down Mother* and *Keep Tightly Closed in a Cool Dry Place*.

JOSEPH CHAIKIN (1935–2003)

After a period working and studying as an actor, Chaikin joined the Living Theatre in 1959, performing in seminal productions such as *The Connection* and *Man is Man*. In 1963, he founded the Open Theatre in order to continue to explore non-naturalistic theatre practice and collaborative creation. Key productions with the Open Theatre included: *The Serpent*, *Terminal* and *America Hurrah*.

See also: **Bertolt Brecht, Jerzy Grotowski.**

SUGGESTED FURTHER READING

Chaikin, J. (1991) *The Presence of the Actor*, New York: Theatre Communications Group.

Hulton, D. (2010) 'Joseph Chaikin and Aspects of Actor Training: Possibilities rendered present', in Hodge, A. (2010) *Actor Training*, London & New York: Routledge.
Pasolli, R. (1970) *A Book on the Open Theatre*, New York: Avon.

Chapter 36

Konstantin Stanislavsky

THE SUPERTASK AND
THROUGHACTION

THE SUPERTASK OF THE WRITER'S WORK

TORTSOV POINTED TO THE inscription on the placard hanging in front of us.

'The Supertask?!' Vanya mused with a tragic expression on his face.

'I'll explain,' said Tortsov to help him. 'All his life Dostoievski looked for God and the Devil in people. That drove him to produce *The Brothers Karamazov*. That is why the search for God is the Supertask in this work.

'Tolstoi strove for self-perfection all his life and many of his works grew from that seed, which formed their Supertasks.

'Chekhov fought against vulgarity and petty-mindness and dreamed of a better life. This struggle, this striving towards it became the Supertask of many of his works.

'Don't you feel how readily these great, life-giving goals which men of genius set themselves can become stimulating, compelling Tasks for an actor, and how they can pull together all the individual Bits of the play and the role?

'Everything that happens in a play, all its individual Tasks, major or minor, all the actor's creative ideas and actions, which are analogous to the role, strive to fulfil the play's Supertask. Their common link with it, and the sway it holds over everything that happens in the play, is so great that even the most trivial detail, if it is irrelevant to the Supertask, becomes harmful, superfluous, drawing one's attention away from the essential meaning of the work.

'This pursuit of the Supertask must be continuous, unbroken throughout the whole play and the role.

'Apart from its continuity you must discern the quality and origin of that pursuit.

'It can be histrionic, mere form, and only provide a more or less credible, overall direction. Efforts of that kind cannot bring the whole work alive, nor arouse you to dynamic, genuine, productive, purposeful actions. The stage does not need these kinds of creative efforts.

'But there is another kind, which is genuine, human, active, and which tries to achieve the basic goal of the play. This continuous pursuit, like a major artery, feeds the actor's entire organism and the character he is playing and gives it, and the whole play, life.

'Genuine living pursuit stirs the special quality of the Supertask itself and its power to compel.

'A masterly Supertask has great drawing-power, is strong, but when it is ordinary, its pull is weak.'

'And when it's bad?' Vanya asked.

'When it's bad an actor must take pains to give it strength and depth.'

'What are the qualities we need in the Supertask?' I asked.

'Do we need a wrong Supertask which doesn't correspond to the ideas the author expresses in the play, even if it is interesting in itself and to the actor?' Tortsov asked.

'No! We can do without it! Moreover, it is dangerous. The more compelling a wrong Supertask, the further it leads the actor away from the author, the play and the role,' said Tortsov in answer to his own question.

'Do we need a cerebral Supertask? We can do without a cold, cerebral Supertask too. But we do need a *conscious* Supertask, that comes from our intelligence, from an interesting creative idea.

'Do we need an emotional Supertask, that arouses our whole nature? Of course we do, in the highest degree like air and sun.

'Do we need a volitional Supertask, which will draw together all our mental and physical qualities? Yes, very much so.

'And what are we to say about a Supertask which stimulates our creative imagination, which attracts our total attention, satisfies our feeling of truth and stimulates our power to believe as well as the other elements in the actor's state of self-awareness? We need every Supertask, which stimulates the inner drives, the Elements, as we need bread and nourishment.

'So it appears that we need a Supertask which is analogous to the writer's thoughts but which unfailingly evokes a response in the actor's personality. That is what can evoke not formalistic, not cerebral but genuine, living, human, direct experiencing.

'Or, in other words, you must look for the Supertask not only in the role but also in the heart and mind of the actor.

'The same Supertask, which every actor playing the role must accept, has a different resonance for each person. You get a Task which is the same and not the same. For example, take the most real of human aspirations, "I want to live happily". How many different, elusive nuances there are in the same wish and the different ways of achieveing it and in the same representation of happiness. There is a great deal which is personal, individual in all of this which we can't always appreciate at a conscious level. If you then take a more complex Task, the individual peculiarities of each human being/actor will be even more pronounced.

'These individual nuances in the personalities of different people playing the same role are of great importance for the Supertask. Without their subjective experiences, it is arid, dead. It is essential to find a response in the actor's personality if the Supertask and the role are to become living, vibrant, resplendent with all the colours of genuine, human life.

'It is important that the actor's attitude to the role should lose nothing of his individual sensibility and at the same time not diverge from the author's ideas. If the actor doesn't invest his own nature as a human being in the role, then what he creates will be dead.

'The actor must find the Supertask for himself and take it to his heart. If it is indicated to him by others, he must filter it through himself and stir it to life emotionally with his own personality and feelings. In other words, he must be able to make each Supertask his own. That means, finding the things in it which have an essential affinity to his own personality.

'What is it that gives the Supertask its special, elusive attraction which stimulates every actor playing the same role? In the majority of cases this special quality gives the Sueprtask the special something we feel in it, something which is hidden in the subconscious.

'The Supertask should be in the closest affinity with it.

'You see now how long and hard we must look for a Supertask which is substantial, stimulating and profound.

'You see how important it is to feel its presence in the author's work and to discover a response to it in one's own heart and mind.

'How many potential Supertasks we have to reject and then nurture once more. How many times we have to take aim and miss before we achieve our goal.'

*   *   *

'I am going to use graphics to make you appreciate the significance of the Supertask and the Throughaction more fully,' said Tortsov going to a large blackboard and taking a piece of chalk.

'Normally all the Tasks and the short lines of life within the role are directed, without exception, in one single direction – i.e. to the Supertask. So:'

Tortsov traced on the blackboard:

 Supertask

'A long series of small, medium and large lines of life in the role all go one way, towards the Supertask. The short lines of life in the role and their tasks, alternate and are linked to each other in logical sequence. Thanks to that, one continuous through line is created, running through the entire play.

'Now, imagine for a moment that the actor has no Supertask, that each of the short lines of life in the role he is playing is moving in a different direction.'

Tortsov once again illustrated his idea with dashes that broke up the unbroken line of the Throughaction:

'Here's a series of large, medium and small tasks and little bits in the life of a role pointed in different directions. Can they create a continuous, straight line?'

We acknowledged they couldn't.

'Then, in that case, the Throughaction is destroyed, the play is broken down into bits, going off in different directions, and each of its parts is obliged to exist on its own account, in the absence of the whole. In that form, beautiful as they may be, the individual parts are of no use to the play.

'I'll give you a third case,' said Tortsov continuing his explanation. 'As I have already told you, in every good play the Supertask and the Throughaction emerge organically from the work itself. That's something you cannot infringe with impunity, without destroying the work itself.

'Imagine there are people who want to introduce an extraneous goal or slant which has nothing to do with the play.

'In that case the organic link between the play and the Supertask and the natural Throughaction which has been created remains in part but is, at moments, deflected by the slant that has been introduced:

 | Supertask

'A broken-backed play like that cannot live.'

*   *   *

'Every action meets a counter-action and the second evokes and strengthens the first. So, in every play, parallel to the Throughaction, there is an opposing counter-Throughaction coming from the opposite direction to meet it.

'That's good and we should welcome such a phenomenon because a reaction naturally provokes a whole series of new actions. We need this constant clash. It produces struggle, opposition, strife, a whole series of corresponding problems and ways of resolving them. It stimulates our energy, action, which are the fundamentals of acting.

'If there were no counter-Throughaction in the play and everything just worked out, there would be nothing for the cast and the characters to do, and the play itself would be actionless and therefore untheatrical.

'So, if Iago didn't weave his treacherous plot, then Othello would not be jealous of Desdemona, and kill her. But as the Moor yearns for his beloved with all his being, and Iago stands between them with his counter-Throughaction, you get a five-act, highly active tragedy which ends in catastrophe.

'Need we add that the line of the counter-Throughaction is made up of individual moments and the small lines of life in the actor/role. I will try and illustrate what I have said using Brand as an example.

'Let's say we have established Brand's watchword, "all or nothing" as the Supertask (whether that's right or not doesn't matter for the present example). In a fanatic this principle is terrifying. It admits of no compromise, concession or weakening in the fulfilment of his ideal in life.

'Now try and link the individual Bits of the extract "with the abandoned child", which we analysed earlier, to the Supertask of the whole play.'

In my mind I tried to use the abandoned child as the starting point and set my sights on the Supertask, 'all or nothing'. Of course my imagination and my ideas helped me establish the link between them, but I could only do it with a great deal of strain, which is crippling to the play.

It is much more natural if you have resistance instead of compliance from the mother, and so in this Bit Agnes does not follow the Throughaction but the counter-Throughaction, going not towards the Supertask but against it.

When I did the same thing with Brand, and looked for the link between his Tasks – 'to persuade my wife to give up the abandoned child, so as to make a sacrifice' and the Supertask – 'all or nothing' – I was able to find it at once. It was natural for the fanatic to demand everything for the sake of his ideal in life. Agnes' counter-Throughaction provoked stronger action from Brand. Hence the struggle between two basic principles began.

Brand's sense of duty is in conflict with a mother's love. Ideas fight feelings. The fanatical pastor against the grieving mother, the male principle against the female.

So, in this particular scene the line of the Throughaction is in Brand's hands and the counter-Throughaction comes from Agnes.

By way of conclusion Tortsov gave us a brief schematic summary of the things he had said over our whole year of study.

This short overview helped me put all the things I had learned in the first year of study in order.

'Now give me all your attention as what I am going to say is very important,' Tortsov stated. 'All the stages in our programme, from the beginning of our work here in the school, all the investigations of the individual Elements, we have undertaken this year, have been done so that we can achieve the creative state.

'That's what we have been working for the whole winter. That's what demands and always will demand your undivided attention.

'But at this stage in your development, your creative state is not ready to cope with the subtle, intense search for the Supertask and the Throughaction. The creative state we have developed needs one major addition. It holds the great secret of the "system", one which justifies the most important principle of our school of acting: *the subconscious through the conscious.*

'We shall turn to the study of this addition and its principles in our next class.'

PART V

Presence

Introduction to Part V: Presence, Physicality, Play and Communion

Dick McCaw, Royal Holloway, University of London, UK

THE MINUTE YOU WALKED THROUGH THE DOOR

FOR THE FIRST FIFTEEN YEARS of my professional life I worked as a producer with two touring theatre companies. This explains why from 1979 through until 1992 I would spend one or two weeks a year auditioning actors. It was always a case of 'the minute you walked through the door': some actors just had 'it', whatever 'it' is, and it was immediately apparent. Let us say for the moment that it was a certain quality of presence – they were just more 'there', more 'now', their reaction to the space and to us was quicker and more alive than the others. I never recall an actor gradually becoming present after their entrance had been a non-event. Guiltily, I once asked a friend, the late John McGrath (writer and director for film and stage), whether he had the same experience. Absolutely, he replied. I was reassured that it was not my partner and I simply making snap judgements, and though I have made no wider survey, the question has remained with me. In 1993 I was appointed Artistic Director of The International Workshop Festival and inherited a project from my predecessor, a collaboration with the South Bank Centre in London that would focus on the Martial Arts. It took me over a year to find a framing device for the programme of professional workshops and presentations, and finally it came to me: we would explore that question of presence. The project was called *The Performer's Energy*, and, by some strange synchronicity, in the same year Eugenio Barba's ISTA (International School for Theatre Anthropology) was organising a project called *The Performer's Bios*. We both agreed that energy or *bios* was an essential element in the performer's presence. It is the vital energy that seems to light up the actor from within, that gives them power on stage, that sets them more presently before us. If Eugenio and I were organising practical workshops for performers around the questions of energy and presence, you can infer that we both felt that these can be developed through training. I believed then and still believe that in many forms of Martial Arts there is something that we can draw upon for the training of actors.

WHAT IS PRESENCE?

The word 'presence' is in the titles of books by Chaikin and Zaporah which indicates its centrality to the training and practice of the actor. Mnouchkine states quite simply that 'There are actors who are present, and others less. It comes with talent' (Féral, Mnouchkine & Husemoller 1989: 93). Chaikin goes further by arguing that 'This "presence" on the stage is a quality given to some and absent from others. All of the history of the theatre refers to actors who possess this "presence" ' (1991: 20). This underlines my first intuition that presence is what theatre is and always has been about (does this apply to all forms of performance?) and that some actors have and some don't have it. The crucial question in the context of this essay is whether one can develop this talent for presence.

Certain themes emerge from the texts in this section from which we can discern an approach to actor-training which will help develop this central but elusive quality of theatre. I list these in no particular order because they all work and feed each other simultaneously: an ability to play off and to play with others; a sense of ensemble or communion which is in turn related to a quality of attention; a sensitivity to others, be they your fellow actors or the audience; finally, there is a capacity for openness or for 'explosion' (Mnouchkine uses the image of a grenade), the ability to open yourself physically, to go beyond your own limits, again for both your partners and the audience. Throughout the passages quoted there is a concern for your understanding of yourself as a physical being.

TRAINING TO BE PRESENT

Before dealing with these themes I want to point out a problem with the very word 'training'. All the practitioners in this section warn the student that there are two very different approaches to training, one which is to do with the accumulation of tricks, skills and solutions, the other being a much more reflective and subtle process of negotiation between your present capacities and the particular needs of your artistic project. Educationalist Paulo Freire calls the first kind of training the 'banking form of education' where the student begins empty – an empty account – and is progressively filled with knowledge (educational capital). It is a quantitative notion of education based on the principle that the more you have, the better you are. Littlewood challenges this principle by forbidding actors to 'use the tricks that have kept them in work before' (Marowitz and Trussler 1967: 115); Mnouchkine warns that there is one thing worse than an actor having nothing in their bag, and that is the one who arrives 'with many things in their bag' (in Féral 1989: 86). Chaikin points out that the actor often 'mistakenly assumes that his preparation should consist of filling himself with broad emotional experiences' (1991: 66), but what is really required is a receptive emptiness. Common to all these passages is the metaphor of fullness and emptiness. They argue that far from being a good thing, the full 'bag' is simply baggage that prevents the actor from being creative.

Copeau passionately rejects 'What is called "vocation" for the theatre' which 'nine times out of ten, does not warrant being encouraged' (in Rudlin and Paul 1990: 10) and is indeed, 'Rotten to the core' (ibid.). This is structurally related to the question of training. If one already knows what theatre is, then one needs simply to acquire the skills that it demands. It is precisely these assumptions about what theatre is, that directors like Copeau, Littlewood and Chaikin challenge. They demand a new theatre and a new form of training that can make it possible. The question is as much about aesthetics as pedagogy. We are dealing with theatre directors who challenge the norms of theatre: where it is performed, for whom, by whom, and what it consists of. The work of Copeau and Brook can be found in James Roose-Evans' book *Experimental Theatre*. Although none of our author-practitioners makes the point explicitly, the implication is that if theatre is constantly evolving then training must also be. In this situation of constant evolution what can be meant by the phrase 'An Actor Prepares'? Chaikin explains:

> All prepared systems fail. They fail when they are applied, except as examples of a process which was significant, at some time, for someone or some group. Process is dynamic: it's the evolution that takes place during work.
>
> (1991: 21)

Chaikin makes a very useful distinction between training as the repetition of something already learned – for a theatre whose aesthetic parameters are already set – and training as a dynamic and constantly evolving process. As Staniewski states, an actor will often have to solve a problem or face a situation in which 'their methodology no longer works' (2004: 110). Probably 'methodology' is the wrong word, since we are not dealing with a discussion of method (what methods are appropriate for what situations), but the application of a particular method, what Littlewood called the 'bag of tricks'. Stanislavsky broadens the question further by putting it in the context of the actor's creative life:

> Remember: every exacting actor, however great, at certain intervals, say every four or five years, must go back and study anew. It is also necessary for him periodically to place his voice – it changes with time. He must also rid himself of those habits which have adhered to him like dirt, as for example, coquetry, self-admiration, etc. As an artist, it is necessary for him constantly to widen his culture. Now, do you understand the task which confronts you? I repeat once more: Do not think of performance – think only of training, training, training.
>
> (Toporkov 1999: 155)

The metaphor of fullness and emptiness resonates throughout the different discussions of actor training. Rather than being about the acquisition of new skills, training for experimental theatre activates hitherto unrealised creative potentiality within the person of the student actor. Zaporah argues that:

> Most of us go through our daily lives unaware of how we do what we do. For example, our speech is probably locked into a pattern that we don't even recognise; it has a particular rhythm, inflection, tone. We've never really listened to our voices.
>
> (1995: 10)

Just as 'trained' actors are locked into fixed responses they have acquired through their vocational training, so most of us are locked into similarly fixed responses to the world of which we are unaware. Stanislavsky writes about how an actor has to relearn basic human movements precisely because few of us are aware of how we perform them:

> We forget everything, how we walk, how we sit, eat, drink, sleep, talk,
> look, listen – in a word, how we act internally and externally. We have to
> learn all this anew, on the stage itself, precisely in the same way a child
> learns to talk, look and listen.
>
> (Stanislavsky 2008: 57)

As children we learn to walk before we learn to speak. The whole process is
negotiated without conscious prompting or reflection. Like any movement skill, it is
mastered when you can perform it without thinking. Imagine if you had to think
about every aspect of walking: our gait would be very uneven and painfully slow.
The actor has to revisit these basic movement functions, because on stage they
become significant for the audience. Our style of performing everyday functions like
coming to sit or stand, how we walk, is as unique as our signature in writing. The
actor-as-person has 'forgotten' how he or she walks and needs to relearn these
primary functions, so that the actor-as-artist can then use this knowledge to be able
to walk, sit down and get up in as many ways as there are characters in the world.
Training is about recognising their own patterns to be able to develop a fuller range
of movement and speech.

Far from the person of the student actor being 'empty' at the beginning of their
training, many of our practitioners argue that the actor has vast and unrecognised
physical and mental resources which it is the job of the trainer to open up. Brook
observes 'an actor, like every human being, has a very thin part of himself which he
uses all the time, and which he considers to be himself', but, '[t]here is a vast area
which is himself that he doesn't know' (Brook 1993: 10). Chaikin agrees with Brook
that the actor 'has to be available to himself – has to be able to discover and call on
himself – and he also has to direct himself and guide his own process' (1991: 22),
and what gets in the way of that process of opening and discovery is tension. Tension
'directs him to particular choices, limiting possibilities and concealing alternatives'
(ibid.): this is another way of saying that when we become tense, or self-conscious, or
frightened, we fall back on those tricks in our bag which we know have worked in the
past. And what is more frightening than the unknown?

Zaporah agrees that 'We're always on guard' (1995: 20) against the new and
unknown but argues that in her form of improvisation problems and weaknesses can
actually be exploited creatively: 'What was denied becomes acceptable and demons
become creative resources. Condemning beliefs turn out to be negotiable – or, at least
– intriguing limitations that transform into intricacies' (1995: 5). Johnstone agrees
with Zaporah, noting that once you have accepted that sanity is pretence, then even
your own hang-ups can be used as creative material. One of the worst mistakes is to
make a conscious attempt to be creative because you 'always arrive at the same
boring old answers' (1981: 88), however, '[i]f they said the first thing that came into
their head, there'd be no problem' (ibid.).

Johnstone argues that actors can expand their range by being empty and receptive
rather than laden with unnecessary baggage: 'The actor who will accept anything
that happens seems supernatural: you are suddenly in contact with people who are
unbounded, whose imagination seems to function without limit' (1981: 100). Brook
points out that this creative emptiness also applies to work on a character: if an actor
thinks he or she is superior to the character then 'he is working from himself as he
knows himself, and he believes himself superior to the part' (1993: 10). Once again,
we have the actor bringing in the already-known, the tried and tested solution, the
learned skill or trick, but, he continues 'if you take the opposite view, whatever the

part is, when you start, the part is greater than you [. . .] if you believe that, then you are experimenting all the time, going towards the character, realising that you can't reach the character' (1993: 10). We are back with the continuing process of creation that Chaikin was writing about above. The different kinds of opening discussed here are ways of realising one's innate creative potential.

PLAY AND PRESENCE

Mnouchkine and Gaulier describe a much more dramatic form of expansion. Watching Japanese theatre reminded Mnouchkine of Shakespeare:

> There I sensed that the goal of the actor should be to open up a man like a grenade. [. . .] Whereas in the West actors are more often taught to grit their teeth and not show what's happening.
>
> (Mnouchkine in Pavis 1996: 95)

This is a far more spectacular and memorable account of the distinction between the contained and routinized body and the uncontained, limitless body. She insists that the muscle that allows for this opening is the imagination: 'Let your imagination come to you. The difficult thing is to let yourself do while doing. You are either *in doing* or *in the letting yourself do* where you do nothing' (in Féral 1989: 85). Once again it is about letting go rather than holding on. The actor needs to be fearless, needs, very literally, to show some guts. Gaulier is equally unafraid in his use of metaphor: he demands from an actor 'the movements of nature which explode around you at Eastertime' (2006: 193), as nature comes back to life in sound and colour. He observes that 'When a "great" actor opens his mouth, gives voice, the audience hears the explosion of the Big Bang, the song of birds in the Amazonian forest, the trumpeting of copulating elephants' (2006: 194). Far better this cosmic bang than the apologetic and miserable fart that issues from an actor who cannot open up physically or creatively. An empty body resonates far more readily than one that is constipated and full of itself.

In their very choice of vocabulary – grenades, farts, elephants copulating – Gaulier and Mnouchkine indicate that they are open to play. Anyone trained by Gaulier or Lecoq will know the importance of the concept of *jeu*, a French word that means both play, playing, and game. *Jeu* is at the heart of their sense of theatre and of the actor's creativity: Gaulier insists that 'Play is as vital a function as breathing or laughter', or again, 'Theatre equals the pleasure of the game plus a play' (2006: 193). Gaulier's story of playing hide and seek with his son makes an extremely subtle point: like a child the actor must occupy two different realities, the imaginary world of the stage and actual time and space of the auditorium.

> An actor who is performing enjoys pretending that not a single member of the audience is looking at them or listening to them, and yet the impulses which they give to their voice are addressed entirely to the audience. The blanket which my son hid under plays the same role as the fourth wall, the imaginary wall which the actor builds each evening in place of the red curtain.
>
> (2006: 194–195)

Freud made a very useful observation about the nature of a child's attitude towards the world of play in his article 'Writers and Day-Dreaming'.

> It would be wrong to think he does not take that world seriously; on the contrary, he takes his play very seriously and he expends large amounts of emotion on it. The opposite of play is not what is serious but what is real.
>
> (Freud 1959: 144)

We must take our play seriously, but in the joyous, noisy, colourful, abandoned way suggested by Gaulier. The same playful seriousness lies behind Johnstone's story of Fred Karno flicking ink from an imaginary pen at an auditionee: if the person dodges the imaginary ink – thereby accepting the offer to play – then he would take them on. Once again, it is about being open to a creative offer. Gaulier seems to be remembering Copeau's words: 'Children teach us authentic inventiveness' (in Rudlin and Paul 1990: 12). He advises the actor to 'observe children at play. They teach us. Learn everything from children' (ibid.). Staniewski also highlights the importance of playfulness in training: 'This kind of dynamic flexibility of the body cannot be approached ostentatiously or with pompous seriousness. There has to be space for fun, for chance, as well as incident' (2004: 93). (There is, however, an important difference between actors and children: the actor has the experience to recognise the value of this way of looking at the world; the child is simply doing what children do.)

The interviews with actors who worked with Joan Littlewood reveal a different kind of playing. In order to help her actors enter into the world of the prison she got them to play certain actions, again and again. 'Although it was just a kind of game, the boredom and meanness of it all was brought home' (in Marowitz and Trussler 1967: 116). Bit by bit, 'It began to seem less and less like a game, and more like real' (ibid.). It is precisely this use of game-playing that Clive Barker (who also worked with Littlewood) advocates in his book *Theatre Games*. Milne and Goodwin note how Littlewood's method was a mixture of Stanislavsky and Rudolf Laban, and how she would break the play up into bits, all of which led to the superobjective, that is, the point of the play. They don't mention that her use of games bears a remarkable similarity to Stanislavsky's later work on Physical Actions where he gets actors on their feet with very little discussion of the play text and gets them to play out scenes in their own words. Gone were the long discussions about motivation and character analysis – this was a process of finding out through doing. In a glossary at the end of *Stanislavsky Directs*, Miriam Goldina offers an explanation of the term Étude:

> An improvisation created by the director on the same theme as the play, with the actors in the characters they are portraying. The situation must be close to the actors' personal experience and of the same nature as the situation in the play.
>
> (Gorchakov 1954: 399)

Vasily Toporkov's *Stanislavsky in Rehearsal* (1999) gives a vivid account of some of these improvised études which demanded a considerable imagination to be able to enter into the given circumstances of the character.

Mnouchkine offers a less positive account of Stanislavsky's approach to acting:

> I believe that theatre is the art of the present for the actor. [. . .] When I
> see young students work on what they call the "Stanislavsky method," I
> am surprised to find how much they go back to the past all the time. Of
> course Stanislavsky talks about the character's past: Where does he come
> from, what is he doing?
>
> (Mnouchkine in Féral, Mnouchkine and Husemoller 1989: 91)

This isn't a reference to Stanislavsky's Physical Actions but his earlier approach
to acting which was based on the actor's finding common ground between the experience of their character and similar experiences from their own lives. This was sometimes called Affective Memory or Emotional Memory and it was a huge inspiration
to Lee Strasberg and what he called his Method Acting. When Mnouchkine refers to
the 'Stanislavsky's method', I think she is actually referring to Strasberg. Stanislavsky
always referred to his approach less dogmatically as a System. Toporkov elegantly
describes the transition from Affective Memory – acting in the past – to Physical
Actions – acting in the present. 'The importance of the transference of the actor's
attention from the search for feelings inside himself to the fulfilment of the stage task
which actively influences his partners is one of Stanislavsky's greatest discoveries'
(1999: 58). Stanislavsky puts the point crisply in a note to Toporkov: 'No. I don't
want your feelings, tell me how you behaved' (Toporkov 1999: 114). Or again, 'Do
not speak to me about feeling. We cannot set feeling; we can only set physical action'
(Toporkov 1999: 160). While the search for feelings took the actor into their past,
the work on physical action kept the actor firmly in the present.

Stanislavsky provides a bridge between this improvisational approach to acting
and the next subject we will approach: ensemble or communion. Again, he is giving
notes to Toporkov: 'Don't *act* anything, just play each action. Don't do anything for
us, do everything only for your partner. Check your partner's reaction' (Toporkov
1999: 86) to see whether you are acting well. Elsewhere he notes: 'The only judge of
whether what I am doing on the stage is correct or incorrect is my partner. I myself
cannot judge this' (Toporkov 1999: 190). Stanislavsky describes the dynamic of
playing with a partner as being 'like a chess game. You cannot anticipate all the
moves: you can only watch the voice, the intonation, the look and the movements of
each muscle of your partner. According to them, you determine how you should
proceed. Then it will be genuine acting' (Toporkov 1999: 191–192). These are
fantastic notes about how to play as an ensemble and how to remain in the moment.
But this insistence on addressing the other actor in the world of the play goes back to
one of the main elements of Stanislavsky's revolution in theatre. He demanded that
actors stop playing straight out into the audience and learn how to address and
respond to each other on stage. From this came the imaginary fourth wall that
Gaulier talked about above. Even in the 1950s there was still a temptation to address
the audience, as Littlewood points out: 'You *cannot* play alone, stop wanting the
audience to adore you and you only, they do anyway. People love actors and actresses,
so relax and let them have a look at the play for a change' (in Marowitz and Trussler
1967: 121).

All the writers in this section agree upon the importance of the actors firing off
each other creatively. Johnstone makes the case very eloquently: 'If an improviser is
stuck for an idea, he shouldn't search for one, he should trigger his partner's ability
to give "unthought" answers' (1981: 82). Each actor has a responsibility for the
other's creative responsiveness: 'The improviser has to understand that his first skill
lies in releasing his partner's imagination' (ibid.: 93). One of the guiding concepts of

his book *Impro* is that one actor doesn't block another's offers but learns to say 'yes' rather than 'no'. 'Those who say 'Yes' are rewarded by the adventures they have, and those who say 'No' are rewarded by the safety they attain' (1981: 92). Saying 'no' is 'blocking', that is, preventing any process from happening. More simply, Zaporah states, 'There is no "mine" and no "yours" ' (1995: 20). Her statement can be summed up in the word 'mutuality', one which carries much weight in Staniewski's lexicon, and which is very feelingly described by Chaikin, the only person to use the word 'empathy'. It is about feeling with the others on stage, tuning in to what is happening, directing one's attention towards that place. ('Acting always has to do with attention, and with where the attention is' (Chaikin 1991: 59).) The word 'attention' brings us back to Stanislavsky who devotes Chapter 5 of *An Actor's Work* to 'Concentration and Attention'.

TIMING AND PRESENCE

Chaikin and Stanislavsky also agree on the importance of rhythm in the actor's work. Sensitivity to rhythm is at the heart of ensemble work. When Chaikin discusses the characteristic rhythm of a person, and how a room can be charged with a rhythm, he seems to be echoing Stanislavsky very closely:

> Nobody is aware of the rhythm and tempo of their lives. And yet I would have thought all human beings should be aware of the pace, or some other way of measuring their movements, actions, feelings, thoughts, breathing, pulse, heart rate and general state.
>
> (Stanislavsky 2008: 488).

Stanislavsky argues that an actor has to develop an ability to tune into the rhythm of a performance, that is, to the creative work of the ensemble. He explains that every performance has its unique tempo and recounts that 'Tradition has it that our great predecessors like Shchepkin, Sadovski, Shumski and Samarin always went to the wings long before their entrance so that they could tune into the tempo of the perform-ance' (Stanislavsky 2008: 486).

I would argue that this ability to tune into the rhythm of a performance, or to find the appropriate rhythm for their character or for a scene is an essential part of the actor's work. It may not be a skill, as much as a sensitivity, to use Brook's distinction. Whatever one calls this ability to tune into characteristic forms of human behaviour, it is something that we develop at a very early age. In his book *The Interpersonal World of the Infant* the late psychologist Daniel Stern shows how both mother and infants 'attune' to each other by picking up on the rhythms of their movements:

> First, the parent must be able to read the infant's state from the infant's overt behaviour. Second, the parent must perform some beha-viour that is not a strict imitation but nonetheless corresponds in some way to the infant's overt behaviour. Third, the infant must be able to read this corresponding parental response as having to do with the infant's own original feeling experience and not just imitating the infant's behaviour.
>
> (Stern 1998: 139)

This seeking for a correspondence to another's behaviour is very close to what Stanislavsky and Chaikin were writing about above. Attunement is at the heart of what we have earlier called empathy or mutuality, it is that awareness of others that allowed Peter Brook's audience at the National Theatre to stand up and sit down together.

Lecoq evokes this feeling for rhythm when he describes how he would mime the movement of the sea: it is about 'feeling the most secret rhythms to make the sea come to life in me, and little by little, to become the sea. Next, I discover that those rhythms emotionally belong to me; sensations, sentiments, and ideas appear' (2006: 69). Lecoq has transposed the feeling for rhythm from an interpersonal sensitivity to a form of kinaesthetic awareness whereby the actor can attune their physical movement to that of the sea. Johnstone adds that a physical movement can just as easily call up an image: rather than thinking about a significant gesture he asks an actor to raise his arm and then asks what he is doing – holding onto a strap whilst in the tube, milking a giraffe? Once again, we are dealing with an actor being alert to the possibilities of their own action – in this case its rhythmic contours. This alertness brings us back to the question about presence:

> First the actor must be present in his body, present in his voice. Secondly, the body must be awake – all of it, the part and the whole – and it must be sensitive to reaction through imaginary and immediate stimuli.
>
> (Chaikin 1991: 66)

Actors have to be awake to everything that is happening both within and between themselves – always on the lookout for resonances, associations, and images.

Theatre is interpersonal, and thus the actor needs to develop that facility or skill for attunement with fellow actors and with the audience. Actor training is about heightening a person's sensitivity to the stage environment. Peter Brook gives very memorable expression to the relation between training and sensitivity:

> When one does exercises, it isn't to make people more powerfully skilful, it's to make everybody from the start more sensitive. Once a group becomes more sensitive, each person feels the reward. [. . .] Step by step, through exercise, through preparation, one begins to see that everything that matters in the theatre is a collective process.
>
> (1993: 7)

These words were delivered after a practical exercise that Peter Brook conducted with the audience at the National Theatre. He simply asked them to get up and then sit down *together*, without any cue from him. In other words, they had to feel the moment. After their first attempt, he offers three bits of advice (which could easily have come from the movement practitioner Moshe Feldenkrais, with whom he worked): he firstly asks, 'adjust yourselves, the way you're sitting, so that you're ready without any waste of energy to be able to get up' (1993: 6); next he asks them to exercise their peripheral vision, 'bring into your field of vision as many people as possible on either side. Know that you can feel the people around you' (ibid.). The third piece of advice is to 'listen'. Just as Chaikin demands attention from his actors, so Brook advises that the audience 'be completely prepared' (ibid.). This is an exercise that I do with every group of first year students and demonstrates the skill of rhythmic attunement. Ensemble is not something given, it is the result of training, indeed it is a form of activity, could one call it 'ensembling'? Most of the writers in this section have shown how an ensemble is the result of each member of the group learning to attune to the rhythm of the others.

Very far from a bag of repeatable tricks, the training being described by Chaikin and Brook is one of heightened sensitivity to the way we do things, developing a feeling for the rhythm of actions. This awareness can be directed outwards towards other performers, or inwards as Lecoq's description of miming the sea. Zaporah gives another example of how the actor can tune into one's own activity, finding a moment between action and awareness:

> Once we become aware of ourselves laughing, we notice a space between our awareness and the laughter – between the one who is doing and the action that's being done. It's from this perspective that we're able to play with the sound of laughter, and even the feel of it.
>
> (1995: 18)

This 'space between' is an extremely subtle thing indeed and requires a kind of super-sensitivity that marks the difference between the trained and the untrained. Once again we are dealing with an actor's awareness of what is happening in the moment of performance or creative process. But it takes patient and sustained practice to be able to find these spaces between, which is another way of describing rhythm. As Lecoq points out, a physical training makes us aware of 'the innumerable little gestures that we do automatically without thinking about it' and so we realise 'that we did not know what we were doing and everything gains importance as it is recreated' (2006: 73). His words echo those of Stanislavsky quoted earlier – training is about recreating the body as an instrument of listening quite as much as communicating.

So, have we identified what it is in actor training that might help develop the quality of presence? On the one hand it is about getting rid of baggage – old tricks and solutions, or social inhibitions – that will prevent the actor from being able to make a creative response. Stanislavsky describes actor training as a constant process of creative hygiene; every five years or so they need to renegotiate their creative skillset. Blocking can be internal or external. The actor cannot explode like a grenade or a dawn chorus if they are tense; they need to be open and playful, to have fun in his or her training. The actor needs to be open to the ideas of others, to be able to tune into the rhythms of others. Thus the actor is alive and awake to stimuli that are both internal and external, is able to connect with what is happening around them. The more actors can develop their sensitivity and awareness, the better they can identify and negotiate their own habits and patterns of doing, and thus develop new choices for themselves. It is this alertness, this quality of being awake and aware of what is on offer and being ready and prepared to respond that defines an actor who is present. What we have in the readings in this section is different notions of training that can help a person arrive at such a quality of presence.

PROVOCATIONS

1   David Zinder asks how the following is possible:

An actor standing absolutely still in front of an audience, not moving a muscle, rendering an expression, nor uttering a sound, yet affecting the spectators to tears or laughter.

(Zinder 2002: ix)

2   I once watched Phelim McDermott explore what Michael Chekhov calls 'Radiation' – he became more present before our eyes. How does he do this?

3   Stanislavsky advised that in order to make a meaningful movement an actor should feel energy coursing through their body: 'Try moving, try sitting down, while feeling your *prana* coursing through you' (Stanislavsky 1998: 327). Is this what McDermott and Chekhov are talking about?

4   Peter Brook tells the story of when he and his long-standing actor Yoshi Oida are watching a bad play. Brook turns around to suggest they leave to find Oida had already left. How did Oida achieve this discrete removal of his presence?

Bibliography

Brook, P. (1993) *Platform Papers: 6. Peter Brook*, London: National Theatre.
Brook, P. (1993) *There Are No Secrets*, London: Methuen.
Chaikin, J. (1991) *The Presence of the Actor*, New York: Theatre Communications Group.
Féral, J. (1989) 'Mnouchkine's Workshop at the Soleil: A lesson in theatre', TDR, Vol. 33, No. 4, 77–87.
Féral, J., Mnouchkine, A. and Husemoller, A. (1989) 'Building Up the Muscle: An interview with Ariane Mnouchkine', TDR, Vol. 33, No. 4, 88–97.
Freud, S. (1959) *Complete Works, Volume Nine*, trans. J. Strachey, London: Hogarth Press.
Gaulier, P. (2006) *The Tormentor: le jeu, light, theatre*, Paris: Filmiko.
Gorchakov, N. (1954) *Stanislavsky Directs*, trans. M Goldina, New York: Funk and Wagnalls.
Johnstone, K. (1981) *Impro*, London: Methuen.
Lecoq, J. (2006) *Theatre of Movement and Gesture*, ed. and trans. D. Bradby, London & New York: Routledge.
Marowitz, C. and Trussler, S. (eds) (1967) *Theatre at Work: Playwrights and productions in the modern British theatre*, London: Methuen.
Pavis, P. (ed.) (1996) *The Intercultural Performance Reader*, London & New York: Routledge.
Roose-Evans, J. (1984) *Experimental Theatre*, London: Routledge & Kegan Paul.
Rudlin, J. and Paul, N. (eds) (1990) *Copeau: Texts on theatre*, London & New York: Routledge.
Staniewski, W. (2004) *Hidden Territories: the theatre of Gardzienice*, London & New York: Routledge.
Stanislavski, K. and Pavel R. (1998) *Stanislavski on Opera*, trans. & ed. E. Reynolds Hapgood, London & New York: Routledge.
Stanislavski, K. (2008) *An Actor's Work*, trans. J. Benedetti, London & New York: Routledge.
Stern, D. (1998) *The Interpersonal World of the Infant*, London and New York: Karnac.
Toporkov, V. (1999) *Stanislavski in Rehearsal*, London & New York: Routledge.
Zaporah, R. (1995) *Action Theater: The improvisation of presence*, Berkeley, CA.: North Atlantic Books.
Zinder, D. (2002) *Body Voice Imagination*, London & New York: Routledge.

Chapter 37

Peter Brook

THERE ARE NO SECRETS: THOUGHTS ON ACTING AND THEATRE; PLATFORM PAPERS

THERE ARE NO SECRETS

QUALITY IS FOUND IN detail. The presence of an actor, what it is that gives quality to his listening and his looking, is something rather mysterious, but not entirely so. It is not totally beyond his conscious and voluntary capacities. He can find this presence in a certain silence within himself. What one could call 'sacred theatre', the theatre in which the invisible appears, takes root in this silence, from which all sorts of known and unknown gestures can arise. Through the degree of sensitivity in the movement, an Eskimo will be able to tell at once whether an Indian or African gesture is one of welcome or aggressivity. Whatever the code, a meaning can fill the form and understanding will be immediate. Theatre is always both a search for meaning and a way of making this meaning meaningful for others. This is the mystery.

A recognition of mystery is very important. When man loses his sense of awe, life loses its meaning and it is not for nothing that in its origins the theatre was a 'mystery'. However, the craft of the theatre cannot remain mysterious. If the hand that wields the hammer is imprecise in its movement, it will hit the thumb and not the nail. The ancient function of theatre must always be respected, but without the sort of respect that sends one to sleep. There is always a ladder to be climbed, leading from one level of quality to another. But where is this ladder to be found? Its rungs are details, the smallest of details, moment by moment. Details are the craft that leads to the heart of the mystery.

* * *

PLATFORM PAPERS

When a group is meeting for the first time, they certainly are not sensitive to one another in the whole of their body. I was very recently in Germany and I asked actors in the big German theatres, "Do you do any exercises?". Either they said, "No, never", or they said "Oh yes, once or twice a week we have gymnastic classes and we work on our bodies". But the interesting thing is that such classes help no-one except the individual, because the real exercise with a group of actors is not for the person by himself. It isn't to make him cleverer or a better actor, or a better athlete or dancer. It's to make a group more sensitive to itself. Something quite different. When one does exercises, it isn't to make people more powerfully skilful, it's to make everybody from the start quite simply more sensitive. Once a group becomes more sensitive, each person feels the reward. He begins to find (as does the director, especially if he does exercises with the actors) that as you study the work you're doing, you are actually seeing this work better, more fully, than when you sat at home trying to do it all by yourself. Step by step, through exercise, through preparation, one begins to see that everything that matters in the theatre is a collective process. Then you come to the point where a group who have had time to prepare something meets a group like yourselves, who have come from all different corners and are sitting in seats. Then you see that the most rewarding aspect of all theatre is when, in an extraordinary way, the audience also becomes more sensitive than it has been when it's in the foyer or the street. That is what, to me, the whole of the theatre process is about. In big buildings, in small buildings, in the open air, in cellars – no matter where – with plays, without plays, with a script, with improvisation, no matter – it is about giving everyone who is together at the moment when there's a performance a taste of being finer in their feelings, clearer in their way of seeing things, deeper in their understanding, than in their everyday isolation and solitude.

What I've learned and observed is that an actor, like every human being, has a very thin part of him which he uses all the time, and which he considers to be himself. And there's a very deep part of him, which isn't only the Freudian sub-conscious but something infinitely more than that. There is a vast area which is himself that he doesn't know. If the actor uses too soon what he thinks is himself, he doesn't go beyond that area. He invents, he creates, sometimes very strikingly, but within this narrow area that he thinks to be himself. If, by all sorts of methods of work, you can create a climate of confidence, security and trust, not only between the actor and the director, the actor with the other actors, but the actor with himself, by his feeling he can experiment and take risks, then a new process starts. The challenge of the role begins to open up what one actor once called a "number of drawers" in himself that he has never opened. This is something very simple and clear. An actor takes a part, for instance a Shakespeare part, and before the first rehearsal, starts having ideas about it. "What can I do with this part?" And that always has in it a touch of superiority. I'm playing, maybe, Osric, or Rosencrantz, or even a part like Othello. I look down on him and say "A poor misguided man". I've met actors playing King Lear who say "Well I had to find out why the poor old bugger did such an idiotic thing in the first scene". If the actor does that, he is working from himself as he knows himself, and he believes himself superior to the part. But if you take the opposite view, whatever the part is, when you start, that part is greater than you, otherwise it isn't worth playing. If you're playing a fool, he is more richly foolish than you. If you're playing a mean person he is more intensely mean than you. And if you're playing a very rich and extraordinary character, that character has feelings and passions and depths that are well beyond you. If you believe that, then you are experimenting all the time, going towards the character, realising that you can't reach the character. Then the character comes towards you and says "No, there is something that you thought you could never understand but you're beginning to find it".

PETER BROOK (1925–)

Brook made his name with a number of influential Shakespeare productions, before becoming one of the founding directors of the Royal Shakespeare Company in 1962. After several landmark productions including: *King Lear, Marat/Sade, US* and *A Midsummer Night's Dream*, Brook left the RSC to set up a centre for international theatre research in Paris. With this group he has directed productions such as: *Ubu, Les Ik, The Conference of the Birds*, the *Mahabharata, The Tempest, The Man Who*, and *Qui est La?*.

See also: **Jerzy Grotowski, Yoshi Oida.**

SUGGESTED FURTHER READING

Brook, P. (1968) *The Empty Space*, Harmondsworth: Penguin.
Brook, P. (1993) *There Are No Secrets*, London: Methuen.

Hunt, A. and Reeves, G. (1995) *Peter Brook*, Cambridge: Cambridge University Press.
Marshall, L. (2006) *Peter Brook*, London & New York: Routledge.
Marshall, L. and Williams, D. (2010) 'Peter Brook: Transparency and the invisible network', in Hodge, A. (2010) *Actor Training*, London & New York: Routledge.

Chapter 38

Joseph Chaikin

THE PRESENCE OF THE ACTOR

PRESENCE ON STAGE

JUST BEFORE A PERFORMANCE the actor usually has additional energy, like an electric field. It's a free-heightened space in which the actor stands. If the actor becomes at all tense, he is applying this unused energy by holding on—the way one holds onto a suitcase. The tension will form in the body of the actor as well as in the mind.

This question of tension is fundamental. I know that the opportunity of being present with a given audience is only once at a time, and I want to be there, available to the occasion. I feel myself straining and pushing when it's not intended. I'm experiencing now the imbalance of me and what I do. I'm overeager to be "understood," which is already a form of tension, a fear that if I understand what's intended, nobody else will understand it unless I shove it at them.

The actor has to allow himself—has to be available to himself—has to be able to discover and call on himself—and he also has to direct himself and guide his own process. Tension directs him to particular choices, limiting possibilities and concealing alternatives. You can't understand simply by trying—but nor can you *not* try to understand. In this sense "trying" is a form of tension.

I have a notion that what attracts people to the theater is a kind of discomfort with the limitations of life as it is lived, so we try to alter it through a model form. We present what we think is possible in society according to what is possible in the imagination. When the theater is limited to the socially possible, it is confined by the same forces which limit society.

THE ENSEMBLE

Technically speaking, I understand ensemble work to have two principles. The first is empathy: one actor, instead of necessarily competing with another, instead of trying to take attention away from him, would instead support the other. (Acting always has to do with attention, and with where the attention is.) There comes a point where you no longer know exactly which actor is in support and which actor initiated the action; they are simply together.

The other has to do with rhythm, with dynamics, and with a kind of sensitivity which could be rhythmically self-expressed. For example, there is a kind of inner rhythm going on all the time in any single person. If you would let the body go with the rhythm, you would discover that there is a pattern and a dynamic and an intensity that would change as experience changed during the day, a quality which, if you knew somebody else well, you could say is the theme of that person's rhythm. This is the rhythm in a room and it affects the room and it charges the room and it charges the people. Sometimes there is a kind of rhythmic battle that goes on between people when they might be quite in accord on what they're talking about. There is a kind of clash of certain rhythms, and sometimes rhythms and inner dynamics get together and sometimes they counterpoint. This work has been the second main concern in building the ensemble.

The basic starting point for the actor is that his body is sensitive to the immediate landscape where he is performing. The full attention of the mind and body should be awake in that very space and in that very time (not an idea of time) and with the very people who are also in that time and space.

The industrial mainstream of society is always a pressure to make of us "achievers," to make of us "goods." Many of our appetites are developed by the industrial society, and most of our models are not freely picked by us.

We are trained and conditioned to be "present" only in relation to the goal. When I go from my house to the grocer, I'm not present. Once I arrive at the grocer, I'm not present until I'm back at the house. Going from point A to B we are in a kind of nonlife, and from B to C the same. This is one of our earliest lessons . . . to be in relation to the goal. This teaches us to live in absent time.

The actor must compose the rules he goes by. The technique of the actor is an inner discipline. The first step in preparation for an actor, and very often the longest step, is for the actor to find in himself one clear place. Quite often the actor mistakenly assumes that his preparation should consist of filling himself with broad emotional experiences. Instead, the actor must find an empty place where the living current moves through him uninformed. A clear place. Let's say the place from where the breath is drawn . . . not the breath . . . but from where the inhalation starts. An actor who is fully emotionally prepared is overwhelming his internal life, is filling the cleared space, and all this functions against discovery.

There are streams of human experiences which are deep and constant, moving through us on a level below sound. As we become occupied with our own noises, we're unable to be in the stream. The more an actor boasts of his feeling as he feels it, the farther he is from the current.

First, the actor must be present in his body, present in his voice. Second, the body must be awake—all of it, the parts and the whole—and it must be sensitive to reaction through imaginary and immediate stimuli. The voice must be alive and exist in its life within the space in the room. It must be sensitive to stimuli in the room from the mind and deep in the body. The voice originates inside the body and comes to exist in the room. The senses must be awake to what's happening and to what's being created, transforming the space, always able to return to the quiet inner starting point. That quiet inner place is always there, whether you are in contact with it or not.

See p. 163.

Chapter 39

Jacques Copeau

TOWARDS A NEW CONCEPT OF
THEATRICAL INTERPRETATION

(Ideas for the founding of a Vieux Colombier School)

O UR OWN CHILDREN. We have our eyes on them. We should take them right now and devote all our care to them, if we want to see the dawn of a dramatic renaissance. For I predict that when they go up on the stage, we shall see things that we have never seen before . . .

So let us welcome our pupils from the ages of 10–12.

From all social strata, children from the working class, the middle class or from artistic parents. City, provinces, countryside.

Someone objects: What! Without waiting for a sense of vocation to develop?

Precisely in order to prevent such a sense developing.

What is called 'vocation' for the theatre, nine times out of ten, does not warrant being encouraged. Such a vocation is already a deformation. [. . .] I knew, once, a stupid young lady, unable to recognise 'a doublet from a pair of breeches' who wrote Comedy with a 'K' and Conservatoire with a double 'S'. She had a penchant for 'declaiming'. She took medication to acquire a tragic pallor and her vocation began with her make-up.

This is the kind of candidate we have for the theatre. Rotten to the core.

We are intervening in the children's lives in order to prevent them becoming like that.

Once registered in the Vieux Colombier School we would take complete charge of them.

You object: But how can you be sure that, from a twelve-year old child, a dramatic vocation will develop?

I answer: The school's atmosphere will propitiate such a development.

It will not be a school for actors, but for theatre artists: dancers, musicians, mimes, stage managers, scene-painters, costume designers, carpenters, stage-hands, etc.

There will inevitably be drop-outs.

Objection: Even supposing that I can make use of my pupils' natures, through the influence of education and atmosphere, this will reduce the part played by individual talent to a minimum.

Answer: The great actor of the future will not come from this school. I am not looking for *the great personality, the great individualist.*

There is only one great personality, one great individual who has the right to dominate the stage: that is the poet; and through him the dramatic work itself.

My aim is to propitiate, to exalt the work, and for that purpose to form a brotherhood of artists who will be its servants.

I care little for the great actor. If pressed I should say that in every age the great actor was the enemy of dramatic art. For great dramatic art what is needed is not a great actor, but *a new conception of dramatic interpretation.*

Do not suppose that I am going to give them a technical education, hypnotise them with the fact that they are being called on to become actors. On the contrary.

Preserve them from theatricality.

Keep them normal.

Give them an all-round upbringing.

And draw them towards the great art of theatre without their suspecting it, so to speak.

General education. Not a special branch of teaching more arid than the others. Class hours mixed with play-time, manual work and games. [. . .] From the diversity of teaching will come amusement, emulation, joy. All instruction to be like a big game, where one feels more and more carried away by the development of one's faculties.

Let it not smack of pedagogy.

Play should remain as free as possible.

The entire experience of the child comes from playing.

He chooses a game according to his inclination, his personality.

He is sincere and true to himself.

The more a child is tutored, the richer his imagination, the more musical he becomes and the more he imagines things plastically, the more he is able to make things with his hands, and, in addition, the more his body becomes supple, trained, rich in responses, the more his play will be rich in adventures, inventions, and the more it will be varied and *dramatic.*

Few pupils.

So as not to have to direct them from too great a distance.

Rather like a family.

While looking at my own children.

Playing.

Children teach us authentic inventiveness.

Enhance their games, excite them without joining in too much.

Help them.

If their imagination slackens for lack of an accessory, suggest a prop they might use.

Edi's sword. No patience to make a beautiful one. I help her make it. She sees my patience, my care. I let her wait a long time for it.

Dreams will grow around the sword. From the love she has for it is born the character of the Knight.

We observe the children at play. They teach us. Learn everything from children. Impose nothing on them. Take nothing away from them. Help them in their development without their being aware of it . . .

All this is difficult to describe, because it is still in a state of experimentation, nothing dogmatic. Inspired from life and human contact. Full of promise. Labour of patience. Already begun.

Aim for nothing less than making the actor, not only the medium, but the source of all dramatic inspiration.

[From Copeau's notes for the third lecture (given in French) at the Little Theatre, New York, 'L'Ecole du Vieux Colombier', 19 March 1917, reprinted in *Registres IV*, pp. 507–13]

See p. 4.

Chapter 40

Philippe Gaulier

TRUTH KILLS THE JOY OF IMAGINING

WHEN I AM HOLDING forth about the 'Game', I am not talking about a strategy such as someone might employ against someone else in order, for example, to extort money. I am talking about the movements of nature which explode all around you at Eastertime. Have you watched the hundreds of wild horses who play in the countryside near Brisbane (Australia), galloping to their hearts' content, copulating, whinnying with joy? They play. Cats, dogs, monkeys, and so on – everyone plays, so as to discover life, nature, sex and light. Play is as vital a function as breathing or laughter.

Extremely learned people have told me that flowers, which at first glance seem rather prim, upright and prudish, take flight with the advent of the first days of Spring, and not just in any old way, but assuming the most scandalous, lewd and pornographic of positions. When I talk about the game, I am talking about an immense desire for life, the same desire which makes us breathe.

The game of hide and seek: hiding behind a door, or under a mask or a disguise. Enjoying disappearing. When the joy of the game wavers, the character in the play appears heavy, true, too true to be honest: theatre dies.

Theatre equals the pleasure of the game plus a play. When the play is beautiful, the game of hide and seek unfolds, simply and freely.

There are people who speak so abruptly it was as if they were farting. In French we call them dry-farts. Their lips part a fraction, allowing a little string of words to slip out of their mouth. Then, like an anus which has just swallowed a glycerine-coated suppository, their lips close up again. The dry-fart has let off an idea.

Too many desperate cases (in police departments, postal services and all the bureaucracy that deals with cash) are non-stop dry-farters.

In the theatre, a true dry-fart wouldn't earn a penny, and rightly so. Playing with the lips and the mouth, the sounds, the words which were certainly born from a deafening cacophony, is the delight of the actor, of someone who enjoys giving life to characters which slumber beneath typefaces in books. In a book, characters vibrate in our imagination. On stage, they thunder in our bodies.

When a 'great' actor opens his mouth, gives voice, the audience hears the explosion of the Big Bang, the song of birds in the Amazonian forest, the trumpeting of copulating elephants, the howl of the Mistral and the Sirocco and the sounds which were at the origin of the word. The sensual movements of the mouth and the lips, which the actor skilfully brings into play, as if they were tasting delicious food, or relishing the finest Côtes de Beaune, add carnal delights to the music.

A game: My son Balthazar (and two years later, Samuel) says to me 'Daddy, I'm hiding under the blankets. Come into the bedroom. Look for me.'

My child dives under the sheets. I can make out his body from the little bulge he makes in the bed.

'Where has my son got to? Oh! Oh! I can't see him anywhere. Balthazar, where are you?'

From under the blanket, come bursts of little laughter. This is my reward for playing this game for two years.

'Balthazar, I've lost you. Answer me now. I'm getting really worried.' (Laughter). 'Balthazar? He's gone.' (Laughter). 'Gone for ever.' (Laughter).

I accentuate the ends of the sentences. I leave them high and hanging in the air, the way you enjoy playing with an echo in a cave. My son, under the blanket, laughs uproariously. My voice, hanging in the air, in search of laughter, is like that of an actor in the theatre who takes pleasure in making words resonate. He gives the words to the audience, crisp, luxurious and sensuous.

At the end of the game, my son shouts 'Hi, it's me.' We kiss one another. He had been frightened. Had I forgotten him? You never know. We kiss as if we'd been apart for years.

An actor who is performing enjoys pretending that not a single member of the audience is looking at them or listening to them, and yet the impulses which they give to their voice are addressed entirely to the audience.

The blanket which my son hid under plays the same role as the fourth wall, the imaginary wall which the actor builds each evening in place of the red curtain.

An actor enjoys pretending the impossible. Beneath their disguise, they imagine they are inaccessible, gone for ever, that no one (not even their parents) could recognise them. The bouquet of plastic roses in their hands smells as sweet as real flowers.

The red curtain is an insurmountable wall, as menacing as the wall which divided the two Germanys (beware all those who might think of clambering over it).

A question: in your school do you use the game 'I'm hiding under the blankets: look for me!'?

Yes. Students often forget to show a fixed point. They have to pretend to listen to the child's laugh. Without this time of listening, this suspended pause, the audience cannot find a way into the game or the story. A suspended pause? Now the audience, as if one man, dives into the play.

Another game which is more basic than the blanket game: the baby enjoys hiding behind the bath towel, then rushing out from behind it, saying 'Hey. It's me.' Hiding behind anything: Mardi Gras masks (they smell strongly of glue and cardboard), the red curtain, costumes, make-up etc.

It is the love of the game (of acting) which makes the difference between a good actor and a bad one. The love of the game? It goes back to childhood and is nourished by the joy of light, the love of life, sensuality, the pleasures of the flesh, and humour.

PHILIPPE GAULIER (1943–)

Philippe Gaulier trained with Jacques Lecoq at his school in Paris, where he later taught for several years. He is renowned for his clown performances, and as a master teacher and pedagogue. He has taught around the world, and is the founder of École Philippe Gaulier, a theatre school in Étampes, outside Paris.

See also: **Jacques Lecoq, Jacques Copeau.**

SUGGESTED FURTHER READING

Gaulier, P. (2006) *The Tormentor*, Paris: Éditions Filmiko.

Murray, S. (2010) 'Jacques Lecoq, Monika Pagneux and Philippe Gaulier: Training for play, lightness and disobedience', in Hodge, A. (ed.) (2010) *Actor Training*, London & New York: Routledge.

Chapter 41

Keith Johnstone

SPONTANEITY

I SOMETIMES SHOCK STUDENTS who have been trained by strict 'method' teachers.

'Be sad,' I say.

'What do you mean, be sad?'

'Just be sad. See what happens.'

'But what's my motivation?'

'Just be sad. Start to weep and you'll know what's upset you.'

The student decides to humour me.

'That isn't very sad. You're just pretending.'

'You asked me to pretend.'

'Raise your arm. Now, why are you raising it?'

'You asked me to.'

'Yes, but why might you have raised it?'

'To hold on to a strap in the Tube.'

'Then that's why you raised your arm.'

'But I could have given any reason.'

'Of course; you could have been waving to someone, or milking a giraffe, or airing your armpit . . .'

'But I don't have time to choose the best reason.'

'Don't choose anything. Trust your mind. Take the first idea it gives you. Now try being sad again. Hold the face in a sad position, fight back the tears. Be unhappier. More. More. Now tell me why you're in this state?'

'My child has died.'

'Did you think that up?'

'I just knew.'

'There you are, then.'

'My teacher said you shouldn't act adjectives.'

'You shouldn't act adjectives without justifying them.'

If an improviser is stuck for an idea, he shouldn't search for one, he should trigger his partner's ability to give 'unthought' answers.

If someone starts a scene by saying 'What are you doing here?' then his partner can instantly say, without thinking, 'I just came down to get the milk, Sir.'

'Didn't I tell you what I'd do if I caught you again?'

'Oh Sir, don't put me in the refrigerator, Sir.'

If you don't know what to do in a scene, just say something like, 'Oh my God! What's that?'

This immediately jerks images into your partner's mind: 'Mother!' he says, or 'That dog's messed the floor again', or 'A secret staircase!' or whatever.

ORIGINALITY

Many students block their imaginations because they're afraid of being unoriginal. They believe they know exactly what originality is, just as critics are always sure they can recognise things that are avant-garde.

We have a concept of originality based on things that already exist. I'm told that avant-garde theatre groups in Japan are just like those in the West—well of course, or how would we know what they were? Anyone can run an avant-garde theatre group; you just get the actors to lie naked in heaps or outstare the audience, or move in extreme slow motion, or whatever the fashion is. But the real avant-garde aren't imitating what other people are doing, or what they did forty years ago; they're solving the problems that *need* solving, like how to get a popular theatre with some worth-while content, and they may not look avant-garde at all!

The improviser has to realise that the more obvious he is, the more original he appears. I constantly point out how much the audience like someone who is direct, and how they always laugh with pleasure at a really 'obvious' idea. Ordinary people asked to improvise will search for some 'original' idea because they want to be *thought* clever. They'll say and do all sorts of inappropriate things. If someone says 'What's for supper?' a bad improviser will desperately try to think up something original. Whatever he says he'll be too slow. He'll finally drag up some idea like 'fried mermaid'. If he'd just said 'fish' the audience would have been delighted. No two people are exactly alike, and the more obvious an improviser is, the more himself he appears. If he wants to impress us with his originality, then he'll search out ideas that are actually commoner and less interesting. I gave up asking London audiences to suggest where scenes should take place. Some idiot would always shout out either 'Leicester Square public lavatories' or 'outside Buckingham Palace' (never '*inside* Buckingham Palace'). People trying to be original always arrive at the same boring old answers. Ask people to give you an original idea and see the chaos it throws them into. If they said the first thing that came into their head, there'd be no problem.

* * *

There are people who prefer to say 'Yes', and there are people who prefer to say 'No'. Those who say 'Yes' are rewarded by the adventures they have, and those who say 'No' are rewarded by the safety they attain. There are far more 'No' sayers around than 'Yes' sayers, but you can train one type to behave like the other.[1]

'Your name Smith?'

'No.'

'Oh . . . are you Brown, then?'

'Sorry.'

'Well, have you seen either of them?'

'I'm afraid not.'

Whatever the questioner had in mind has now been demolished and he feels fed up. The actors are in total conflict.

Had the answer been 'Yes', then the feeling would have been completely different.

'Your name Smith?'

'Yes.'

'You're the one who's been mucking about with my wife then?'

'Very probably.'

'Take that, you swine.'

'Augh!'

Fred Karno understood this. When he interviewed aspiring actors he'd poke his pen into an empty inkwell and pretend to flick ink at them. If they mimed being hit in the eye, or whatever, he'd engage them. If they looked baffled, and 'blocked' him, then he wouldn't.

There is a link with status transactions here, since low-status players tend to accept, and high-status players to block. High-status players will block any action unless they feel they can control it. The high-status player is obviously afraid of being humiliated in front of an audience, but to block your partner's ideas is to be like the drowning man who drags down his rescuer. There's no reason why you can't play high status, and yet yield to other people's invention.

'Is your name Smith?'

'And what if it is?'

'You've been making indecent suggestions to my wife.'

'I don't consider them indecent!'

Many teachers get improvisers to work in conflict because conflict is interesting but we don't actually need to teach competitive behaviour; the students will already be expert at it, and it's important that we don't exploit the *actors'* conflicts. Even in what seems to be a tremendous argument, the actors should still be *co-operating*, and coolly developing the action. The improviser has to understand that his first skill lies in releasing his partner's imagination. What happens in my classes, if the actors stay with me long enough, is that they learn how their 'normal' procedures destroy other people's talent. Then, one day they have a flash of *satori*—they suddenly understand that all the weapons they were using against other people they also use inwardly, against themselves.

Once you learn to accept offers, then accidents can no longer interrupt the action. When someone's chair collapsed Stanislavsky berated him for not continuing, for not apologising to the character whose house he was in. This attitude makes for something really amazing in the theatre. The actor who will accept anything that happens seems supernatural; it's the most marvellous thing about improvisation: you are suddenly in contact with people who are unbounded, whose imagination seems to function without limit.

By analysing everything into blocks and acceptances, the students get insight into the forces that shape the scenes, and they understand why certain people seem difficult to work with.

These 'offer-block-accept' games have a use quite apart from actor training. People with dull lives often think that their lives are dull by chance. In reality everyone chooses more or less what kind of events will happen to them by their conscious patterns of blocking and yielding. A student objected to this view by saying, 'But you don't choose your life. Sometimes you are at the mercy of people who push you around.' I said, 'Do you avoid such people?' 'Oh!' she said, 'I see what you mean.'

Note

1   When I meet a new group of students they will usually be 'naysayers'. This term and its opposite, 'yeasayers', come from a paper by Arthur Couch and Kenneth Kenison, who were investigating the tendency of people answering questionnaires to be generally affirmative, or generally negative in attitude. They wrote in Freudian terms:
    'We have arrived at a fairly consistent picture of the variables that differentiate yeasayers from naysayers. Yeasayers seem to be "id-dominated" personalities, with little concern about or positive evaluation of an integrated control of their impulses. They say they express themselves freely and quickly. Their "psychological inertia" is very low, that is, very few secondary processes intervene as a screen between underlying wish and overt behavioural response. The yeasayers desire and actively search for emotional excitement in their environment. Novelty, movement, change, adventure—these provide the external stimuli for their emotionalism. They see the world as a stage where the main theme is 'acting out' libidinal desires. In the same way, they seek and respond quickly to internal stimuli: their inner impulses are allowed ready expression . . . the yeasayer's general attitude is one of *stimulus acceptance*, by which we mean a pervasive readiness to respond affirmatively or yield willingly to both outer and inner forces demanding expression.
    'The "disagreeing" naysayers have the opposite orientation. For them, impulses are seen as forces requiring control, and perhaps in some sense as threats to general personality stability. The naysayer wants to maintain inner equilibrium; his secondary processes are extremely impulsive and value maintaining forces. We might describe this as a state of high psychological inertia—impulses undergo a series of delays, censorships, and transformations before they are permitted expression. Both internal and external stimuli that demand response are carefully scrutinised and evaluated: these forces appear as unwelcome intruders into a subjective world of "classical" balance. Thus, as opposed to the yeasayers, the naysayers' general attitude is one of *stimulus rejection*—a pervasive unwillingness to respond to impulsive or environmental forces.' ('Yeasayers and Naysayers', *Journal of Abnormal and Social Psychology*, Vol. 160, No. 2, 1960.)

KEITH JOHNSTONE (1933–)

Whilst working as a playreader, director and teacher at the Royal Court Theatre, London, in the late 1950s, Johnstone explored various strategies in order to generate more spontaneous responses from actors and writers he was working with. He has since become an international expert in improvisation. He founded London-based improvisation company Theatre Machine in the 1960s and after moving to Canada set up a number of other initiatives including Theatresports, Lifegames and the Loose Moose Company.

See also: **Ruth Zaporah.**

SUGGESTED FURTHER READING

Johnstone, K. (1979) *Impro*, London: Methuen.
Johnstone, K. (1999) *Impro for Storytellers*, London: Methuen.

Dudeck, T. R. (2013) *Keith Johnstone: A critical biography*, London: Methuen.

Chapter 42

Jacques Lecoq

MIME, THE ART OF MOVEMENT

THE ACTOR-MIME USES talent to allow us to see what is invisible: hidden meaning. If I mime the sea, it is not about drawing waves in space with my hands to make it understood that it is the sea, but about grasping the various movements into my own body: feeling the most secret rhythms to make the sea come to life in me and, little by little, to become the sea. Next, I discover that those rhythms emotionally belong to me; sensations, sentiments, and ideas appear. I play it again, on a second level, and express the forces in it by giving my movements more precise shape: I choose and transpose, my physical impressions. I create another sea – the sea played with this 'extra' that belongs to me and which defines my style.

Constraints will force the mime to fix what is lacking from the real with compensations, recreating it. The freedom of 'everything is possible' will allow the invention of a world with laws other than those of reality.

The constraint of the non-object is about recreating, by imaging, the presence of a piece of scenery or an object and interacting with them in a sensitive way. It is also a relationship of action favouring the illusion of the expanse, of the situation, of resistance and of weight (look at it, touch it, move it).

The constraint of silence forces one to make oneself understood without speech being involved: when words are no longer possible or are not yet possible, recovering the territory of the unsaid that the discourse of words had forgotten. These two constraints develop a sense of space for the actor improvising.

> If I open a door, I must close it without changing its location. To take an object and maintain the illusion of its shape, material, weight, without naming it, forces one to recognise it and recover the very sensation of its feeling and its function.
>
> If we try to mime all the actions that we do every morning from waking up to having breakfast, the innumerable little gestures that we do automatically without thinking about it, we realise that we did not know what we were doing and everything gains importance as it is recreated.

Since the reformers of the theatre, Stanislavski, Meyerhold, Copeau, theatre pedagogues have developed silent improvisation, seeking to return sensitivity to the perception of the body for the performing actor, eliminating real objects in order to perceive them better. But to recreate an action, an object with illusion (action mime) allows the imagination to invent what does not really exist, to change its dimensions, its weight, to overturn gravity and to play with the infinite possibilities that allow the actor-mime to take flight towards other worlds, wherever the imagination might lead them.

PEDAGOGY OF THE CONSTRAINT

A measure of constraint is indispensable but exaggerating prohibitions can lead to the negation of expression, to the point of absurdity.

> I have seen pedagogical constraints lead to making an actor wear a hat with a little bell on it; the objective was to move without letting the bell tinkle. This is like the instruction given to an actor to not move while speaking, or to hold the hands tied; thus speech has to be stronger and have maximum intonation.

Nevertheless, constraints are necessary as rules of the game for acting. A high jumper would not jump so high if there was no obstacle to clear. The pedagogue must know where to place the bar at exactly the right height to make it a positive provoca-tion and improve the actor's play. After all, ultimately, anything can be mimed.

Constraints favour style; too much constraint leads to virtuosoism, to feats. Not enough constraint dilutes the intentions and the gestures in the soup of natural gestures.

This bar of constraint, this necessary obstacle, is placed at different heights according to the pressure expressed in the strength of the intentions and the actor's play. The most difficult thing is to find the right measure of constraint so that the life presented expresses itself in a style that remains alive; otherwise the bar, if set too high, can result in a bruising that snuffs out its life.

Constraints are necessary for transposing life into representations of life, for creating another life that is stronger. They are born of the demands of poetry.

STYLE

Style results from the economy of means employed between a desire and a constraint. It results from a convention, from a rule of the game. The necessary obstacle is indis-pensable in pedagogy as it is in learning to be free. It must vary from person to person.

It is not in the armchair that adapts to your body that you will be best off, but rather in one that resists it a little, but not too much. In that armchair you will be better off. In the first case the body gets stuck in a form that receives it, in a sympathy that cancels it. In the second case, the body thrives in a living immobility provoked by a little 'extra'.

The most difficult thing is to know how to choose constraints in a way where they are not only a simple exterior given but are born of the desire of artists, of their own special playfulness.

THE RULES OF THE GAME

The rules of the game in poetic creation are in the playing itself, which seeks for constraints to help improve its quality.

> Children who play with a ball of rags, kicking it around, bit by bit produce rules that are obligations, and limit the game, in order to make it more interesting: they set boundaries on the playing field, agree on the width of the goal. This is how the old game of soule became rugby football. Soule was a game played between the able-bodied men from two villages. A large ball, made of rags (the *soule*) was placed between the two villages and, when the signal was given, the players started the attack, and had to get hold of the ball and place it in the opposing village square. Everything was allowed, or nearly everything.

One must not fall into the trap of formal exterior constraints that impose a particular style on to something that does not justify it: 'in the style of'. Rather, one should find the strictness of the constraint in the very heart of the theme at play. One should not be afraid, faced with a great theatre text, to push it around a little in order to reveal the structure that organises it; this can be done without premeditation, without an opinion, as if it were being discovered for the first time. A weak text cannot resist when it is pushed around. The rules of the game belong to the author. One cannot produce a play without going to meet him or her.

See p. 43.

Chapter 43

Joan Littlewood

WORKING WITH JOAN: THEATRE WORKSHOP ACTORS TALKING TO TOM MILNE AND CLIVE GOODWIN

Theatre Workshop found a permanent home at the Theatre Royal, Stratford East, in 1953, under the direction of Joan Littlewood. At the peak of its influence and prestige – just one year before Joan Littlewood's departure – Tom Milne and Clive Goodwin talked to a group of actors from the company. The collage of opinions and attitudes which they assembled from these interviews first appeared in Encore *during 1960.*

[*Editor's note: The extracts below are the words of the anonymous actors who had worked with Littlewood who were interviewed by Milne and Goodwin for their article. Their words have been extracted here in order to give the reader a direct flavour of her approach to working with actors. Each extract represents the words of a different actor.*]

WHEN I WENT ALONG for my audition she gave me a script and she said, 'Read all the parts – play all the characters.' I said, 'I can't do this' – and she said, 'Go ahead and do it. You are either an actor, or you can't!' Well, I did it. Women, children, old men, young men. I was terrible – I felt such an idiot. She said, 'Well, at least you don't mind making a fool of yourself – and any man who has courage on the stage and is willing to make a fool of himself can, in fact, become a good actor.' I stayed with Joan, and although I'm not sure whether I'm a good actor yet, now I'm playing a lead in the West End for her.

* * *

This thing about releasing the actor. Sometimes you have to do things on the stage which you find personally embarrassing, and you don't want to do them, but when you try them out, they work. I think her greatest asset is her ability to draw people out, to give them confidence and build them up. The thing an actor needs most is courage – the courage to get down to the footlights and do something silly, something which will make him look ridiculous. If an actor has enough guts and confidence to do this, then he's capable of doing wonderful things. She can even take a man off the street and get him to give a good performance. There was one bloke in *The Quare Fellow*, I remember – an American director said to me, 'Either this man is the most marvellous bloody actor I've ever seen, or a rank amateur.' But you see, you couldn't tell.

*   *   *

A lot of actors have found that the first two or three shows they have done with her, they haven't understood what she's getting at. But then something dawns. I didn't know much before I joined her but I think you have to be prepared to chuck out an awful lot you *have* learned when you work with her. Some actors claim that their confidence is undermined because she won't let them use the tricks which have kept them in work before. But that's ungenerous. I think it's a result of not trusting her. What you have to be prepared to do, completely, is to take her word for it. You learn to understand that her ideas are good – that she is right – for an actor I would say she is right all the time. Her greatest capacity is to know the limitations of each individual actor – to know what he can do – and even more important, to know what he can't do. She doesn't come to the first rehearsal knowing all the answers. She's obviously done a lot of work on the script, of course, but I think she's genuinely curious how far the group can go in any particular direction. If it takes them to a point that is satisfactory, she'll use it, but she will be surprised herself by what you do on the stage.

*   *   *

For the first week of rehearsals of *The Quare Fellow* we had no scripts. None of us had even read the play. We knew it was about prison life in Dublin, and that was enough for Joan. None of us had ever been in prison, and although we could all half-imagine what it was like, Joan set out to tell us more – the narrow world of steel and stone, high windows and clanging doors, the love-hate between warder and prisoner, the gossip, the jealousy, and the tragedy – all the things that make up the fascination of dreariness. She took us up on to the roof of the Theatre Royal. All the grimy slate and stone made it easy to believe we were in a prison yard. We formed up in a circle, and imagined we were prisoners out on exercise. Round and round we trudged for what seemed like hours – breaking now and then for a quick smoke and furtive conversation. Although it was just a kind of game, the boredom and meanness of it all was brought home. Next, the 'game' was extended – the whole dreary routine of washing out your cell, standing to attention, sucking up to the screws, trading tobacco, was improvised and developed. It began to seem less and less like a game, and more like real. By degrees the plot and the script were introduced, although some of us never knew which parts we were playing until half-way through the rehearsals. The interesting thing was that when she gave us the scripts we found that many of the situations we had improvised actually occurred in the play. All we had to do was learn the author's words.

*   *   *

It isn't strictly true, you know, that Joan never gives you a move. She might say to you, 'In this scene you're coming out of a cellar, and fighting your way down a long, dark passage. You can't see, but you just know you have got to get out and through the door at the end.' Well, that's not saying to someone, 'Here you move from right to left,' which isn't giving a move at all, just placing someone in a particular position. No, Joan *really* gives you a move – she explains the particular effort required to get into a particular position. I would say that she gives people *movement*, she gives actors an objective, and a motive to get there. And it's a very strong pattern of movement, because it grows out of what the play means and what the character is after. Some people have remarked on the beautiful grouping in her classical productions, but she never arranges us on the stage: somehow the grouping just grows out of the action.

If the characters are right, the feelings are right, and the motivations are right, the grouping must be right.

* * *

As a young 'actress' I was told 'stick your behind out, dear, it's always good for a laugh'. Well, this show of ours, at the moment, is one big behind.

We may as well go the whole hog and start throwing whitewash at the audience and custard pies at the obtruding behinds, only that would need better timing.

Can we stop regarding the audience as morons, cut out the rubbish, get back a bit of tension, pace and atmosphere in Act II. Can we stop wriggling our anatomies all over the script, over-acting, bullying laughs out of the audience and playing alone, for approbation. This latter, which looks like selfishness, is mere insecurity and lack of trust in yourselves and each other. You *cannot* play alone, stop wanting the audience to adore you and you only, they do anyway. People love actors and actresses, so relax and let them have a look at a play for a change.

[Editor's note: The extract above is taken from notes given by Joan Littlewood to the cast of one of her productions.]

* * *

When we had a long period together as a group we used to improvise and take classes. And it wasn't just singing scales – we made definite, quite surprising vocal experiments. We had fascinating classes in voice and movement, the combining of efforts, moving sticks and shifting weights – and you surprise yourself – you find a lot out about your own personality.

She's a tremendous believer in technique. People get the idea that it's all terribly Method, but if she had her way, all her actors could sing, dance, fence, and mime. If she had her way she'd have a group training like mad. A fact that's often glossed over is that it just isn't economically possible for her to do this. Of course in any sensible community, the Government would stand up and say to Joan 'Look, here's a handsome subsidy, go and do what you want to do,' and she would build a theatre group that would make London the envy of the world.

JOAN LITTLEWOOD (1914–2002)

After training at RADA, Littlewood moved to Manchester, where she met Jimmie Miller (later known as Ewan MacColl) and joined the socialist theatre company, Theatre of Action. In 1945, with others from her former company, she started Theatre Workshop, which toured for eight years until eventually finding a base in Stratford, East London. The company produced many landmark productions until eventually, disillusioned with the English theatre system, Littlewood retired from theatre in 1975.

See also: **Bertolt Brecht, Rudolf Laban.**

SUGGESTED FURTHER READING

Littlewood, J. (1994) *Joan's Story*, London: Methuen.

Barker, C. (2010) 'Joan Littlewood', in Hodge, A. (ed.) (2010) *Actor Training*, London & New York: Routledge.
Holdsworth, N. (2006) *Joan Littlewood*, London & New York: Routledge.
Leach, R. (2006) *Theatre Workshop: Joan Littlewood and the Making of Modern British Theatre*, Exeter: University of Exeter Press.

Chapter 44

Ariane Mnouchkine

BUILDING UP THE MUSCLE;
WORKSHOP AT THE SOLEIL;
THE THEATRE IS ORIENTAL

BUILDING UP THE MUSCLE

I **BELIEVE THAT THEATRE** is the art of the present for the actor. There is no past, no future. There is the present, the present act. When I see young students work on what they call the "Stanislavski method," I am surprised to find how much they go back to the past all the time. Of course Stanislavski talks about the character's past: Where does he come from, what is he doing? But the students are not able to simply find the present action. So they go back and I always tell them. "You enter leaning backwards, weighted by all this past, while in the theatre only the moment exists."

I think that the greatest law is probably the one that governs the mystery between inside and outside, between the state of being (or the feeling as Jouvet would say) and the form. How do you give a form to a passion? How do you exteriorize without falling into exteriority?

How can the autopsy of the body—I mean the heart—be performed by the body? My slip of the tongue is revealing because the autopsy of the heart must be performed by the body. An actor or actress worthy of the name is a kind of autopsy-er. His or her role is to show the inside.

FÉRAL: We talk a lot about a concept we borrowed from the East which people like Eugenio Barba use in their work with the actor: the actor's presence. It is a very difficult notion to grasp but as a spectator I can identify an actor who has presence and one who hasn't.

MNOUCHKINE: Presence is something you state, but I myself have never worked with this idea. I would not be able to tell an actor to "be present." On the other hand, what I do know, what I try to tell the actor, is that he should be in his present, in his action, in his emotion, in his state of being, and in the versatility of life as well. These are the lessons Shakespeare gives. With him we can begin a verse in a murderous rage, have a moment of forgetfulness of this rage to simply be happy about something in the text, then fall back into a strong desire for vengeance, and all of this in two verses—in a few seconds, therefore in the present. The actor truly playing such a verse is "hyperpresent." Present to the second.

As for the actual concept of the actor's presence . . . There are actors who are present, and others less. It comes with talent. There are no bad actors who have presence, unless it's bad presence, and presence increases with the capacity of the actor to be naked.

FÉRAL: How do you help an actor to be in the present? Do you use a technique? Do you have a method? Is your method a form of listening?

MNOUCHKINE: I believe that there are no techniques. There are methods and I believe every director has one, maybe an unconscious one. I believe I have one, but I do not know it.

The last word you said is very important: "listening." I believe that I know how to do that well. There, that is the only thing that I can say. I think I know—no—I would not even say that I know, but I love, I love to listen, and I love to look at the actors. That I love with a passion. I think that is already a way to assist them. They know that I never tire of listening to them, of watching them, but how do I help them? I do not know.

FÉRAL: In one of your texts you wrote, "You must build up the muscle of the actor's imagination." This nourishment you feed the imagination is a form of assistance.

MNOUCHKINE: I encourage the expression "building up the muscle." When I work with very young actors one of the first questions I ask is, "What do you think is the actor's most important muscle?" Of course no one thinks of it, and so I tell them it is the imagination. And it can be conditioned, worked on.

FÉRAL: How do you proceed?

MNOUCHKINE: With sincerity, with emotion. By acting, really by acting. Not by the memory, I don't believe in that. You have to be able to have visions little by little, to be a visionary, to see what they talk about, to see where they are going, where they are, to see the sky above them, the rain, to take in the emotion of another and to believe in it.

We are trying to talk very seriously and very severely about theories of theatre, but really the essential theory is that you have to believe in it: believe in what we act, what we are, what we incarnate; and believe in what another incarnates, believe in the emotional trouble, in one's strength, one's anger, one's joy, one's sensuality, one's love, one's hatred, whatever you want . . . but you have to believe in it.

The common misinterpretation of Brecht is that we thought he said you shouldn't believe in it. Brecht never said that. He said you should not deceive.

I think there is something in the actor's work that obliges him or her not to fall back into childhood but enter childhood. He must divest himself of all made-up images which go against the work of the imagination. These made-up images are clichés or crutches where there is no emotion.

FÉRAL: But this imagination must nourish itself somewhere. It is not enough for the actor to say to himself. "I will believe in it" to believe in it.

MNOUCHKINE: There has to be a true situation to start from. I will not say a pretext because we know that it is possible to improvise from this. But there has to be a theatrical situation and a desire to create a character. There has to be invention, discovery.

*   *   *

WORKSHOP AT THE SOLEIL

For the Acting

Look for your little interior music that gives rhythm to your actions. Let your imagination come to you. The difficult thing is to let yourself do while doing. You are either in doing which blocks you or in the letting yourself do where you do nothing.

Use your imagination. The imagination is a muscle. It can be built up, enriched, nourished, by looking at others with mischievousness but without meanness. The actor is an active receptacle: this is not a contradiction but a difficulty. He must be concave and convex. Concave to take in and convex to project.

Avoid moving around all the time. If you move constantly, I don't see you. You must find your stops and your rhythm. The stops give movement, the states of being give life. In order for me to see you, you must stop. Only do one thing at a time. If you jump for joy, good. So jump, then speak, but do not do both at the same time. Sometimes you have acted out two things: your despair and your mistrust. You have not been able to act one thing at a time. So we haven't seen anything. Complete your gestures. Take the time to finish everything. Do not stammer with your gestures. Complete your stops. Also, avoid slowness that tries to be profound. It's often too slow to be honest. Do not fall into true slowness. You have to act out this slowness, but at a quicker pace. Slowness is an enemy. After several seconds there is nothing left of the previous illumination.

Avoid overacting and being idea-filled. Verbiage is as gestural as it is verbal. Avoid decorating. Some people do not realize the physical exertion this demands. Do not adorn your acting when you haven't got the essential down. There are people who arrive and who don't have anything in their bag. And others who arrive with many things in their bag and it is worse. It's fake. Proceed in a simple way.

You are so rushed that you explain yourself to us instead of living. Do not comment on your gestures constantly. The public is not stupid, it understands. You do not take the time to act out your desires and your anger. You are not in the present. You are here already and I do not see your desires. I want to know what you want before you get here.

One of your only weapons is action. But while you are in the doing alone, nothing can happen to you. You need states of being, presence. It is the state of being that justifies actions. The most important thing is to find your state of being. You need a pure state of being, a series of pure states of being. Is it enough to work on the state of being? Are we sure that if we work on a state of being, the state of being will follow? No!—a lot comes from what you believe or do not believe. But to believe is most important. You believe that space is outside of you. This is wrong, it is in you. I can only take in space if I see you take it in. I only see this distance by your look. We are the ones who see you seeing. You must be visionaries. It is essential. As long as we have illustrative entrances, figurative ones, you cannot fly off. If you illustrate space, there is no stage, there is no theatre. You have to see to believe. You want to create by intelligence, no.

Give yourself time. The problem is a rapport between the interior and the exterior. If you are not able to translate this rapport, you do little things, instead of daring to tell us, instead of making signs. Signs ask the question. If you haven't at a given moment felt both the emotion and the externalization by the sign, you haven't found it. Do not hide yourself, reveal yourself. You have to dare to discover. You are being figurative instead of metaphorical, instead of finding the sign.

Your problem will be to translate your state of being. Dramatic acting is a translation. Translate something immaterial, an emotion in a body. It is through the body that this emotion operates. The actor is a double translator, because his own translation must be translated also.

"The mask is essential for training the actor"

During the course of the workshop it was shown that the mask is essential for training the actor because it does not allow lies and it uncovers all the weaknesses of the actor: lack of imagination, knowing how to act more than how to be, lack of presence, lack of listening power, etc. By its very nature, the mask uncovers all complacencies, all weaknesses. It goes against the actor who doesn't enter it and uses it to hide herself. Inversely, it can become sublime and bring forth theatrical moments of rare intensity. Behind the mask, thanks to it and its support, characters emerge and are led into extraordinary adventures.

It is true that the use of the mask imposes a certain form of acting which other less typed theatrical forms do not. But it is evident that the rules of theatre which apply themselves to the mask are valid everywhere.

During the course of the classes, certain simple principles came back again and again although it was always difficult to apply them: The distinction between easy and simple, decorative and necessary, fakeness and trust, big and little, solitude and listening, displacement and action, illustrativeness and state of being, exteriority and externalization.

Some of the advice Mnouchkine gave to the actors ended up having the strength of maxims: Finding the true and precise little detail; looking for the little to find the big; not mixing up displacement and expression, apoplexy and dynamism, slowness and depth; refusing moves for the sake of moves in theatre; not acting counter to the mask; not accepting a versatility during the improvisation; and knowing when to give up what we had planned on and accept what might present itself. But more than anything Mnouchkine untiringly stressed the importance of the vision we bring to things, the vision that teaches, listens, and recalls. The necessity of apprenticeship by observation.

Despite the numerous failures, the rare successes, this workshop was a deep lesson in theatre. Mnouchkine reminded us at the end that the laws of theatre undoubtedly exist but during the night they hide and the next day no one knows where they have gone.

—*Translated by Anna Husemoller*

*   *   *

THE THEATRE IS ORIENTAL

What interests me in the Asian tradition is that the actor there is a creator of metaphors. His art consists of putting passion on display, of narrating the interior of the human being . . . and also stories, of course. I once made a trip to Japan, a bit hippie-style. Seeing the theatre there I said to myself, "It's like Shakespeare", even though I understood nothing of the themes or the language. And it was because the actors were wonderful. There I sensed that the goal of the actor should be to open up a man like a grenade. Not so as to put his guts on display, but to depict them, to transform them into signs, forms, movements, rhythms. Whereas in the West actors are more often taught to grit their teeth and not show what's happening.

"Why", I wondered, "does a Kathakali actor speak to me so directly?" "How does it come about", people ask me today, "that people who know nothing of Kabuki can like your productions?" The answer is the same: Because it's theatre! That is to say, "translation into" something. My "taste for the Orient" as it is called has nothing to do with, for example, the fact of having been influenced by some German director or other. For the theatre, Asia is a constant! Brecht constantly touched on that. And as for Artaud, he simply said, "The theatre is Oriental".

The Kabuki in Japan, like the *commedia dell'arte* in Italy at one time, is going through a bad period today; it is suffering from a certain immobility and will have to revive itself. But for us, that has no importance because it is not our tradition. We are not experiencing its internal conflicts. We try to understand what impulses have created that tradition. And tradition doesn't mean decadence. With decadence you only fix on the external sign. We don't know its grammar; our connection with this theatre is therefore a relationship of absolute respect but not of servility to the techniques.

When we decided to perform Shakespeare, a recourse to Asia became a necessity. Because Shakespeare is located within the metaphor of human truths. So we seek ways of staging him which avoid the realistic and the prosaic at all costs.[1]

Note

1   Quoted in an interview by Catherine Dégan, "L'Acteur est un scaphandrier de l'âme", *Le Soir*, 20–22 July 1984.

ARIANE MNOUCHKINE (1939–)

Mnouchkine studied psychology at the Sorbonne in Paris, before travelling in Asia on a year out. In 1964 she founded Théâtre du Soleil, but their break-through production was *The Kitchen* in 1967. Mnouchkine studied with Lecoq, and has subsequently created a highly physical style for the company, based on a fusion of different global theatrical forms. Landmark productions include: *1789, L'Age d'Or, Richard II, The Oresteia* and *Tambours sur la Digue*.

See also: **Bertolt Brecht, Jacques Lecoq, Jacques Copeau.**

SUGGESTED FURTHER READING

Kiernander, A. (2008) A*riane Mnouchkine and the Théâtre du Soleil*, Cambridge: Cambridge University Press.
Miller, J. (2007) *Ariane Mnouchkine*, London & New York: Routledge.
Richardson, H. (2010) 'Ariane Mnouchkine and The Théâtre du Soleil: Theatricalising history; the theatre as metaphor; the actor as signifier', in Hodge, A. (2010) *Actor Training*, London & New York: Routledge.

Chapter 45

Wlodzimierz Staniewski

TECHNIQUE

TRAINING

FOR EACH NEW THEATRE project it is necessary to prepare new lines of life, new aesthetics for the voice and body. The majority of the training methods are carefully developed and verified by time. They form the letters of an exercise alphabet which I apply in practical work. Obviously, body and voice exercises keep the actor fit and maintain a level of performance skill. But I want to stress that they can have considerable contribution to one's health, both mental and physical. Through this kind of training, the actor can get acquainted with herself.

The partnership work can also help this process where the actor can not only develop a deep understanding of the partner but also gain greater knowledge, through the partner, of herself. This is mutuality. In such practice it is impossible to avoid the boundary between work which serves theatre and work which serves the human being. On the one hand we are dealing with the joy of movement – aspiring towards lightness, dreaming about flying – and on the other, when we work in pairs, we cannot stop wondering about each other. In the joyful dynamics of approaching and departing, in antiphony, in the quasi-gymnastics in which we are constantly surprised by the stream of new images of our partner, new figures, gestures, aspects of the other person, in the running towards and away, in whirling, lifting, jumping, we reach a certain level of synchronicity. In all these moments we stop perceiving the activity as acrobatics. We only think in terms of metaphors. It is as if we were dancing poetry.

And then we want to be better – for the other person, for our partner, for the one with whom our body is synchronized. We want to be better than we are because we have to be more considerate, humble and precise. We cannot make mistakes because it can be physically harmful.

The very nature of 'causing an effect' in each other is a purifying process, offering a sense of a happy encounter with another person together with a harmonious conclusion. Within the stream of encounters, increasingly sophisticated manoeuvres evolve; even violent and aggressive gestures occur which are acceptable within the form. It is like fencing, when those who cross their swords know that their thrusts cannot hurt. There has to be playfulness. This kind of dynamic flexibility of the body cannot be approached ostentatiously or with pompous seriousness. There has to be space for fun, for chance, as well as incident. Nothing can be forced from a partner. It can only be drawn out, evoked, as if calling the partner. This calling has to elicit an adequate answer. This is antiphony – a dialogue of call and response.

MORNING EXERCISES

As I have said, working with the body in our training is a form of health practice. From the very beginning at the Centre for Theatre Practices we have cultivated a belief that one should start the day with physical exercises. These exercises should take place outdoors, in an open space, in relation to nature. It is not only a matter of breathing fresh air, awakening your body to life, unblocking bio-energy, or ulti-mately experiencing the joy of exercising together, although all these aspects are significant. It is a matter of energy, which is of a completely different nature to that experienced indoors.

Energy broadens our inner space, our 'uncultivated garden' in which our body lives, and allows more beautiful flowers to bloom. Perhaps it is partly because our inner life is influenced by our perception of the landscape, astonishing skies, wind on our skin, sound of birdsong, smell of the earth, and all our senses are exercised in this process.

The morning exercises are intended to be difficult and demanding. They encourage us to be brave. They provoke us. First of all they have to guarantee safety. So we focus on assisting the partner, offering safe arms, secure contact. Everyone within the group has to fully concentrate even if they are not actively involved in the immediate physical exchange. It is a situation in which there is both movement, concentration and concentration in movement.

The rest of the group has to be ready to make an assisting movement or gesture. This form of attention evokes a sense in those assisting that the same exercise lives in them, provoking inner animation. It enables you to assimilate the movement, to make one, two, three steps and to stretch out your hands at precisely the right moment, to support the acrobatic move. But it also allows your body to foresee, instinctively, a moment of danger, threat or fall.

The purpose of these exercises is also to focus on the way in which the body finds itself in the most unexpected positions. So the acrobatic training is very dynamic and teaches the actor how to both find and freeze the momentum in the most unex-pected and surprising, vital kinetic movement.

NIGHT RUNNING

My father was a very speedy man. I will always hear, to the end of my life, the way in which he ran up the stairs in our house. I always remember running as a moment of being very happy. Either that, or I was running in order to become happy. Night running is probably about happiness.

After introducing this as part of the daily life of the group, I began to do some research, and discovered that running is a ritual in many cultures, or that it functions like a ritual. I made a great effort for many years to experience such a ritual and I went to Mexico to Sierra Madre Occidental, to Tarahumara country, to visit the Indian tribe there. I participated in the Raramuri running practice with the Indians.

Running is a *petite mort* – a small death – like making love. It brings you to a climax and at the same time to the border of life. When you run for happiness and happiness is never accessible, you run faster, you chase, but happiness runs away from you. Instead of capturing happiness you are touching death because you touch the extremes: the extremity of your breath, of your physical opportunities and possibilities. Achilles' pursuit of Hector around the walls of Troy belongs to the same symbolic sphere.

It is very practical. Your breathing is altered and your muscles are stretched. Your mind is also affected: you experience the way the landscape is passing, and you are no longer *observing* but *perceiving* the things that you pass. The amount of detail which you perceive and the impact you are getting from experience is completely different.

I am not talking about running around the streets of New York. I am talking about Gardzienice's meadows, forest, or (with the Tarahumara) through canyons, along the rocky paths where they run day and night. The practice in which I took part was sixteen hours of non-stop running.

Two teams run. I was only able to run for some dozen minutes and then I collapsed but they came back after about 12 kilometres (7 miles) and I tried to join them again. A lot of things happen during the running that belong to ritualistic practice. To some it looks like a sport, but for me it is a transcendent ritual, a sort of mystery.

Running is an extremely realistic, existential practice and it can also be a sort of rehearsal. If you introduce different moves, different gestures and exercises during the running, they are more realistic, but at the same time they incorporate 'figures'. So the practice becomes artistic and aesthetic.

The group is anything between eight and twenty people. Not a crowd because then the chemistry is bad and it cannot be stimulated properly. The leader, as in the ancient Greek choir, proposes the theme, the subject, the exercises of the voice, the theatrical momentum. An existential physiological act, which is very realistic, becomes artistic, aesthetic. It can become almost mystical. Suddenly the ground is not the ground, but something like a mystical ladder which you are climbing. There are emotions within the group which can affect you deeply.

Running can create an incredible pulsation of the given song that we are working on in the training. This pulsation is rhythmicized and evokes voices which would never be evoked in a static situation within a theatre space. Because you pump your diaphragm, you open your throat and it happens naturally. You don't have to use artificial methods. You are naturally opening yourself and you hear the song in a way that would be unreachable on the stage. That's why I have introduced the audible pulse of breathing in the performance, which is a reflection of the running.

TRANSCENDING YOUR CULTURE

Ideally, the expeditions are where the actor is learning to perceive. It is an art, and is much deeper than just looking.

In the early expeditions the cultural references were often Gypsies. We were not so much taking themes from their dances, but certain electrifying gestures – a hand movement – that seemed a particularly significant expression of a person through their body. The gesture was already found. The actor is seeing the crux of this gesture as a separate phenomenon, not as a part of the whole body. Through the training process, I would encourage an actor to 'exercise' this gesture and to reorganize all the dynamics of the rest of the body around it so that the gesture is a source for the rest of the movement. It means somehow to re-compose the body, to teach the body new dynamics which are influenced by this gesture, then to sculpt the actor.

The actor is always starting with the particularity of their own culture. But then you are working in the way that is in reference to that which is old, ancient, forgotten or hidden, which can mean it is somehow universal. The actor has to have the ability to transcend his or her own culture. If somebody is saying, 'But I am Swedish and that's me!', I am saying it means that you are limiting yourself. All that you can do is probably only possible within the constraints of today. It means that you are nothing else but a replica of a contemporary cliché. Ideally, I am going further, not only demanding that the actor transcends their own culture, but transcends their own sex.

Real 'acting out' occurs when the man is able to break through the limitation of his male conditions and assumptions to reach the secret and the enigma of the female body. Of course you cannot get it without identifying with the female soul, and vice versa. This is the old knowledge of Eastern theatre and of ancient Greek theatre, but now it is extremely difficult to reach it. Through transcending your own state and culture, you have much more knowledge about what you have just broken through.

REPETITION

If something has been discovered, trained and fixed as a meaningful element of the given scene in a performance, it has to be trained continuously to keep it on the proper level. In this I am closer to music than to theatre and acting. Concert musicians know how dangerous it is not to train, and how easily – even if you are a great artist – you can get out of tune. So they train all the time, concentrating especially on difficult passages. The actor has to do the same.

I believe that a certain momentum can create a causing effect, giving rise to mysterious results and consequences. Certain gestures, tunes, turns of the body have to be done precisely, because they are causing a special chemistry to which partners must react properly and to which the public must also respond. The audience easily recognizes when something has lost its correct momentum.

To reach the correct momentum you have to train a particular means of expression repetitively – whether it is the voice, the gesture, a certain movement or a moment of harmony.

When people talk about theatre there is often much glibness because theatre seems to give people the idea that it is all about freedom of expression. The actor declares, 'I am expressing myself!' What does it mean, 'I am expressing myself'? It means, 'Today I feel like this, another day I feel that.' In music this is not the case, nor is it in dance. Because the feeling is something else; it is like an angel above you. So make the angel open the wings, but your body, your voice, your gesture, has to be precisely to the tune, to the point.

You can try to make a system out of the process of artistic work. But the system is only as good as the extent to which it can keep the work within the discipline you have prescribed. When actors have to solve a problem, they often have to work beyond their methodology. In some situations it is evident that their methodology no longer works. In the face of a particular challenge, it just produces clichés. My advice is, don't work methodologically. If you do follow a method you are killing the work itself, and then you can only work in order to demonstrate. You can never retrieve the actor's organic potential.

WLODZIMIERZ STANIEWSKI (1950–)

Staniewski was a former collaborator with Jerzy Grotowski. He joined Grotowski in 1971 and worked on a number of his paratheatrical projects. In 1977 he founded Gardzienice, the Centre for Theatre Practices. The company has achieved international acclaim for its work, which is centred on a return to a more direct engagement with nature and people, and involves song and a strong sense of musicality.

See also: **Jerzy Grotowski, Eugenio Barba.**

SUGGESTED FURTHER READING

Staniewski, W. (2003) *Hidden Territories: The theatre of Gardzienice,* London & New York: Routledge.

Allain, P. (1997) *Gardzienice: Polish theatre in transition,* Amsterdam: Harwood Academic Press.
Hodge, A. (2010) 'Wlodzimierz Staniewski: Gardzienice and the naturalized actor', in Hodge, A. (ed.) (2010) *Actor Training,* London & New York: Routledge.

Chapter 46

Ruth Zaporah

ACTION THEATER

ENSEMBLE

ENSEMBLE REFERS TO A group of people who collectively and simultaneously construct theater work wherein each of them is considered only in relation to the whole. There are different kinds of ensembles. An Action Theater ensemble improvises theater collaboratively with no script, no director, no choreography. The individuals serve the collaborative intention. Who leads and who follows is irrelevant, and changes continually depending on the material presented. The group is single-minded, one organism.

Imagine a group of pelicans flying together in a "V." The members of an ensemble are like the individual birds. As the pelicans create their "V" in flight, so do the ensemble members create their scene of action. The pelicans don't think, "Now, I'm making a 'V'," and the performers don't think, "Now, I'm making a scene." Both respond to their moment to moment experience relative to their intention. Both get the job done. Both are aware of their environment: sensing, discovering, relaying information, while at the same time, adapting to changes from within the group.

Ensemble work reflects how performers interact with their environment and each other. In an ensemble, performers constantly pass cues back and forth. To see and hear these cues, the performers require clear attention, freed of personal needs or wants.

They must:

1 Notice what the others are doing.
2 Believe what the others are doing is real.
3 Let the others' reality become their context.
4 Act from inside the context.

Inevitably, patterns enacted in ensemble are repeated outside the studio and vice versa. How aware are we of the spaces we inhabit? The other people in it? How does it feel to be moving closely with a group of people? How flexible can we be in changing places as follower and leader? Can we free ourselves from distracting judgments and preferences?

As the work evolves in the course of these twenty days, students change the way they relate to their internal voices. What was denied becomes acceptable and demons become creative resources. Condemning beliefs turn out to be negotiable—or, at least, intriguing limitations that transform into intricacies.

* * *

LANGUAGE

Most of us go through our daily lives unaware of how we do what we do. For example, our speech is probably locked into a pattern that we don't even recognize; it has a particular rhythm, inflection, tone. We've never really listened to our voices. As a result, when we hear ourselves on a tape recorder we're surprised.

Autobiographies introduces students to a new way of listening to themselves, others, and themselves in connection with others. They listen from *inside and outside* of the sound. There's no trick to it. All that's required is to turn attention toward the flow of sound: the mouth and ear experience.

Students collaborate, listening and relating through what they hear in timing, tone and attitude. What they hear affects what they do and what they do affects what they hear. Pieces of their stories intersperse with pieces of others'. Affected by what they hear from others in the group, students recast the emotional value of their own autobiographies. Their investment in who they are and what they're talking about changes. They might speak with sensuality about the death of a baby brother, with military cadence about the breaking of bones, or with a particular glee about the pressing urgency of a job.

Students are learning to hear form (how they speak) separate from, yet linked, to content (what they say). They start to see that any emotional reaction to phenomena is self-created and can be changed. This realization leads to flexibility in how they interpret occurrences in their lives, much less on stage. It also points to the infinite possibilities of meaning.

Each session ends with a score. A score is a performance structure, and is different from an exercise. An exercise focuses inward and is specifically designed to develop a skill. In an exercise, the participants are not consciously sharing their event with an audience. They're not directing their expression to anyone other than to a partner. A score, on the other hand, encompasses the skills practiced in exercises and plays them out for an audience.

* * *

As we take apart and examine forms of expression, be it movement, sound or speech, we become more aware of ourselves in relation to our experience. Clearly, we are not our experience. We're the consciousness that witnesses that process. We're not our feelings. Feelings, emotions, and thoughts pass through us. When we laugh, we're not laughter, we're experiencing laughter; we're aware of it: we hear it and feel it. Once we become aware of ourselves laughing, we notice a space between our awareness and the laughter—between the one who is doing and the action that's being done. It's from this perspective, that we're able to play with the sound of laughter, and even the feel of it.

The awareness that our every action is a construct of some constellation of influences can be devastating at first. We don't know what's ours, and what's been handed down to us. We don't know who we are. Eventually, this understanding frees us. We let go of all that we've been holding and realize that we never had anything anyway.

When we're improvising, personal material may occasionally surface. We have a choice—whether to allow the images or feelings to be expressed or to push them back into the shadows of the psyche. If it's fear that causes us to repress this material, we're constantly working under this limitation. This affects everything we do. We're always on guard. If, on the other hand, we hold these images and feelings, with curiosity and an understanding that they're only images and feelings, and we still choose not to express the image or feeling because of their appropriateness to the moment, we're free to move along. In other words, we detach from what we call our own, what's preciously ours. Opportunities are infinite once we can freely explore our psyches. The overwhelming panic that we have nothing to say becomes panic to play with. The "unacceptable" flaw which we keep hidden is already familiar. The grace that we envy in others is available to us. There is no "mine" and no "yours."

* * *

WHO ARE WE?

One of Action Theater's objectives is to detail perception by expanding awareness:

- of the energy and tension of the body
- of feeling and imagination's link to the body
- of ourselves from the inside out

We don't use the word "character" in Action Theater. Sometimes we say "entity" or "physical presence." Or we say "being." "Character" produces stereotypes. It asks us to be somebody other than who we are. A somebody that can be described, "a cranky judge," "a bored wife," "a hard-talking waitress." Instead, we manifest a vast array of entities, parts of ourselves that are, up until then, hidden in our psyches. We build upon our uncovered components to create "beings" who are whole and complete.

The detailed perception we acquire through practice is reflected by precise expression. In order to express ourselves in detail, we must know and control our body and mind. If we are still and empty, we become a blank canvas on which to project the nature of our psyches.

* * *

CREATIVITY

"Being creative" is not something beyond us, nor do we have to become it. "Creative" is an idea that compartmentalizes and limits our experience. When we start thinking about being creative, we break from the present. Our bodies are in one place (present) and our minds are in another (future).

Another way to look at creativity is to say that it's not about being creative, but simply about being. "Being creative" implies being *other* than who you are, when actually creativity is being *more* of who you are.

We can find this by quieting down, relaxing, letting go of the future and simplifying our actions. What's the least you need to do to communicate exactly what you mean? Clear, spontaneous expression is not the result of how much you do, but rather, the quality of attention you give. Thus we ask the student to intentionally do very little and discover fullness in that smallness. Slow down their mind and pay attention to each moment of change. Adding more action won't compensate for lack of attention. Simplify. Bare the bone. Don't build with more action, build with more attention. Then, you'll be "creative."

Communication relies on intention and skill. I may want to communicate something to you but I don't have the skills for it. For example: I want you to know that I'm feeling sad, but I don't have the language or expression to transmit that information. Or, I get so wrapped up in my experience that I forget to notice whether you're listening and understanding what I'm saying. A lift of an eyebrow can be a powerful communication if one intends it to be so.

*   *   *

KNOWING WHEN

How does the percussionist know when to stop hitting the drum? How does she know to pause, to be silent? How does she know to pick-up again with a bell?

How does the improvisor know when to shift, transform or develop?

She doesn't, in a thinking sense. She doesn't evaluate, speculate, desire or fear.

The percussionist and the improvisor pay attention. They listen, or stand by. They watch the event from the inside. They follow their actions: they allow the sounds to come to their consciousness, sensations to be noticed, feelings to manifest, images to occur, the memories to become realized, and thoughts to erupt. Of course, the freer the percussionist and the improviser are, the more able they are to stand by without interference. The more skilled they are, the more they can live through their instrument, whether it's the drums and clackers or the body itself. Freedom doesn't often show itself on the fourteenth day of the training. Students may have to say to themselves, "Shift," "Transform," or "Develop." They may have to fight their self-consciousness into this process. They may not quite trust their impulses, trust that they, in fact, do know what to do next.

Each student has to come to terms with each condition on some level, before he can shift out of it. A student must have experienced the condition before they can free themselves from it. Each condition has to be lived; it becomes something else and, then, something else again through the process.

Inside of self-consciousness, students can notice the next step. Rather than fight against struggle, they may stay with struggle and develop it. Or, they may transform the condition's experience, and work through the inside of it. Or they may shift out of it.

If the student really shifts, transforms, or develops, with no holding back, she will be liberated from what held her back.

RUTH ZAPORAH (1936–)

Zaporah trained in ballet and in modern dance. She began her career working with experimental San Francisco Bay Area dance groups. Her Action Theater approach grew out of working with drama students, where she had to create techniques for movement and improvisation that were relevant for theatre performance. Working through awareness and play, Action Theater aims to develop strong, clear and spontaneous communication.

See also: **Keith Johnstone.**

SUGGESTED FURTHER READING

Zaporah, R. (1995) *Action Theater: The improvisation of presence*, Berkeley, CA: North Atlantic Books.
Zaporah, R. (2003) 'Dance: A Body with a Mind of Its Own', in Albright, A. C. and Gere, D. (eds) (2003) *Taken by Surprise: A Dance Improvisation Reader*, Middletown, CT: Wesleyan University Press, 21–26.

PART VI

Epilogue

Chapter 47

Yoshi Oida

THE INVISIBLE ACTOR

WHEN WE SPEAK ABOUT teaching, it is simply someone else's experience. Your teacher has walked the path ahead of you, and you look at their tracks in the dust. They might provide you with some hints about where to go next. But these 'tracks' are somebody else's past, they are not your future. All the books and courses are simply maps of other people's pasts. Absorb and use them, but always remember that your own path will be different, and it is this personal path that you must travel. Don't try to exactly copy another person's path; use their knowledge, but remain aware that the particular 'landscape' of your own path is unique. However, the paradox remains: you must discover your own path, but you can't perceive it while you are on it, only after you have travelled it.

There was a famous Kabuki actor, who died about fifty years ago, who said, 'I can teach you the gesture pattern that indicates "looking at the moon". I can teach you the movement up to the tip of the finger which points to the sky. From the tip of your finger to the moon is your own responsibility.'

See p. 47.

AFTERWORD

Mark Evans, Coventry University, UK

ACTOR TRAINING SHOULD NOT be a lonely activity. Please do not leave this volume on the bookshelf – take it with you into class, keep it to read on the bus, lend it to friends and use it to stimulate experiment and innovation with friends, colleagues and fellow actors. Your copy should be battered, well-thumbed, decorated with post-its and pencil marks. We tend not to take books into practical sessions – challenge that assumption.

Hopefully this book will have both inspired and frustrated you. Use it to begin your own journey – perhaps even to collate your own Actor Training Reader, to write your own introductory essays, to compose your own manifesto for training.

Bon voyage!

Index